Redefining
Urban and Suburban
America

JAMES A. JOHNSON METRO SERIES

**JAMES A. JOHNSON
METRO SERIES**

The Metropolitan Policy Program at the Brookings Institution is integrating research and practical experience into a policy agenda for cities and metropolitan areas. By bringing fresh analyses and policy ideas to the public debate, the program hopes to inform key decisionmakers and civic leaders in ways that will spur meaningful change in our nation's communities.

As part of this effort, the James A. Johnson Metro Series aims to introduce new perspectives and policy thinking on current issues and attempts to lay the foundation for longer-term policy reforms. The series examines traditional urban issues, such as neighborhood assets and central city competitiveness, as well as larger metropolitan concerns, such as regional growth, development, and employment patterns. The James A. Johnson Metro Series consists of concise studies and collections of essays designed to appeal to a broad audience. While these studies are formally reviewed, some will not be verified like other research publications. As with all publications, the judgments, conclusions, and recommendations presented in the studies are solely those of the authors and should not be attributed to the trustees, officers, or other staff members of the Institution.

Also available in this series:

On growth and development

Edgeless Cities: Exploring the Elusive Metropolis
Robert E. Lang

Growth and Convergence in Metropolitan America
Janet Rothenberg Pack

Growth Management and Affordable Housing
Anthony Downs, editor

Laws of the Landscape: How Policies Shape Cities in Europe and America
Pietro S. Nivola

Reflections on Regionalism
Bruce J. Katz, editor

Sunbelt/Frostbelt: Public Policies and Market Forces in Metropolitan Development
Janet Rothenberg Pack, editor

On transportation

Still Stuck in Traffic: Coping with Peak-Hour Traffic Congestion
Anthony Downs

Taking the High Road: A Metropolitan Agenda for Transportation Reform
Bruce Katz and Robert Puentes, editors

On trends

Redefining Urban and Suburban America: Evidence from Census 2000, vol. 1
Bruce Katz and Robert E. Lang, editors

Redefining Urban and Suburban America: Evidence from Census 2000, vol. 2
Alan Berube, Bruce Katz, and Robert E. Lang, editors

On wealth creation

Building Assets, Building Credit: Creating Wealth in Low-Income Communities
Nicolas P. Retsinas and Eric S. Belsky, editors

The Geography of Opportunity: Race and Housing Choice in Metropolitan America
Xavier de Souza Briggs, editor

Low-Income Homeownership: Examining the Unexamined Goal
Nicolas P. Retsinas and Eric S. Belsky, editors

Savings for the Poor: The Hidden Benefits of Electronic Banking
Michael A. Stegman

On other metro issues

Evaluating Gun Policy: Effects on Crime and Violence
Jens Ludwig and Philip J. Cook, editors

Redefining Urban and Suburban America

EVIDENCE FROM CENSUS 2000

VOLUME THREE

Alan Berube, Bruce Katz, and Robert E. Lang
Editors

BROOKINGS INSTITUTION PRESS
Washington, D.C.

Library of Congress Cataloging-in-Publication data
Redefining urban and suburban America: evidence from Census 2000 /
Bruce Katz and Robert E. Lang, eds.
   p.   cm.
Includes bibliographical references and index.
   ISBN-13: 978-0-8157-0844-1(cloth : alk. paper)
   ISBN-10: 0-8157-0884-x
   ISBN-13: 978-0-8157-0883-4 (pbk. : alk. paper)
   ISBN-10: 0-8157-0883-1
1. Metropolitan areas—United States. 2. Suburbs—United States. 3. City and town life—United States. 4. United States—Population. 5. Sociology, Urban—United States. I. Katz, Bruce. II. Lang, Robert, 1959—
HT334.U5 R43 2003
307.76'4'0973—dc21   2002151690

9 8 7 6 5 4 3 2 1

The paper used in this publication meets minimum requirements of the American National Standard for Information Sciences—Permanence of Paper for Printed Library Materials: ANSI Z39.48-1992.

Typeset in Minion and Univers Condensed

Composition by Circle Graphics
Columbia, Maryland

Printed by R. R. Donnelley
Harrisonburg, Virginia

Contents

Redefining
Urban and Suburban
America

Introduction

ALAN BERUBE, BRUCE KATZ,
AND ROBERT E. LANG

M uch recent work in the social science arena has examined the growing "placelessness" of modern American society. Experts point to, variously, the Internet, satellite television, globalization of the consumer economy, the increase in long-distance moves, and the decline in measures of "social capital" as evidence that Americans are less attached than ever before to the particular places in which they live.[1]

True enough, few Americans today buy their groceries at the corner market. But the places in which people live—which are defined by both political and social boundaries—still reflect a lot about their inhabitants. In turn, those communities shape the views and experiences of those who inhabit them. In choosing where to live, Americans select not just their neighbors, but also their job opportunities, their children's schools, their commute, their future home wealth, their health care, and their places of worship and congregation.

In other words, place still matters, and *where* we live says a lot about *how* we live. This, the third volume of the Redefining Urban and Suburban America series, examines the contours and implications of the nation's shifting residential landscape. It represents a confluence of the first two volumes,

---

1. See, for example, Edward Relph, *Place and Placelessness* (London: Pion, 1976); Ada Louise Huxtable, *The Unreal America* (New York: New Press, 1997); Manuel Castells, *The Informational City: Information Technology, Economic Restructuring, and the Urban-Regional Process* (Oxford: Basil Blackwell, 1989); David Harvey, *The Condition of Postmodernity: An Enquiry into the Origins of Cultural Change* (Oxford: Basil Blackwell, 1989). For an alternative view, see Dolores Hayden, *The Power of Place: Urban Landscapes as Public History* (MIT Press, 1995).

drawing on both short-form census questionnaire subjects such as population and ethnicity and detailed long-form subjects such as income and educational attainment.

The analytical lens of this volume remains a geographic one, centered specifically on metropolitan areas, cities, and in some cases, neighborhoods. The volume seeks to provide a clearer view of what the results of Census 2000 have revealed about the changing shape of American places, and ultimately, how those results have changed the very idea of the city, the suburb, and the small town. The diversity of outcomes across places—on measures such as population growth, racial and ethnic diversity, employment, and income— reinforces the need to look beyond the national level to discern the impacts of demographic and economic change on a country as large as the United States.

The first four chapters describe how centers of growth in the United States shifted over the 1990s and beyond. Immigration and migration and patterns of development and redevelopment have given rise to population and household growth in a distinct set of places, both new and old.

The next four chapters examine the social consequences of the divergent growth patterns within and across cities, metropolitan areas, and larger regions. The forces of integration and segregation, by income and by race, have produced differing outcomes for different parts of the nation and their inhabitants. These chapters document the shifting arrangement of people and jobs in metropolitan areas and the possible consequences for the social and economic health of those places.

The population dynamics explored in this volume and past volumes have contributed to a changed urban and suburban landscape in the United States. The last two chapters describe how the federal government has modified the very system used to classify U.S. cities and suburbs in response to those dynamics and the likely implications for political and popular views of where Americans live.

SHIFTING GROWTH CENTERS SIGNAL NEW URBAN AND SUBURBAN DESTINATIONS

The rise and fall—and rise again—of major American cities have commanded a great deal of attention among researchers and in the media. So, too, has the post–World War II suburban population boom, which continues in most metropolitan regions today. Yet these general patterns overlook the diverse gains made within cities and metropolitan areas. An emerging set of new growth centers, the subject of the first four chapters of this volume, has forced us to refine our mental map of which communities within metropolitan America drove population growth in the 1990s.

To begin with, although the first volume in this series focused on trends in the nation's largest cities, the resurgence of urban population in the 1990s was hardly limited to those giants. Medium-sized cities like Tallahassee, Florida, and Hayward, California, also captured significant numbers of new residents over the decade. In chapter 1, Jennifer Vey and Benjamin Forman demonstrate that these medium-sized cities, as a group, grew about as fast as the United States as a whole in the 1990s and considerably faster than the 100 largest cities. Vey and Forman draw important distinctions, however, regarding the growth of medium-sized cities in different regions of the country and in different locations within the metropolis. Specifically, Western and Southern cities experienced population booms, and satellite cities not located at the core of their respective metropolitan area tended to grow faster than central cities. That more and more Americans—including many members of racial and ethnic minorities—are living in medium-sized cities highlights an opportunity for their leaders to collaborate on common issues and to lead the way by adopting innovative public policies from which larger cities can learn.

In a number of cities, the locus for growth has recently shifted to some of their oldest sections—their downtowns. In the first volume of this series, Robert Lang and Rebecca Sohmer quantified this "downtown rebound" in a selection of U.S. cities. In chapter 2 of this volume, Eugenie Birch goes further to examine the size and characteristics of the downtown-dweller population in forty-five cities and to explore how they are changing the complexion and economic and social trajectory of the neighborhoods they inhabit. She finds that fewer families with children live downtown today than in decades past but that more downtown households own their homes. She also confirms that downtowns are home to a diverse lot, containing both the young and highly educated and some very low-income residents. In the end, Birch suggests that downtowns fit one of five categories based on their phase in the development cycle. Cities seeking to capitalize on the "living down-town" movement could benefit from studying their development climate, generating additional housing for occupancy by owners, and creating a higher-density style of living that differentiates them from suburban markets.

Despite these city and downtown gains, the suburbs remain at the cutting edge of population growth in metropolitan America. At the heart of suburbia lie some of America's fastest-growing places, which Robert Lang and Meghan Zimmerman Gough call "growth counties" in chapter 3. These 124 counties together captured more than one-third of the nation's population growth over the five decades from 1950 to 2000. They are found within the urban core of rapidly changing Sun Belt metropolitan areas like Houston and

Phoenix, as well as at the exurban fringe of slower-growing Northern areas like Milwaukee and St. Louis. Depending on their location within the metropolis, growth counties and their residents share similar demographic, economic, and even attitudinal characteristics. Because of their fast growth, these areas will be the focus of local policy debates on development, transportation, and fiscal capacity for many years to come. Lang and Gough argue that growth counties can learn much from one another about the opportunities and challenges that growth presents.

Among the fastest-growing large and medium-sized municipalities are several that look more like suburbs than traditional cities. Robert Lang and Patrick Simmons examined these "boomburbs" in the first volume of this series, and Lang is back in chapter 4 of this volume to examine whether these places are still booming. His conclusion: most of the boomburbs continued to gain on traditional cities from 2000 to 2003, accounting for more than half of the population growth of cities in their size category. Growth in some of the older, denser, built-out suburbs—like Anaheim, California, and Tempe, Arizona—has stalled in recent years, however. As today's boomburbs become tomorrow's mature cities, Lang argues, they and their regions must confront issues related to planning, design, and use of natural resources that will determine their long-term sustainability.

METROPOLITAN DECENTRALIZATION AND RESIDENTIAL MOBILITY BRING SOCIAL CONSEQUENCES

Movement of the U.S. population into these new destinations represents more than a geographic phenomenon. As people change their residential locations, so too they change the social characteristics of their communities. The quality of schooling, employment options, and amenities available—even political viewpoints—may be shaped by the location of one's housing. The chapters in this section demonstrate that the continued spreading out of the American population has brought both gains and setbacks in the nation's social progress.

One promising story to emerge from Census 2000 concerned the decline in residential racial segregation over the 1990s, detailed in the first volume of this series. In chapter 5 of this volume, David Fasenfest, Jason Booza, and Kurt Metzger examine the flip side—racial integration in metropolitan America. Focusing on the nation's ten largest metropolitan areas, the authors examine changes over the 1990s in how people of different races organized themselves at the neighborhood level. The trend is unmistakable: the number of predominantly white neighborhoods declined dramatically as the number of mixed-race neighborhoods increased in most metropolitan areas. As a result, white and black Americans today live in more racially heterogeneous communities than in previous decades, signaling improvement in intergroup relations. At the same time, the authors find, fast-growing numbers of U.S. Hispanics and Asians are living in neighborhoods in which their group predominates. Fasenfest, Booza, and Metzger conclude that efforts to study and promote further racial integration in America should look beyond the traditional white-black divide.

What benefits might accrue from increased racial integration in metropolitan America? In chapter 6, Steven Raphael and Michael Stoll focus on one measure of progress: the physical distance between African Americans and jobs. Decades of research have pointed to the existence and negative consequences of a "spatial mismatch" between lower-income blacks, who until recently have lived overwhelmingly in central cities, and job opportunities, which have followed the U.S. population to the suburbs. Promisingly, Raphael and Stoll find that although blacks remain the group most spatially isolated from jobs, the spatial mismatch between them and jobs fell during the 1990s by a greater degree than the comparable measure for whites. Regional differences remain important, and the more residentially segregated metropolitan areas of the Northeast and Midwest exhibit a greater blacks-jobs mismatch than more integrated areas of the South and West. What is most revealing is that the movement of black households into areas nearer to jobs accounted for the entire decline in spatial mismatch. Jobs actually moved farther away from predominantly black neighborhoods, as employment locations continued to decentralize over the decade. Raphael and Stoll's findings suggest that continued efforts to promote residential mobility for black households may contribute to further employment gains for that group.

Americans' movements over the past few decades have produced less positive social outcomes, too. In chapter 7, Todd Swanstrom and colleagues find that among them was the increasing economic segregation of the population into high- and low-income communities. This sorting of households by income was especially pronounced in the 1980s but subsided somewhat in the 1990s. Yet the long term has produced wide and variable income gaps— not just between cities and suburbs but also among suburbs themselves. Fewer suburbs today have a middle-income profile; compared with the metropolitan norm, more and more suburbs, the authors find, look either rich or poor. Swanstrom and colleagues catalog the potential harmful effects of economic segregation in a system in which the quality of public services depends greatly on local fiscal capacity, and they call for a greater public policy focus on the needs of lower-income municipalities, wherever they exist.

One of the underlying causes of the widening economic gap between cities and suburbs lies in the imbalance between household and housing growth in metropolitan areas. Thomas Bier and Charlie Post examine the evidence in chapter 8 and find that metropolitan areas that built more housing than needed to accommodate household growth during the 1980s and 1990s—in effect creating a housing surplus—suffered from increased vacancy and abandonment in their central cities. As more new housing became available, often at the outer suburban fringe, the first housing to be abandoned typically lay within the central city and older suburbs. In the 1990s, for instance, the Pittsburgh region built three new houses for every household the region added, and partly as a consequence, the city of Pittsburgh lost households to its suburbs and saw its vacancy rate rise. Bier and Post show that on the other hand, in areas where household growth outpaced housing growth and where a significant percentage of new housing was located in the central city, city vacancies remained low. The authors describe several policy avenues that could put central cities and their suburbs on more even footing for development and ameliorate the negative consequences of metropolitan overbuilding for city neighborhoods.

NEW CLASSIFICATIONS REDEFINE THE LANDSCAPE—LITERALLY

Geography provides the lens through which this volume tracks the evolution of urban and suburban America. As people move within and across communities, they bring about change, in both their place of origin and their destination. Migration and its consequent growth alter the demographic, economic, and social characteristics of places. Eventually, those changes affect the geographic systems used to classify America itself. Towns expand to become cities, developing rural areas are annexed by nearby jurisdictions, and neighborhoods contract and merge with one another. Because of that, the nation's emerging growth centers have literally redefined the urban and suburban landscape.

With every decennial census (and sometimes between censuses, too) the Office of Management and Budget (OMB) joins forces with the Census Bureau to update metropolitan statistical areas, which are defined by their population and economic characteristics. These areas form the basis for research throughout the Redefining Urban and Suburban America series, as well as for public sector programs and business decisionmaking. Before Census 2000 was conducted, however, OMB and the bureau undertook a much more comprehensive review of how these areas were constructed and recommended significant changes to the classification system. Those changes were designed to reflect the growth of new communities and the increasing economic and social connections across regions. In June 2003, the agencies announced the new system. The last two chapters of this volume examine the system's major features and implications.

In chapter 9, William Frey and colleagues map the major changes embodied in the new system. The system establishes the metropolitan statistical area as the primary unit of analysis but offers researchers other options for how to view and measure change in their local areas. Frey and coauthors find that the majority of the nation's largest metropolitan areas underwent some change in territory and population in transitioning to the new system. The continued suburbanization of America in the 1990s and the movement of population even farther away from the urban core meant that most metro areas expanded in size. The titles of several areas also changed, reflecting the ascendance of boomburbs like Naperville, Illinois (outside Chicago); Scottsdale, Arizona (outside Phoenix); and Fremont, California (outside San Francisco). Perhaps the most significant change involved the naming of more than 500 new "micropolitan areas," which bridge the gap between rural and metropolitan areas. The authors explain how the extensive changes to metropolitan areas and the development of the new micropolitan concept might be expected to affect federal policy, public and private sector research, and popular notions of the places in which we live.

Because micropolitan areas represent the new system's landmark innovation, they have attracted a great deal of attention in the popular press, and the research community has focused on analyzing just what these places represent. In chapter 10, Robert Lang and Dawn Dhavale disentangle the very different types of places subsumed in micropolitan America by their size, growth, and function. They point out that with the advent of micropolitan areas, truly rural areas cover less than half of the continental United States for the first time. While as a universe micropolitan areas are growing somewhat more slowly than the nation as a whole, they vary quite dramatically on size and growth factors. Many of the fastest growing are peripheral outposts of metropolitan development, or they are rich in natural (Silverthorne, Colorado) or man-made (Branson, Missouri) amenities. The fastest-shrinking micropolitan areas—"Dwindlevilles" in Lang and Dhavale's terminology—are typically highly remote areas surrounding big towns and small cities in the South and Midwest. Lang and Dhavale conclude that micropolitan areas might use their new "quasi-metropolitan" status as a tool for economic development or to organize and lobby federal and state governments for program changes that recognize their newly elevated status.

SUMMARY

Although it is now five years on from Census 2000, the findings discussed in this volume highlight abiding long-term trends regarding where Americans live, whom they live with, and what the consequences are for public policy and civil society. The authors demonstrate that places can shape Americans' exposure to racial and ethnic diversity, different groups' access to employment, and the quality of local public services. As growth centers shift, the response of private investment and public resource allocation affects the economic and social trajectory of local communities. Leaders in the political, civic, and business communities therefore will benefit from greater understanding of how, both literally and figuratively, America continues to redefine its metropolitan landscape. This volume presents a compelling field guide to that ongoing transformation.

1

Demographic Change in Medium-Sized Cities

JENNIFER S. VEY AND BENJAMIN FORMAN

The 1990s brought dramatic changes to the metropolitan landscape. For a number of central cities in the United States, the strong economy, coupled with high levels of immigration, led to a resurgence in population and stable fiscal conditions. Other cities, however, were unable to stem the flow of jobs and residents to the suburbs. Research by the Brookings Institution on the 100 largest cities revealed a significant increase in the number of Hispanics living in center cities, a concomitant loss of white residents, and a dominant pattern of decentralization.[1]

A more complete understanding of urban growth dynamics during the 1990s requires a look beyond the nation's most populous cities. Medium-sized cities that serve as "satellites" to larger central cities are home to an increasing fraction of the country's metropolitan population, particularly in the West. More traditional medium-sized central cities have retained their significance in most regional economies, and many have become important immigrant magnets. This chapter examines demographic trends in these two types of medium-sized cities and reveals that they are experiencing significant change: some cities are losing population, whereas others are coping with extreme growth; nearly all are more racially and ethnically diverse than a decade ago. The competitiveness of medium-sized cities hinges on how well they are able to confront the challenges and exploit the opportunities that these changes present.

---

1. Berube (2003a, 2003b).

METHODOLOGY

This chapter uses data from the 2000 Census Summary File 1 to describe population trends in the 1990s for medium-sized cities in the United States. The analysis here follows that in other studies by the Brookings Institution of large U.S. cities, defined as those ranked from 1 through 100 in terms of population.

Definition and Classification of Medium-Sized Cities

We define "medium-sized" cities as those ranked from 101 through 200 on the basis of their population in 1990. As in the other analyses, the cities are measured by their 1990 populations (rather than their 2000 populations) to avoid biasing the analysis toward fast-growing cities. The populations of these medium-sized cities ranged from 98,000 (Columbia, South Carolina) to 170,000 (Worcester, Massachusetts) in 1990. Their combined population in 2000 was 13.8 million.

The medium-sized cities in this analysis are categorized by census region (Northeast, Midwest, South, and West). The distribution of the cities studied here does not precisely match the distribution of the population at large, because these places are significantly overrepresented in the West, which had 21 percent of the population in 1990 but 38 percent of medium-sized cities. California, in particular, has a large number of medium-sized cities; the state is home to twenty-eight, half of which are located in just three metropolitan areas (Los Angeles, Riverside–San Bernardino, and Orange County).

Not all of the cities included in our group conform to traditional notions of what constitutes a "city." "Boomburbs" that emerged as cities in the late twentieth century—places such as Santa Clarita, California, and Overland Park, Kansas—are now the size of older core cities such as Ann Arbor, Michigan, and Providence, Rhode Island.[2] These rapidly growing cities are typically satellites of larger central cities. Their predominance in the West is due in part to the pervasiveness of master-planned community development and the benefits of forming geographically large municipalities around water districts.[3] To disaggregate the experience of satellite cities from traditional central cities we have classified our group as follows:

—*Central cities* are the largest cities in their metropolitan areas. Fifty-four of the cities studied fall into this category. All but one of the Northeastern

2. Used here, the word "boomburbs" refers generally to large, rapidly growing suburban cities that are not the largest city in their metropolitan area. See Lang and. Simmons (2003).

3. Lang and Simmons (2003).

cities are central cities. A large proportion of cities in the Midwest and South are also included in this category: fourteen of twenty and fifteen of twenty-seven, respectively.

—*Satellite cities* are not the largest cities in the metropolitan areas of which they are a part. Although satellite cities are particularly prevalent in the West, they are located in every region (although the Northeast only has one—Elizabeth, New Jersey).[4] Forty-six cities fall in this category.

Analysis of Racial and Ethnic Change

Following conventional practice for analyzing trends in U.S. population diversity, this chapter separates the populations of the medium-sized cities into racial and ethnic categories.[5] The Census Bureau considers race and Hispanic origin to be distinct concepts. On the Census 2000 short form, all respondents were asked whether they were Spanish, Hispanic, or Latino, and then asked to report the race or races they considered themselves to be. All individuals who identified themselves as Spanish/Hispanic/Latino are, for the purposes of this survey, considered to be "Hispanic," regardless of their race. Other race categories discussed in this survey—white, black, Asian/Native Hawaiian/Pacific Islander, American Indian, and "some other race"—include only those individuals who did not identify themselves as Hispanic.[6]

For the first time, the 2000 census gave respondents the opportunity to classify themselves as being of more than one race. This new option potentially complicates efforts to compare 2000 census population counts by race/ethnicity to 1990 counts at the city level. In this chapter, the race categories represent individuals who classified themselves as that race only; individuals who classified themselves as being of more than one race are grouped in a "multiracial" category. Some unknown share of a given city's residents in 1990 could have reclassified themselves as multiracial in 2000; this may introduce a degree of error into the calculation of changes in the population of that city's other race/ethnicity groups. Census 2000 results, however, indicate that the degree of error is likely small.

4. The average density of the forty-six satellite cities (3,285 persons per square mile) is considerably higher than the average density of the fifty-four central cities (2,261 persons per square mile). This is driven to a large degree by the high densities of satellite cities located in the Los Angeles metropolitan area. Inglewood, California, for example, had a density of 12,317 persons per square mile in 2000. This was far higher than the densities of older, medium-sized New England central cities in this analysis.

5. U.S. Census Bureau (2001).

6. Census 2000 established separate Asian and Native Hawaiian/Pacific Islander race categories. In 1990, these were part of the same Asian/Pacific Islander category. This chapter recombines the categories for ease of comparison with 1990 statistics.

FINDINGS

This analysis of medium-sized city population change in the 1990s reveals that growth accelerated from that in the 1980s but that significant differences separated regions of the United States, central and satellite cities, and racial and ethnic contributions to growth.

Medium-Sized Cities Grew Faster than Largest Cities in the 1990s

Population growth over the last decade brought hopeful signs of urban recovery. Medium-sized cities grew by 12.9 percent between 1990 and 2000, outpacing the 100 largest cities by 4 percentage points.

Only twelve medium-sized cities lost population during the 1990s, down from twenty in the 1980s (figure 1-1). Six cities—South Bend, Indiana; Knoxville, Tennessee; Chattanooga, Tennessee; Fort Lauderdale, Florida; Columbia, South Carolina; and Pueblo, Colorado—experienced a true "turnaround," losing population in the 1980s but gaining population in the 1990s. An additional four cities—Cedar Rapids, Iowa; Hollywood, Florida; Pasadena, Texas; and Salt Lake City, Utah—experienced flat growth in the 1980s but grew over 10 percent during the last decade. The "strong growth" category (10 to 20 percent growth) increased from eleven cities in the 1980s to twenty-three cities in the 1990s. Population growth was highly uneven, however. A quarter of the medium-sized cities analyzed either lost population or did not grow at all during the 1990s. For a number of older industrial cities, such as Flint, Michigan, and Syracuse, New York, the 1990s was another decade of serious population loss.[7] Several cities that were growing in the 1980s—Springfield, Massachusetts, and Hartford, New Haven, and Waterbury, Connecticut—lost population in the 1990s (see table 1A-1 in appendix).

At the other extreme were cities that experienced explosive growth. Table 1-1 shows that over one-third of the seventy-five growing cities increased their populations by more than 20 percent. Plano, Texas, led this group of boomers. With the addition of 93,000 residents, Plano's 1990 population swelled by 73 percent.

Significant Regional Disparities Marked Medium-Sized City Growth

Regional growth patterns explain much of the unevenness in growth rates among medium-sized cities. The South and West have been the fastest-

---

7. Flint posted four consecutive decades of population loss, losing 37 percent of its residents since its peak at 197,000 in 1960. After five consecutive decades of population decline, Syracuse lost 28 percent of its residents from its peak population of 206,000 in 1950.

FIGURE 1-1. **Population Growth in Medium-Sized Cities, 1980s and 1990s**

Number of cities

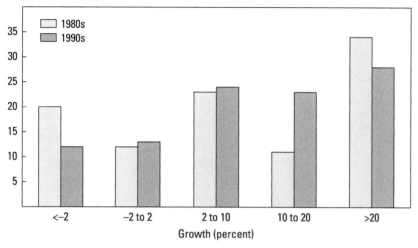

Growth (percent)

Source: Authors' calculations based on data from the 1980 and 1990 Census STF1 and the 2000 Census SF1.

growing regions of the country for several decades.[8] In the 1990s, these regions grew by 17.3 percent and 19.6 percent, respectively. Of the twenty-eight medium-sized cities that grew by more than 20 percent during the 1990s, twenty-six were located in these two regions. Figure 1-2 depicts the growth of medium-sized cities by region relative to the growth of each region overall. This figure shows that medium-sized cities in the South and West grew at almost exactly the same rates as their regions.

Conversely, most declining medium-sized cities were located in the Northeast and Midwest, the country's slowest-growing regions. Unlike the medium-sized cities located in the Sun Belt, however, cities in the Northeast and Midwest grew more slowly than their respective regions. The Northeast region grew by 5 percent; Northeastern medium-sized cities did not grow at all. In the Midwest, medium-sized cities grew by a little more than half the regional growth rate. This trend points to a pattern of metropolitan decentralization, discussed in more detail below.

Figure 1-3 depicts the growth of medium-sized cities by region for both the 1980s and the 1990s. The bars on the left show that, in the aggregate,

8. Perry and Mackun (2001).

TABLE 1-1. **Population Change in Medium-Sized Cities, 1990–2000**

Declining[a]	No growth[b]	Moderate growth[c]	Strong growth[d]	Rapid growth[e]
Hartford, CT	Kansas City, KS	Fort Lauderdale, FL	Clearwater, FL	Tallahassee, FL
Gary, IN	Waterbury, CT	Chattanooga, TN	Amarillo, TX	Eugene, OR
Flint, MI	Bridgeport, CT	Topeka, KS	Fullerton, CA	Mesquite, TX
Syracuse, NY	Huntsville, AL	South Bend, IN	Cedar Rapids, IA	Escondido, CA
Lansing, MI	Peoria, IL	Inglewood, CA	Simi Valley, CA	Sioux Falls, SD
New Haven, CT	Beaumont, TX	Pueblo, CO	Tempe, AZ	Irving, TX
Erie, PA	Livonia, MI	Torrance, CA	Thousand Oaks, CA	Oceanside, CA
Warren, MI	Berkeley, CA	Ann Arbor, MI	Sunnyvale, CA	Hayward, CA
Savannah, GA	Independence, MO	Knoxville, TN	Orlando, FL	Rancho Cucamonga, CA
Evansville, IN	Allentown, PA	Sterling Heights, MI	San Bernardino, CA	Salem, OR
Portsmouth, VA	Lowell, MA	Paterson, NJ	Pomona, CA	Grand Prairie, TX
Springfield, MA	Worcester, MA	Springfield, IL	Salt Lake City, UT	Chula Vista, CA
	Pasadena, CA	Vallejo, CA	Lakewood, CO	Winston-Salem, NC
		Manchester, NH	Hollywood, FL	Irvine, CA
		Rockford, IL	Modesto, CA	Santa Rosa, CA
		Springfield, MO	Alexandria, VA	Chesapeake, VA
		Providence, RI	Garden Grove, CA	Overland Park, KS
		Stamford, CT	Orange, CA	Reno, NV
		Abilene, TX	Columbia, SC	Santa Clarita, CA
		El Monte, CA	Ontario, CA	Durham, NC
		Concord, CA	Pasadena, TX	Salinas, CA
		Hampton, VA	Oxnard, CA	Brownsville, TX
		Elizabeth, NJ	Moreno Valley, CA	Aurora, IL
		Waco, TX		Laredo, TX
				Glendale, AZ
				Boise City, ID
				Scottsdale, AZ
				Plano, TX

Source: Authors' calculations based on data from 1990 Census STF1 and Census 2000 SF1.
a. < –2 percent growth.
b. –2 to 2 percent growth.
c. 2 to 10 percent growth.
d. 10 to 20 percent growth.
e. > 20 percent growth.

growth in the 1990s was similar to that in the 1980s. However, a look at each region reveals a more nuanced picture:

—*West.* Vigorous growth among medium-sized cities in the West (20 percent) continued throughout the 1990s, down slightly from their booming 28 percent growth rate in the 1980s. None of the medium-sized cities located in the West lost population during the 1990s. Growth rates varied, however: Berkeley, California, experienced no growth in the 1990s, whereas Scottsdale, Arizona, grew by 56 percent.

—*South.* Medium-sized cities in the South experienced stronger growth in the 1990s than in the 1980s: 17 percent versus 13 percent. Only two of the twenty-seven Southern cities—Savannah, Georgia, and Portsmouth,

FIGURE 1-2. Population Change in Medium-Sized Cities and Their Regions, 1990–2000

Percent

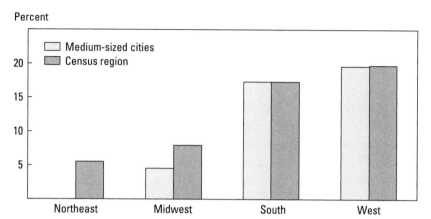

Source: Authors' calculations based on data from the 1990 Census STF1 and the 2000 Census SF1.

FIGURE 1-3. Population Change in Medium-Sized Cities, by Region, 1980s and 1990s

Percent

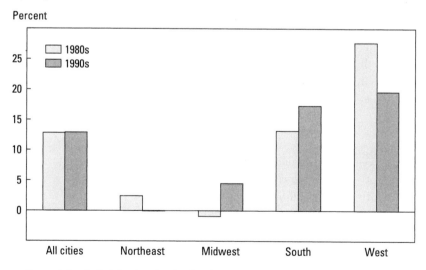

Source: Authors' calculations based on data from the 1980 and 1990 Census STF1 and the 2000 Census SF1.

Virginia—lost population in the 1990s, down from six in the 1980s. Ten cities saw growth rates over 20 percent.

—*Midwest.* Overall, medium-sized Midwestern cities saw an upturn in population during the 1990s, growing on average by 4.5 percent. This moderate growth was a welcome shift from the 1 percent population loss these cities endured during the 1980s. Eight of the twenty medium-sized Midwestern cities lost population or did not grow at all during the 1990s. In sharp contrast to these struggling cities, three medium-sized Midwestern cities grew by more than 20 percent: Overland Park, Kansas, Sioux Falls, South Dakota, and Aurora, Illinois.

—*Northeast.* Signs of recovery remained elusive for much of the Northeast. Cities in this region grew an average of 2.5 percent in the 1980s but experienced no growth during the 1990s. Nearly half of the fifteen medium-sized cities in this region lost population. Only a few medium-sized cities in the Northeast grew, including Stamford, Connecticut (8 percent) and Elizabeth, New Jersey (10 percent).

What drives the differences in growth rates among medium-sized cities both within and between regions? We analyzed a number of variables to see how the attributes of a particular city influenced the growth of that city during the 1990s. Demographic analysis of medium-sized cities shows that cities with a large percentage of foreign-born residents in 1990 tended to grow faster during the decade than cities with mostly native-born residents. Cities that had a high proportion of residents with bachelor's degrees in 1990 also grew faster over the decade. As one might expect, places with aging populations generally grew more slowly during the 1990s.[9]

Growth patterns also appear to influence growth rates. Medium-sized satellite cities, for example, showed a significant growth advantage during the 1990s. They grew 18 percent overall, twice as fast as medium-sized

---

9. These findings were obtained using multiple regression. Our basic model is as follows: $Growth_i = 6.70 - 1.41 * Density_i + 0.45 * ForeignBorn_i - 0.73 * Over65_i + 0.59 * Degree_i + 10.68 * Annex_i + 7.09 * Satellite_i$. *Growth* equals the city's population change expressed in percentage points. *Density* refers to the population density of city i in 2000 divided by 1,000; *ForeignBorn* refers to the percentage of the population in city i that was foreign-born in 1990; *Over65* refers to the percentage of the population of city i that was over age sixty-five in 1990; *Degree* refers to the percentage of persons over age twenty-five in city i holding a bachelor's degree; *Annex* is a variable that refers to whether city i increased its land by more than 5 percent over the decade by annexation; *Satellite* is a variable that refers to whether city i is the largest city in its metropolitan area. All of the coefficients in this formula were statistically significant. The model was able to example 37 percent of the overall variation in growth rate in our sample of 100 medium-sized cities.

FIGURE 1-4. Population Change in Medium-Sized Central Cities and Satellite Cities, by Region, 1990–2000

Percent

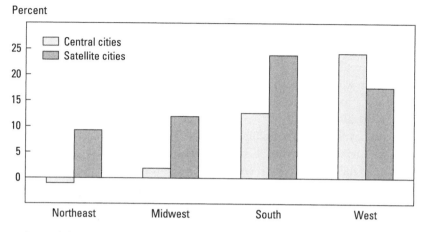

Source: Authors' calculations based on data from 1990 Census STF1 and Census 2000 SF1.

"central cities." There was some regional variation in this trend. Figure 1-4 illustrates that satellite cities in the West actually grew more slowly than Western central cities. However, in both the Midwest and the South, satellites grew considerably faster than the medium-sized central cities. This trend may reflect the sprawling growth patterns of these areas.[10]

Annexation of land also exhibited a significant relationship to medium-sized growth in the 1990s. All other factors being equal, a city that annexed land in the 1990s was considerably more likely to gain population. In every region except the Northeast, medium-sized cities annexed a significant amount of land during the 1990s; the land area encompassed by medium-sized cities as a group increased by 11 percent. Central cities annexed more land than did satellite cities, 13 percent versus 8 percent. The median increase in land area was highest in cities in the South (5 percent), followed by those in the Midwest (1.1 percent) and the West (0.7 percent).[11]

10. Fulton and others (2001). According to this study, between 1982 and 1997 metropolitan areas in the Midwest grew by 7 percent; at the same time, urbanized land area in the Midwest increased by more than 32 percent. This type of decentralization was also consistent with growth patterns in the South, where metropolitan population grew by 22 percent, whereas urbanized land area increased by 60 percent.

11. Annexation was determined by comparing land area values from 1990 census geography files to the land area values provided in 2000 census geography files.

Satellite City Growth Outpaced Metropolitan Area Growth While Central Cities Lagged

On average, medium-sized central cities grew by 9 percent during the 1990s, whereas their metropolitan areas grew by 14 percent. Figure 1-5 shows the relationship between the growth of central cities and their metropolitan areas for each region. The growth gap was particularly apparent in the Northeast, where the population of medium-sized central cities declined by 1 percent, but their metropolitan areas grew an average of more than 4 percent. Central cities in the Midwest grew by 1.5 percent, but they too were outpaced by their metropolitan areas, which grew by 10 percent. Growth in the South was stronger overall, but here central cities added residents at half the rate of their metropolitan areas (12.4 percent versus 23.1 percent). This pattern of decentralization is consistent with the growth patterns observed in the metropolitan areas where the largest cities were located.[12]

Western central cities were an exception to this finding. As a group, they grew faster than their metropolitan areas. The most likely explanation is that many of these cities are relatively young and have grown in size through annexation. Irvine, California, for example, had less than 65,000 residents when it was incorporated in 1980; since that time, it has more than doubled its population, and its land area increased by almost 10 percent during the 1990s. In fact, Western central cities were most aggressive in terms of adding land area in the 1990s. The median Western central city increased its land area by 4.2 percent; the median Western satellite city added only 0.5 percent.

Nevertheless, in every region of the country satellite cities grew at a faster rate than their metropolitan areas (19 percent versus 17 percent overall). Satellites also grew at more than double the rate of their principal cities (9 percent). The relationship between the growth of satellite cities and their metropolitan areas in each census region is displayed in figure 1-6. In the Midwest, satellite cities grew by an average of 12 percent, whereas their metropolitan areas grew by 9 percent. Southern satellite cities grew by 24 percent, outpacing their metropolitan areas, which grew by 22 percent. In the West, satellites grew by 18 percent, a shade faster than their metropolitan areas (17 percent). Although we have not analyzed migration trends in these metropolitan areas, these growth patterns indicate that satellite cities may be absorbing population from their core cities. New residents of these metropolitan areas may also be choosing to live in these satellite cities over other parts of the region.

12. Berube (2003a).

FIGURE 1-5. Population Change in Medium-Sized Central Cities and Their Metropolitan Areas, 1990–2000

Percent

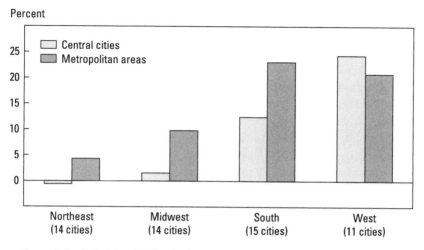

Northeast (14 cities)   Midwest (14 cities)   South (15 cities)   West (11 cities)

Source: Authors' calculations based on data from the 1990 Census STF1 and the 2000 Census SF1.

FIGURE 1-6. Population Change in Medium-Sized Satellite Cities and Their Metropolitan Areas, 1990–2000

Percent

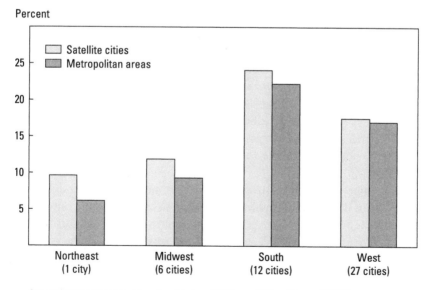

Northeast (1 city)   Midwest (6 cities)   South (12 cities)   West (27 cities)

Source: Authors' calculations based on data from 1990 Census STF1 and Census 2000 SF1.

Asians and Hispanics Fueled Growth in Medium-Sized Cities

Both the Asian and the Hispanic populations of medium-sized cities more than doubled during the last decade (table 1-2). This rapid growth compensated for the 5 percent decline in the non-Hispanic white population. As the pie charts in figure 1-7 illustrate, these trends brought about a significant change in the racial and ethnic composition of medium-sized cities:

—*White Population.* Despite positive growth rates overall, more than two-thirds of medium-sized cities lost non-Hispanic whites during the 1990s. Although the number of white residents living in medium-sized cities declined in all regions, the white population of medium-sized cities in the Northeast experienced the most serious loss (21 percent). Southern medium-sized cities suffered the least; as a group, their white population decreased by just over 1 percent. Cities that were able to attract white residents generally had very high rates of growth overall. The average growth rate across the seventeen cities that gained white residents was 37 percent.

Non-Hispanic white residents remained the majority in medium-sized cities in all regions but the Northeast. The proportion of white residents dropped dramatically in Northeastern cities, from 63 percent in 1990 to 50 percent in 2000 (table 1-3). Medium-sized cities in the Midwest continue to have the highest proportion of white residents, 73 percent.

—*Black Population.* The percentage of black residents in medium-sized cities increased by 14 percent overall. Cities in the South saw the largest increase, at 22 percent. Despite this increase, from 1990 to 2000 the share of black residents in medium-sized cities remained at 14 percent. Southern cities continue to be home to the largest proportion of blacks (36 percent).

—*Hispanic Population.* Every medium-sized city but two—Gary, Indiana, and Flint, Michigan—saw an increase in its Hispanic population. On average, medium-sized cities experienced higher Hispanic growth rates (67 percent) than the 100 largest cities (43 percent). In medium-sized cities, nearly 70 percent of the new net residents between 1990 and 2000 were Hispanic.

A number of medium-sized cities that are not typically thought of as immigrant destinations had large increases in their Hispanic population during the 1990s. In North Carolina, Winston-Salem and Durham are notable for their remarkable growth from a very small base. In Winston-Salem, for example, the addition of 15,000 Hispanic residents during the decade increased their share of the population to almost 9 percent, up from 1 percent in 1990. Durham's Hispanic population was only 1,700 in 1990; by the end of the decade, the city had more than 16,000 Hispanic residents.

TABLE 1-2. Population Growth in Medium-Sized Cities, by Region and Race/Ethnicity, 1990–2000

Percent

Region	Total	White	Hispanic	Black	Asian
All cities	13	−5	67	14	58
Northeast	0	−21	51	5	53
Midwest	5	−4	89	8	80
South	17	−1	79	22	99
West	20	−2	64	13	51

Source: Authors' calculations based on data from 1990 Census STF1 and Census 2000 SF1.

FIGURE 1-7. Racial and Ethnic Composition of Medium-Sized Cities, 1990 and 2000

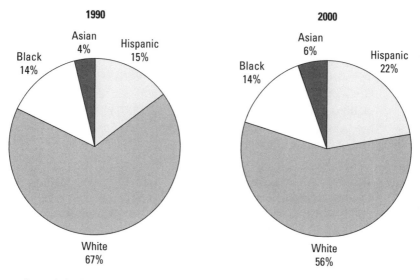

Source: Authors' calculations based on data from the 1990 Census STF1 and the 2000 Census SF1.

TABLE 1-3. Racial/Ethnic Composition of Medium-Sized Cities, by Region, 1990 and 2000

Percent

Region	White 1990	White 2000	Hispanic 1990	Hispanic 2000	Black 1990	Black 2000	Asian 1990	Asian 2000
Northeast	63	50	16	24	17	18	2	4
Midwest	79	73	4	6	15	16	1	2
South	59	52	1	9	39	36	1	1
West	64	52	21	29	6	6	8	9
All cities[a]	67	56	15	22	14	14	4	6

Source: Authors' calculations based on data from 1990 Census STF1 and Census 2000 SF1.
a. $N = 100$.

Providence, Rhode Island, and Allentown, Pennsylvania, were two Northern cities that saw significant growth in their Hispanic populations. In 1990, Providence was less than 15 percent Hispanic; by 2000, the share of Hispanic residents had more than doubled. Allentown's population increased by 1 percent during the 1990s, but were it not for a 120 percent increase in its Hispanic population, the city would have lost 12 percent of its overall population. Kansas City, Kansas, and Salem, Oregon, were also among the medium-sized cities that emerged as magnets for Latino residents, increasing their Hispanic populations from 10,000 to 25,000 and from 6,000 to 20,000, respectively.

The proportion of Hispanic residents in medium-sized cities increased in all regions. Hispanic residents now make up, on average, approximately one-quarter of all residents in Northeastern medium-sized cities (up from 16 percent in 1990) and nearly 30 percent of residents in Western medium-sized cities.

—Asian Population. All but three medium-sized cities—Gary, Indiana, Flint, Michigan, and Inglewood, California—had gains in their Asian populations. The Asian population in these cities grew by 58 percent, outpacing the 38 percent increase in the 100 largest cities. Asians now make up 6 percent of medium-sized city populations, up from 4 percent in 1990.

The two bars in figure 1-8 contrast the racial and ethnic composition of medium-sized cities with that of the top 100 cities. Medium-sized cities have become nearly as diverse as the top 100 cities in terms of the proportion of residents that are Hispanic or Asian. They are, however, less diverse overall. In comparison to the largest cities, non-Hispanic whites still constitute the majority (56 percent) of residents in medium-sized cities. Medium-sized cities are also home to proportionately fewer black residents than the top 100 cities (15 percent versus 24 percent respectively).

CONCLUSION

Evidence from Census 2000 points to uneven patterns of growth and decline in medium-sized cities in the 1990s, with some cities losing residents, others posting moderate growth, and a number seeing rapid population increases. Medium-sized cities throughout the country also experienced shifts in their racial and ethnic composition. The individual challenges that these cities will face in the years ahead will depend largely on these demographic trends. Possible implications for medium-sized cities:

—Managing population loss. Cities such as Hartford, Connecticut, which lost 54,000 residents between 1950 and 2000, face an uphill battle

FIGURE 1-8. Racial and Ethnic Composition of Large and Medium-Sized Cities, 2000

Percent

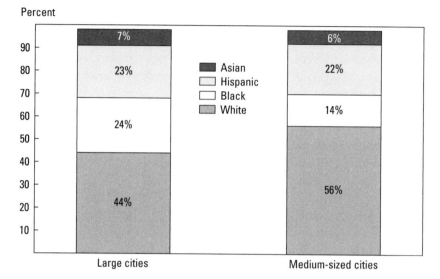

Source: Authors' calculations based on data from 1990 Census STF1 and Census 2000 SF1.

against continued disinvestment and decline. The ability of these cities to stem the flow of businesses and residents to the suburbs depends on their ability to create viable markets in which a local economy can thrive. Abandoned housing and vacant lots, visible evidence of population loss and decreased density, have become a persistent problem in declining cities. Turning these liabilities into opportunities for growth and development—through land acquisition and assembly—should be a high priority for policymakers in Hartford and other cities facing severe population loss.

—*Managing rapid growth.* A large number of medium-sized cities in the South and West are dealing with explosive growth. In Glendale, Arizona, for instance, there are now 16,000 more children under age 18 than there were in 1990. Rapid growth presents immediate infrastructure demands—schools, roads, utilities—that present physical, as well as fiscal, challenges for municipal governments. This will require urban leaders to look for equitable solutions that meet short-term needs without comprising the long-term health of the city.

—*Responding to increasingly diverse populations.* The demographic composition of many medium-sized cities has changed markedly, with growing numbers of Hispanic and Asian residents and shrinking numbers of whites. This will require cities to understand the household structures of new populations, many of which may be younger and of larger size, and develop strategies that respond to changing needs. City leaders must work to provide jobs, housing, schools, services, and amenities that are appropriate and attractive to families and individuals of varying race and ethnicity.

—*Promoting regional cooperation.* Medium-sized cities in all areas of the country cannot operate in isolation from their metropolitan areas. Rapidly growing satellite cities in the West and South, for example, must work cooperatively with the other cities in their metropolitan areas to cope with issues such as traffic congestion and affordable housing. For those cities in the Northeast and Midwest that continue to lose population, forming coalitions with older suburban areas to stimulate reinvestment and economic development is critical.

T A B L E   1 A - 1 . **Population Change in Medium-Sized Cities, 1980–2000**

				Change (percent)		
Region and City	*1980*	*1990*	*2000*	*1980–90*	*1990–2000*	*1980–2000*
Northeast						
Central cities						
Manchester, NH	90,936	99,567	107,006	9.5	7.5	17.7
Stamford, CT	102,000	108,056	117,083	5.9	8.4	14.8
Lowell, MA	92,418	103,439	105,167	11.9	1.7	13.8
Providence, RI	157,000	160,728	173,618	2.4	8.0	10.6
Paterson, NJ	138,000	140,891	149,222	2.1	5.9	8.1
Worcester, MA	162,000	169,759	172,648	4.8	1.7	6.6
Waterbury, CT	103,000	108,961	107,271	5.8	−1.6	4.1
Allentown, PA	104,000	105,090	106,632	1.0	1.5	2.5
Springfield, MA	152,000	156,983	152,082	3.3	−3.1	0.1
New Haven, CT	126,000	130,474	123,626	3.6	−5.2	−1.9
Bridgeport, CT	143,000	141,686	139,529	−0.9	−1.5	−2.4
Hartford, CT	136,000	139,739	121,578	2.7	−13.0	−10.6
Erie, PA	119,000	108,718	103,717	−8.6	−4.6	−12.8
Syracuse, NY	170,000	163,860	147,306	−3.6	−10.1	−13.3
	1,795,354	**1,837,951**	**1,826,485**	**2.4**	**−0.6**	**1.7**
Satellite cities						
Elizabeth, NJ	106,000	110,002	120,568	3.8	9.6	13.7
Subtotal	**1,901,354**	**1,947,953**	**1,947,053**	**2.5**	**0.0**	**2.4**
Midwest						
Central cities						
Sioux Falls, SD	86,332	100,814	123,975	16.8	23.0	43.6
Springfield, MO	133,000	140,494	151,580	5.6	7.9	14.0
Springfield, IL	100,033	105,227	111,454	5.2	5.9	11.4
Cedar Rapids, IA	110,000	108,751	120,758	−1.1	11.0	9.8
Rockford, IL	140,000	139,426	150,115	−0.4	7.7	7.2
Ann Arbor, MI	108,000	109,592	114,024	1.5	4.0	5.6
Topeka, KS	119,000	119,883	122,377	0.7	2.1	2.8
South Bend, IN	109,727	105,511	107,789	−3.8	2.2	−1.8
Evansville, IN	130,000	126,272	121,582	−2.9	−3.7	−6.5

(*continued*)

TABLE 1A-1. **Population Change in Medium-Sized Cities, 1980–2000 (*continued*)**

Region and City	1980	1990	2000	1980–90	1990–2000	1980–2000
				Change (percent)		
Lansing, MI	130,000	127,321	119,128	−2.1	−6.4	−8.4
Kansas City, KS	161,000	149,767	146,866	−7.0	−1.9	−8.8
Peoria, IL	124,000	113,504	112,936	−8.5	−0.5	−8.9
Flint, MI	160,000	140,761	124,943	−12.0	−11.2	−21.9
Gary, IN	152,000	116,646	102,746	−23.3	−11.9	−32.4
	1,763,092	**1,703,969**	**1,730,273**	**−3.4**	**1.5**	**−1.9**
Satellite cities						
Overland Park, KS	82,000	111,790	149,080	36.3	33.4	81.8
Aurora, IL	81,293	99,581	142,990	22.5	43.6	75.9
Sterling Heights, MI	109,000	117,810	124,471	8.1	5.7	14.2
Independence, MO	112,000	112,301	113,288	0.3	0.9	1.2
Livonia, MI	105,000	100,850	100,545	−4.0	−0.3	−4.2
Warren, MI	161,000	144,864	138,247	−10.0	−4.6	−14.1
	650,293	**687,196**	**768,621**	**5.7**	**11.8**	**18.2**
Subtotal	**2,413,385**	**2,391,165**	**2,498,894**	**−0.9**	**4.5**	**3.5**
South						
Central cities						
Laredo, TX	91,000	122,899	176,576	35.1	43.7	94.0
Tallahassee, FL	82,000	124,773	150,624	52.2	20.7	83.7
Chesapeake, VA	114,000	151,976	199,184	33.3	31.1	74.7
Brownsville, TX	85,000	98,962	139,722	16.4	41.2	64.4
Orlando, FL	128,000	164,693	185,951	28.7	12.9	45.3
Abilene, TX	98,000	106,654	115,930	8.8	8.7	18.3
Amarillo, TX	149,000	157,615	173,627	5.8	10.2	16.5
Columbia, SC	101,202	98,052	116,278	−3.1	18.6	14.9
Waco, TX	101,000	103,590	113,726	2.6	9.8	12.6
Huntsville, AL	143,000	159,789	158,216	11.7	−1.0	10.6
Fort Lauderdale, FL	153,000	149,377	152,397	−2.4	2.0	−0.4
Knoxville, TN	175,000	165,121	173,890	−5.6	5.3	−0.6
Beaumont, TX	118,000	114,323	113,866	−3.1	−0.4	−3.5
Savannah, GA	142,000	137,560	131,510	−3.1	−4.4	−7.4
Chattanooga, TN	170,000	152,466	155,554	−10.3	2.0	−8.5
	1,850,202	**2,007,850**	**2,257,051**	**8.5**	**12.4**	**22.0**
Satellite cities						
Plano, TX	72,000	128,713	222,030	78.8	72.5	208.4
Mesquite, TX	67,053	101,484	124,523	51.3	22.7	85.7
Durham, NC	101,000	136,611	187,035	35.3	36.9	85.2
Grand Prairie, TX	71,462	99,616	127,427	39.4	27.9	78.3
Irving, TX	110,000	155,037	191,615	40.9	23.6	74.2
Winston-Salem, NC	132,000	143,485	185,776	8.7	29.5	40.7
Clearwater, FL	85,170	98,784	108,787	16.0	10.1	27.7
Alexandria, VA	103,217	111,183	128,283	7.7	15.4	24.3
Pasadena, TX	118,000	119,363	141,674	1.2	18.7	20.1
Hampton, VA	123,000	133,793	146,437	8.8	9.5	19.1
Hollywood, FL	121,000	121,697	139,357	0.6	14.5	15.2
Portsmouth, VA	105,000	103,907	100,565	−1.0	−3.2	−4.2
	1,208,902	**1,453,673**	**1,803,509**	**20.2**	**24.1**	**49.2**
Subtotal	**3,059,104**	**3,461,523**	**4,060,560**	**13.2**	**17.3**	**32.7**

(*continued*)

TABLE 1A-1. Population Change in Medium-Sized Cities, 1980–2000 (*continued*)

Region and City	1980	1990	2000	Change (percent) 1980–90	Change (percent) 1990–2000	Change (percent) 1980–2000
West						
Central cities						
Irvine, CA	62,000	110,330	143,072	78.0	29.7	130.8
Salinas, CA	80,000	108,777	151,060	36.0	38.9	88.8
Boise City, ID	102,000	125,738	185,787	23.3	47.8	82.1
Reno, NV	101,000	133,850	180,480	32.5	34.8	78.7
Santa Rosa, CA	83,000	113,313	147,595	36.5	30.3	77.8
Modesto, CA	107,000	164,730	188,856	54.0	14.6	76.5
Salem, OR	89,233	107,786	136,924	20.8	27.0	53.4
Vallejo, CA	80,303	109,199	116,760	36.0	6.9	45.4
Eugene, OR	106,000	112,669	137,893	6.3	22.4	30.1
Salt Lake City, UT	163,000	159,936	181,743	−1.9	13.6	11.5
Pueblo, CO	102,000	98,640	102,121	−3.3	3.5	0.1
	1,075,536	**1,344,968**	**1,672,291**	**25.1**	**24.3**	**55.5**
Satellite cities						
Rancho Cucamonga, CA	55,250	101,409	127,743	83.5	26.0	131.2
Scottsdale, AZ	89,000	130,069	202,705	46.1	55.8	127.8
Glendale, AZ	97,000	148,134	218,812	52.7	47.7	125.6
Oceanside, CA	77,000	128,398	161,029	66.8	25.4	109.1
Chula Vista, CA	84,000	135,163	173,556	60.9	28.4	106.6
Escondido, CA	66,460	108,635	133,559	63.5	22.9	101.0
Ontario, CA	89,000	133,179	158,007	49.6	18.6	77.5
Pomona, CA	93,000	131,723	149,473	41.6	13.5	60.7
Oxnard, CA	108,000	142,216	170,358	31.7	19.8	57.7
San Bernardino, CA	119,000	164,164	185,401	38.0	12.9	55.8
Thousand Oaks, CA	77,000	104,352	117,005	35.5	12.1	52.0
Hayward, CA	94,000	111,498	140,030	18.6	25.6	49.0
Tempe, AZ	107,000	141,865	158,625	32.6	11.8	48.2
Simi Valley, CA	77,500	100,217	111,351	29.3	11.1	43.7
El Monte, CA	81,119	106,209	115,965	30.9	9.2	43.0
Orange, CA	91,000	110,658	128,821	21.6	16.4	41.6
Garden Grove, CA	123,000	143,050	165,196	16.3	15.5	34.3
Lakewood, CO	114,000	126,481	144,126	10.9	14.0	26.4
Fullerton, CA	102,000	114,144	126,003	11.9	10.4	23.5
Sunnyvale, CA	107,000	117,229	131,760	9.6	12.4	23.1
Inglewood, CA	94,000	109,602	112,580	16.6	2.7	19.8
Pasadena, CA	113,000	131,591	133,936	16.5	1.8	18.5
Concord, CA	104,000	111,348	121,780	7.1	9.4	17.1
Torrance, CA	130,000	133,107	137,946	2.4	3.6	6.1
Berkeley, CA	103,000	102,724	102,743	−0.3	0.0	−0.2
Moreno Valley, CA[a]	-	118,779	142,381	-	19.9	-
Santa Clarita, CA[b]	-	110,642	151,088	-	36.6	-
	2,395,329	**3,087,165**	**3,628,510**	**28.9**	**17.5**	**51.5**
Subtotal	**3,470,865**	**4,432,133**	**5,300,801**	**27.7**	**19.6**	**52.7**
Total	**10,844,708**	**12,232,774**	**13,807,308**	**12.8**	**12.9**	**27.3**

Source: Authors' calculations based on data from 1990 Census STF1 and Census 2000 SF1.

a. Moreno Valley was not incorporated until 1984 and is excluded from totals and subtotals.

b. Santa Clarita was not incorporated until 1987 and is excluded from totals and subtotals.

REFERENCES

Berube, Alan. 2003a. "Gaining but Losing Ground: Population Change in Large Cities and Their Suburbs." In *Redefining Urban and Suburban America: Evidence from Census 2000,* vol. 1, edited by Bruce Katz and Robert E. Lang. Brookings.

———. 2003b. "Racial and Ethnic Change in the Nation's Largest Cities." In *Redefining Urban and Suburban America: Evidence from Census 2000,* vol. 1, edited by Bruce Katz and Robert E. Lang. Brookings.

Fulton, William, and others. 2001. "Who Sprawls the Most? How Growth Patterns Differ across the U.S." Brookings.

Lang, Robert E., and Patrick A. Simmons. 2003. "Boomburbs: The Emergence of Large, Fast-Growing Suburban Cities." In *Redefining Urban and Suburban America: Evidence from Census 2000,* vol. 1, edited by Bruce Katz and Robert E. Lang. Brookings.

Perry, Marc, and Paul Mackun. 2001. "Population Change and Distribution." Census 2000 Brief. U.S. Department of Commerce.

U.S. Census Bureau. 2001. "Overview of Race and Hispanic Origin, 2000." Census 2000 Brief. U.S. Department of Commerce.

Who Lives Downtown?

2

EUGENIE L. BIRCH

Over the past few decades, public and private officials have tried to reinvent their downtowns by using a variety of tactics. One of the most popular—and arguably most successful—strategies of recent years has been downtown residential development. The call to create vibrant downtowns that maintain their urban appeal twenty-four hours a day, seven days a week, has become a mantra for those working to inject life into struggling main streets and business districts.

Many downtowns boast a large number of assets that support residential uses. Architecturally interesting buildings, waterfront property, a rich cultural heritage, a bustling entertainment sector, specialized services like health care and higher education, and, of course, proximity to jobs are common attributes. Downtowns also have a new cadre of advocates, exemplified by the directors of business improvement districts, who have made revitalization a top priority.

Certain segments of the population, recognizing these amenities, see downtown living emerging as an alternative to living in the suburbs.[1] In fact, an analysis of metropolitan data reveals that downtown housing represents an increasingly important niche in the residential real estate market. To date, however, its impact has been quite modest: between 1970 and 2000, the forty-five

I would like to thank the Brookings Institution Metropolitan Policy Program for its support; I am especially indebted to senior research associate Jennifer Vey. Additional funding from the Fannie Mae Foundation, the Lincoln Institute of Land Policy, and the University of Pennsylvania supported earlier work.
    1. Fulton (2004) makes the same observation.

downtowns in this study had a net gain of about 35,000 housing units (an 8 percent increase) while their suburbs gained 13 million (a 99.7 percent increase).

Still, however small its relative growth, downtown housing provides visible and tangible evidence of urban vitality that has important psychological and economic effects. The occupation of vacant, centrally located buildings, the increased presence of people on formerly empty streets, and investment in supportive commercial activities and amenities help restore the market's confidence in worn-out downtowns. New residents then follow, creating a virtuous cycle of economic growth and development in the city as a whole.

As interest in downtown redevelopment grows, so too does the need for a more comprehensive understanding of downtown residential patterns. Local officials need to stay abreast of new trends in order to develop more responsive revitalization strategies. Environmentalists and "smart growth" advocates want to tap downtown infill opportunities as a way to help counter suburban sprawl. Economic development experts want to attract the young and well-educated, many of whom appear to value a more urban lifestyle.[2] And real estate entrepreneurs, chamber of commerce leaders, historic preservationists, new urbanists, and others all benefit from a more precise knowledge of where downtown development is occurring and what segments of the population are shaping its growth.

To that end, this study uses U.S. Census Bureau data to provide some insight into downtown demographic trends from 1970 to 2000.[3] It focuses on the growth of the downtown residential market, offering an assessment of which cities and regions have attracted downtown residents. It describes who lives downtown—their household composition, race, age, education, and income level—and compares downtown trends with those in the cities and suburbs. Finally, it discusses what those trends mean for local leaders working to encourage downtown living as a way to reinvigorate their urban core and, ultimately, their surrounding region.

EVOLUTION OF DOWNTOWN RESIDENTIAL TRENDS

The recent movement of households into downtowns signifies a dramatic change in the land use patterns of these areas. Downtowns traditionally contained offices, large warehouses, and occasionally factories. Downtown living

2. Florida (2002); Landry (2000).
3. Since 1990, several studies have reported on the rise in downtown living. See Brookings Institution and Fannie Mae Foundation (1998); John Eckberg, "More People Calling Cincinnati's Downtown Home," *New York Times,* July 30, 2000 p. 5; Haya El Nasser, "Downtowns Make Cities Winners," *USA Today,* May 7, 2001, p. 2; Birch (2002); and Sohmer and Lang (2003).

usually was restricted to hotels, clubs with sleeping facilities, flophouses, and jails.[4] By the 1920s, downtowns reached their economic peak and began to change.[5] Many downtown business functions began migrating to "uptowns" or "midtowns" within cities and later to "edge city" and "edgeless city" locations outside town.[6] This movement accelerated in the post–World War II period as favorable tax and mortgage insurance practices and massive federal investment in the nation's interstate highway system helped fuel the flight to the suburbs.

By mid-century, public officials and private investors had already begun to employ multiple federal programs to buttress declining downtowns. In the decades since, they have used urban renewal, subsidized interest programs, and U.S. Treasury–sanctioned private-activity bonds for specified redevelopment projects.[7] With these and other state and local funds they have built festival malls, stadiums, convention centers, hotels, and other attractions.[8]

Over the years, cities also began to use public housing, urban renewal (with associated low-interest financing), community development block grants, and, later, low-income housing tax credits to construct housing in or adjacent to downtowns. In the late 1950s and early 1960s, several cities consciously deployed urban renewal funds to foster middle-income residential developments as an alternative to the suburbs. Lower Manhattan (Manhattan Plaza), Midtown New York (Lincoln West), Boston (West End), Detroit (Lafayette Village), Philadelphia (Society Hill), San Francisco (Golden Gateway Center), and Los Angeles (Bunker Hill Towers) are just a few examples. Often, these places provided the seeds of today's downtown housing resurgence. However, political opposition brought the projects to a screeching halt by the late 1960s, as opponents viewed them as favoring middle-income residents over the poor.[9]

Despite these investments, attempts to stem the outward movement of traditional downtown activities—especially offices, department stores, and hotels—largely failed. By the latter part of the twentieth century, downtowns still typically contained a cluster of signature or class A office buildings, aligned in an identifiable skyline and displaying the logos of important corporations. Larger downtowns had convention centers, associated hotels, and sports stadiums, and a few still hosted businessmen's clubs. But downtowns also had masses of partially or underoccupied class B and C buildings, heavy

---

4. Murphy (1972).
5. Fogelson (2001); Isenberg (2004).
6. Lang (2003).
7. Redstone (1976).
8. Friedan and Sagalyn (1989); Garvin (2001); Gratz and Mintz (1998).
9. See, for example, Gans (1982); Hartman (1993); Jacobs (1961).

doses of parking, and discontinuous ground-floor retail located along key streets or in the lobbies of major office buildings. Adjacent to the core were warehouses and factories, often abandoned. Detroit in the late 1980s was an extreme example: Hudson's Department Store, the Hilton Hotel, and multiple office buildings stood entirely empty, while nearby the mirrored windows of the Renaissance Center—a 2.2 million-square-foot complex built in 1976 that drained the remaining office, retail, and hotel activities from the surrounding downtown—reflected the devastation.

By the late 1990s, the situation began to change, and downtowns throughout the country began to witness something of a renaissance. In Detroit, for example, Hudson's was demolished and replaced with a mixed-use project, while a new stadium, rehabilitated historic buildings and theaters, and new amenities such as a waterfront promenade began to spark renewed interest in downtown. Still, despite many positive developments, the suburbanization of people and jobs remains the dominant trend. By 1999, for example, only 44 percent of the office space in thirteen of the nation's largest markets was located downtown, ranging from a fairly large percentage in metropolitan areas like New York (64 percent downtown) and Chicago (54 percent), to a very low share in Miami (18 percent), Detroit (21 percent), and Dallas (25 percent).[10]

And so today housing has become a critical piece of evolving strategies for revitalizing downtowns. With an abundant supply of sound but underutilized properties, favorable transportation networks, and "character," many downtowns are successfully competing with their suburbs for certain consumers. Some view this residential approach as "a land use of last resort," while others label it the "SoHo Syndrome," an essential element of grassroots, preservation-based activity that rejuvenates downtown districts.[11]

METHODOLOGY

This analysis employs data from the U.S. Census Bureau to explore population and household growth rates and several demographic characteristics—race and ethnicity, age, education, and income—in three geographic areas: downtown, city, and suburbs. It tracks these characteristics from 1970 to 2000 in forty-four cities for forty-five downtowns chosen for their size and location from among the nation's 243 cities having a population of 100,000

---

10. Lang (2003).
11. David A. Wallace, personal communication, April 2002; Gratz and Mintz (1998).

or more.[12] The sample covers 18 percent of those cities, representing 48 percent of the total population; it includes 90 percent of the top ten cities, 62 percent of the top fifty, and 28 percent of the bottom fifty. The sample downtowns are spread among the four main census regions, and the percentage of downtowns in any one region closely reflects the distribution of the nation's urban population. Thus 16 percent of the sample downtowns are in the Northeast, which has 20 percent of the nation's urban population; 23 percent of the sample downtowns are in the Midwest, which has 23 percent of the urban population; 27 percent are in the West, which has 25 percent of the urban population; and 35 percent are in the South, which has 33 percent of the urban population.

Deriving a spatial definition of "downtown" is the most challenging aspect of this research because no commonly accepted physical standard exists. Some equate downtowns with the central business district (CBD). For several decades, in fact, the U.S. Census Bureau issued CBD data, simply designating one or two census tracts in selected cities as the central business district. However, it discontinued the practice in 1984. Others have attempted to define downtowns as the area within a specified radius (1 mile, one-half mile, and so forth) from a city's so-called 100 percent corner, the intersection that includes the highest-value real estate.[13] This concept poses difficulties when applied uniformly to different-sized cities—among some of the physically smaller of the 100 most populous cities, one-half mile from the 100 percent corner can extend into the suburbs. In the end, this study uses local knowledge and experience, asking public officials in the sample cities to define their own downtowns by census tracts as of 1999–2000. Those boundaries then became the basis of the time series dating back to 1970.[14] They also were checked through field visits.[15]

---

12. Due to size, historical development, and internal geography, New York City is assigned two downtowns: Lower Manhattan and Midtown. Houston was not included in the sample due to the large percentage of prisoners in its downtown population.

13. Downtown Preservation Council (2003); Murphy (1972).

14. This method defines each city's 2000 downtown, whose area may have been different (most likely smaller) thirty years ago. However, given that this analysis focuses on tracking changes in the space now considered a city's downtown, this choice is appropriate.

15. Downtown delineations also were cross-referenced with Downtown Preservation Council (2003). That study focused on forty-eight downtowns, thirty-one of which are included in this research project. The Downtown Preservation Council method is more fine-grained, delineating the downtown boundaries in blocks. As this study is longitudinal, assembling a database from 1970 to the present, it did not have the capacity to collect block data. Instead, the investigator tracked the data of the 2000 census tract boundaries backward, making adjustments where required for changes in tract boundaries. Thus this report is based on an assessment of the changes to the 2000 downtown.

The resulting sample consists of downtowns that vary considerably in population and geographic size. As a group, they provide a general view of downtown living, and individually (or grouped according to size or location) they demonstrate important variations. The sample downtowns range in population from 97,000 (Lower Manhattan) to 443 (Shreveport, Louisiana), and they fall into five population categories: 50,000 or more (11 percent of the sample); 25,000 to 49,999 (13 percent of the sample); 10,000 to 24,999 (24 percent of the sample); 5,000 to 9,999 (24 percent of the sample); and under 5,000 (27 percent of the sample). Taken together they represent under 1 million people (470,000 households) in cities containing 37 million inhabitants surrounded by suburbs of about 65 million residents.[16]

Downtowns in the sample range in size from almost seven square miles (Detroit) to under one-quarter square mile (Shreveport). Nine percent of the sample downtowns measure five square miles or larger; 38 percent, three to five square miles; 36 percent, one to three square miles; and 18 percent, under one square mile. Altogether, the sample downtowns cover 121 square miles, and they are located in cities covering approximately 7,300 square miles surrounded by 149,000 square miles of suburban territory.

Finally, the densities of the sample downtowns differ, ranging from slightly more than two people per acre (Jackson, Mississippi) to seventy-six people per acre (Lower Manhattan). Two of the sample downtowns (Lower Manhattan and Midtown Manhattan) have fifty or more people per acre. The building types accommodating these downtown densities are usually multi-family structures such as a former office buildings or lofts, attached townhouses, or multi-story apartment buildings. Thirteen percent of the downtowns have twenty to forty-nine people per acre; 16 percent have ten to nineteen people per acre; and thirty-one percent have five to nine people per acre. Dwellings at those densities are most likely low-scale converted buildings—lofts, warehouses, and office buildings—whose floor plates allow the capacious dwellings prized by the young, highly educated professionals who form the dominant group of downtown residents. The highest share of the downtowns—36 percent—have population densities of under five people per acre. Their low densities indicate a predominance of the large single-family housing often found in historic districts or in new construction on cleared or formerly vacant sites. Such low densities could also reflect a transition stage in which a former office or loft district is in the process of being converted and as yet has few residents.

16. The sample represents metropolitan areas containing 59 percent of the nation's urban population and 70 percent of the nation's suburban inhabitants.

FINDINGS

This analysis of U.S. downtowns finds that the 1990s brought a resurgence in downtown population after twenty years of decline. Important demographic distinctions separate downtown residents from those in the remainder of a metropolitan area. The varying trajectories of the downtowns studied here suggest a five-part typology characterizing a downtown's stage in the development life cycle.

Downtown Populations Grew in the 1990s

In recent years, population trends in the majority of the sample downtowns have been quite positive. Looking back thirty years, however, one finds that the story is mixed. Between 1970 and 2000, downtown population in the sample U.S. cities declined 1 percent, falling from 930,215 to 919,009. Performance varied considerably in this period: fifteen downtowns (33 percent of the sample) had positive growth rates ranging from 2 percent (Boston) to 97 percent (Norfolk, Virginia). Six downtowns grew by more than 50 percent: Norfolk and Seattle (86 percent), San Diego (73 percent), Los Angeles (62 percent), Lower Manhattan (61 percent), and Portland (56 percent). At the other end of the scale, the cities that saw the steepest drops were St. Louis (−67 percent); Columbus, Ohio (−52 percent); Columbus, Georgia (−48 percent); and Detroit (−46 percent). See table 2-1.

Interestingly, downtown population trends from 1970 to 2000 do not necessarily mirror those of their cities, and some clear regional patterns emerge. On average, downtowns in the West experienced population increases, as did their cities. Northeastern downtowns also grew, but their cities lost population. In contrast, Southern downtowns declined, while their cities expanded around them. In the Midwest, both downtowns and their cities saw their populations decrease (table 2-2).

A look at individual cities and downtowns illustrates the variations between them in growth. A total of twelve downtowns actually outperformed their respective cities. Chicago's downtown grew more than 39 percent, for example, while the city lost over 13 percent of its population. This "downtown up/city down" pattern held true for Norfolk, Cleveland, Atlanta, and Boston as well. Conversely, Orlando's downtown population fell 41 percent while the city grew 89 percent, downtown Charlotte lost 31 percent of its residents while its city grew 125 percent, and Mesa, Arizona, saw its downtown population decline by 25 percent while its city increased a whopping 532 percent.

This thirty-year view of downtown growth, while useful, obscures very distinct decade-by-decade trends: downtown population declined by 10 percent

T A B L E   2 - 1 . Individual Downtown Population Growth by Region, 1970–2000

Region	1970	1980	1990	2000	Change (percent)			
					1970–80	1980–90	1990–2000	1970–2000
Northeast								
Baltimore	34,667	29,831	28,597	30,067	−13.9	−4.1	5.1	−13.3
Boston	79,382	77,025	77,253	80,903	−3.0	0.3	4.7	1.9
Lower Manhattan	60,545	71,334	84,539	97,752	17.8	18.5	15.6	61.5
Midtown Manhattan	56,650	65,078	69,388	71,668	14.9	6.6	3.3	26.5
Philadelphia	79,882	72,833	74,686	78,349	−8.8	2.5	4.9	−1.9
Pittsburgh	9,468	6,904	6,517	8,216	−27.1	−5.6	26.1	−13.2
Washington, DC	30,796	25,047	26,597	27,667	−18.7	6.2	4.0	−10.2
Total	**351,390**	**348,052**	**367,577**	**394,622**	**−0.9**	**5.6**	**7.4**	**12.3**
South								
Atlanta	23,985	18,734	19,763	24,931	−21.9	5.5	26.1	3.9
Austin	5,021	3,084	3,882	3,855	−38.6	25.9	−0.7	−23.2
Charlotte	9,104	5,808	6,370	6,327	−36.2	9.7	−0.7	−30.5
Chattanooga	17,882	16,759	12,601	13,529	−6.3	−24.8	7.4	−24.3
Columbus, GA	12,354	8,669	8,476	6,412	−29.8	−2.2	−24.4	−48.1
Dallas	28,522	20,622	18,104	22,469	−27.7	−12.2	24.1	−21.2
Jackson	10,569	8,152	6,980	6,762	−22.9	−14.4	−3.1	−36.0
Lafayette	3,020	2,193	2,759	3,338	−27.4	25.8	21.0	10.5
Lexington	6,753	4,983	5,212	4,894	−26.2	4.6	−6.1	−27.5
Memphis	7,606	4,878	6,422	6,834	−35.9	31.7	6.4	−10.1
Miami	26,184	15,428	15,143	19,927	−41.1	−1.8	31.6	−23.9
New Orleans	4,040	4,000	2,798	3,422	−1.0	−30.1	22.3	−15.3
Norfolk	1,464	1,206	2,390	2,881	−17.6	98.2	20.5	96.8
Orlando	21,318	16,053	14,275	12,621	−24.7	−11.1	−11.6	−40.8
San Antonio	25,720	20,173	19,603	19,236	−21.6	−2.8	−1.9	−25.2
Shreveport	616	264	377	443	−57.1	42.8	17.5	−28.1
Total	**204,158**	**151,006**	**145,155**	**157,881**	**−26.0**	**−3.9**	**8.8**	**−22.7**
Midwest								
Chicago	52,248	50,630	56,048	72,843	−3.1	10.7	30.0	39.4
Cincinnati	3,472	2,528	3,838	3,189	−27.2	51.8	−16.9	−8.2
Cleveland	9,078	9,112	7,261	9,599	0.4	−20.3	32.2	5.7
Columbus, OH	12,995	8,737	6,161	6,198	−32.8	−29.5	0.6	−52.3
Des Moines	6,207	8,801	4,190	4,204	41.8	−52.4	0.3	−32.3
Detroit	68,226	46,117	38,116	36,871	−32.4	−17.3	−3.3	−46.0
Indianapolis	27,402	33,284	14,894	17,907	21.5	−55.3	20.2	−34.7
Milwaukee	16,427	14,518	14,458	16,359	−11.6	−0.4	13.1	−0.4
Minneapolis	35,537	33,063	36,334	30,299	−7.0	9.9	−16.6	−14.7
St. Louis	22,792	9,942	9,109	7,511	−56.4	−8.4	−17.5	−67.0
Total	**254,384**	**216,732**	**190,409**	**204,980**	**−14.8**	**−12.1**	**7.7**	**−19.4**
West								
Albuquerque	1,673	1,242	1,197	1,738	−25.8	−3.6	45.2	3.9
Boise	4,118	2,938	2,933	3,093	−28.7	−0.2	5.5	−24.9
Colorado Springs	5,520	4,182	3,401	5,035	−24.2	−18.7	48.0	−8.8
Denver	3,120	2,639	2,794	4,230	−15.4	5.9	51.4	35.6
Los Angeles	22,556	33,079	34,655	36,630	46.7	4.8	5.7	62.4
Mesa	3,809	3,117	3,206	2,864	−18.2	2.9	−10.7	−24.8
Phoenix	8,019	6,724	6,517	5,925	−16.1	−3.1	−9.1	−26.1
Portland	8,290	8,084	9,528	12,902	−2.5	17.9	35.4	55.6
Salt Lake City	6,098	4,647	4,824	5,939	−23.8	3.8	23.1	−2.6
San Diego	10,362	10,593	15,417	17,894	2.2	45.5	16.1	72.7
San Francisco	34,999	28,311	32,906	43,531	−19.1	16.2	32.3	24.4
Seattle	11,719	12,030	12,292	21,745	2.7	2.2	76.9	85.6
Total	**120,283**	**117,586**	**129,670**	**161,526**	**−2.2**	**10.3**	**24.6**	**34.3**
TOTAL	**930,215**	**833,376**	**832,811**	**919,009**	**−10.4**	**−0.1**	**10.4**	**−1.2**

Source: Author's analysis of decennial census data.

TABLE 2-2. Downtown and City Population Growth by Population Trend, 1970–2000

Category and area	Change (percent) Downtown	Change (percent) City
Downtown up, city up		
Seattle	85.6	6.9
San Diego	72.7	76.8
Los Angeles	62.4	32.5
Lower Manhattan	61.5	1.5
Portland	55.6	39.5
Denver	35.6	8.7
West region	**34.3**	**49.0**
Midtown Manhattan	26.5	1.5
San Francisco	24.4	9.4
Lafayette	10.5	61.0
Albuquerque	3.9	84.6
Downtown up, city down		
Norfolk	96.8	−23.6
Chicago	39.4	−13.4
Northeast region	**12.3**	**−7.4**
Cleveland	5.7	−35.8
Atlanta	3.9	−14.9
Boston	1.9	−6.6
Downtown down, city up		
Salt Lake City	−2.6	4.6
Colorado Springs	−8.8	170.3
Memphis	−10.1	4.7
Dallas	−21.2	41.8
South Region	**−22.7**	**33.9**
Austin	−23.2	160.7
Miami	−23.9	9.1
Chattanooga	−24.3	31.6
Mesa	−24.8	531.5
Boise	−24.9	149.9
San Antonio	−25.2	76.6
Phoenix	−26.1	129.0
Lexington	−27.5	144.2
Shreveport	−28.1	10.8
Charlotte	−30.5	125.4
Des Moines	−32.3	0.2
Indianapolis	−34.7	6.0
Jackson	−36.0	20.2
Orlando	−40.8	89.1
Columbus, GA	−48.1	21.1
Columbus, OH	−52.3	34.1
Downtown down, city down		
Milwaukee	−0.4	−16.0
Philadelphia	−1.9	−21.4
Cincinnati	−8.2	−25.4
Washington, DC	−10.2	−23.5
Pittsburgh	−13.2	−35.2
Baltimore	−13.3	−27.5
Minneapolis	−14.7	−10.7
New Orleans	−15.3	−17.9
Midwest Region	**−19.4**	**−17.0**
Detroit	−46.0	−36.5
St. Louis	−67.0	−43.3

Source: Author's analysis of decennial census data.

in the 1970s and stagnated (−0.1 percent) in the 1980s before reversing to grow 10 percent in the 1990s. The trends were far from consistent across cities, however (table 2-1).

The 1970s were calamitous for most downtowns. Thirty-seven of the forty-five downtowns in the sample (82 percent) lost population; of those, six downtowns—Shreveport (−57 percent), St. Louis (−56 percent), Miami (−41 percent), Austin (−39 percent), Charlotte (−36 percent), and Memphis (−36 percent)—experienced drops greater than 35 percent. A bright spot in this otherwise grim picture was the growth in eight downtowns: Los Angeles (47 percent), Des Moines (42 percent), Indianapolis (22 percent), Lower Manhattan (18 percent), Midtown Manhattan (15 percent), Seattle (3 percent), San Diego (2 percent), and Cleveland (0.4 percent).

By the 1980s, the downward trend slowed as far fewer downtowns (twenty-one, or 47 percent of the sample) lost population. Nonetheless, five lost one-quarter or more of their residents, including two downtowns—Indianapolis (−55 percent) and Des Moines (−52 percent)—that were growing a decade earlier, as well as New Orleans (−30 percent); Columbus, Ohio (−30 percent); and Chattanooga (−25 percent). At the other end of the scale, almost half of the twenty-four downtowns that gained population—including Norfolk (98 percent) and Cincinnati (52 percent)—saw increases of more than 10 percent.

In the 1990s, the balance shifted. Population grew in more than 70 percent of the sample (thirty-two downtowns), and only thirteen downtowns saw decreases, although six—Columbus, Georgia (−24 percent); St. Louis (−18 percent); Cincinnati (−17 percent); Minneapolis (−17 percent); Orlando (−12 percent); and Mesa (−11 percent)—experienced a drop of more than 10 percent. Five downtowns had gains of more than 35 percent: Seattle (77 percent), Denver (51 percent), Colorado Springs (48 percent), Albuquerque (45 percent), and Portland (35 percent). Notably, the growth in a handful of downtowns, such as Pittsburgh (26 percent), resulted from a significant increase in the incarcerated population. (In Pittsburgh, the growth rate without the incarcerated residents was only 5 percent.)[17]

17. Many cities have historically viewed their downtowns as repositories for locally unwanted land uses, especially prisons, homeless shelters, group homes for delinquents, and treatment facilities for the addicted. Houston, which is not included in this study, is an extreme case: 81 percent of its downtown population is incarcerated. The increase in prisoners in the 1990s yielded a growth rate for the city of more than 200 percent. Subtracting inmates, Houston actually lost downtown population in the 1990s. Downtowns in the sample cities with high proportions of prisoners are Pittsburgh (34 percent), Cleveland (23 percent), Indianapolis (23 percent), San Antonio (22 percent), Charlotte (16 percent), and Milwaukee (12 percent). In the 1990s, these places built more jails, collectively increasing the number of inmates by 53 percent.

In sum, a look at the three decades reveals considerable variation in downtown development among cities. Some places, such as Des Moines, Indianapolis, and Minneapolis, had gains in one decade and losses in another. Others, like Norfolk, displayed enormous percentage gains on small numerical bases. And seven downtowns—Detroit, San Antonio, Orlando, St. Louis, Phoenix, Jackson, and Columbus, Georgia—had losses across all three decades. However, the most important finding is evidence of a much earlier beginning to today's increase in downtown living than previously believed. While only New York's two downtown areas, Seattle, Los Angeles, and San Diego saw increases across all three decades, another 29 percent of the sample has experienced sustained growth since the 1980s.

Household Numbers Grew in Downtowns as Household Composition Shifted

While population trends are important, it is actually *households* that drive the housing market, defining demand for the number, size, and style of housing units. From 1970 to 2000, the number of downtown households grew 8 percent—from 433,140 to 468,308. That growth significantly outpaced the 1 percent population decline during this period and exhibited a different pattern over each decade. In the 1970s, the number of downtown households declined 3 percent, while population fell 10 percent; in the 1980s, households decreased 2 percent and population fell 0.1 percent; and in the 1990s, households rose 13 percent, surpassing the 10 percent population increase.

The double-digit growth in households in the 1990s demonstrates that more consumers are attracted to downtowns today than in the past. At the same time, steeper growth in the number of households than in the number of individual residents indicates a shift in the demographic profile of the downtown population over time. A closer examination of household composition sheds some light on these changes.

Downtowns historically have been dominated by non-family households. But from 1970 to 2000, singles—living alone or together—became an even greater presence downtown.[18] The number of these households in the sample downtowns grew by 24 percent over the three decades—17 percent during the 1990s alone—and their average share of the downtown total jumped from 62 percent in the 1970s to 71 percent in 2000. That is far greater than the 2000 share of non-family households in the sample downtowns' respective cities (41 percent) and suburbs (29 percent) (figure 2-1).

---

18. While the common perception of singles may be young, unmarried people, it is important to note that this group also includes elderly individuals living on their own.

FIGURE 2-1. Household Composition of Downtowns, Cities, and Suburbs, 2000

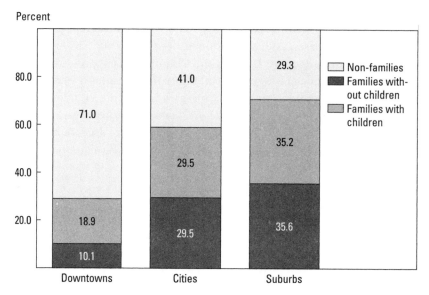

Source: Author's analysis of decennial census data.

By contrast, the number of families living downtown decreased 18 percent over the three decades, and families' overall share of households fell to 29 percent from 38 percent. Trends within this group varied, however.

Overall, downtowns saw a dramatic decrease (–27 percent) in the number of families with children. Of this group, married couples with children experienced the greatest decrease (–40 percent) while single women with children declined more slowly (–12 percent). Notably, single men with children constituted the only family household group to show an increase (150 percent), though their numbers were still very low (3,408 across all forty-five downtowns in 2000).

In light of these shifts, by 2000 families with children made up just 10 percent of all households in downtowns, compared with 30 percent in cities and 36 percent in suburbs (figure 2-1). Married couples with children constituted 5 percent of all downtown households, female-headed households with children made up another 4 percent, and single men with children made up 1 percent.

The number of families without children living downtown also decreased, by 12 percent between 1970 and 2000. Over the three decades, growth trends for this group were volatile, dropping 20 percent between 1970 and 1980 and 6 percent in the following decade. By the 1990s, however, the numbers shot up 17 percent, the second-highest growth rate after that for unrelated singles living together. By 2000 they were still an important component of the downtown population, constituting 19 percent of all downtown households.

All told, these trends reveal that singles (59 percent), unrelated individuals living together (12 percent), and childless families (19 percent) were the major source of demand for new housing units in downtowns across the country. In 2000, these three groups constituted 90 percent of downtowners, up from 85 percent in 1970 and 87 percent in 1990. There was a still considerable variability from place to place, however (table 2-3).

For example, in 2000 more than 90 percent of households in downtown Cincinnati were non-families; 83 percent were singles living alone. The pattern of singles living alone in downtowns with a high percentage of non-families appeared in other Midwestern cities as well, such as Columbus, Ohio, and Milwaukee, and in several Western downtowns, including Portland, Seattle, and San Diego. In contrast, the downtowns with the lowest percentage of singles living alone tended to be concentrated in the South.

The remaining 47 percent of downtowns housed a higher share of families than the sample norm of 29 percent. Families made up nearly half of all households in Lower Manhattan and Columbus, Georgia, and more than 40 percent of households in San Antonio and Miami. Columbus, Georgia, had the highest share of families with children (29 percent), as well as the highest proportion of female-headed families (22 percent). Of all downtowns, Lower Manhattan had the largest shares of both married couples with children (14 percent) and childless families (31 percent). Childless families also were dominant in Miami (26 percent), Norfolk (25 percent), and San Antonio (23 percent).

Downtown Homeownership Rates More Than Doubled over Thirty Years

As the number of downtown households and housing units increased over the past thirty years, so too did homeownership rates. Growth in the number of downtown homeowners was steady across each decade, rising 33 percent between 1970 and 1980, 35 percent from 1980 to 1990, and 36 percent from 1990 to 2000, for a total of 141 percent during the thirty-year period. As the number of homeowners escalated over the three decades, the downtown homeownership rate more than doubled, from 10 percent to 22 percent. Renters still clearly dominated downtown housing markets, however, while the cities and especially the suburbs in the sample boasted comparatively high shares of homeowners (41 percent and 61 percent respectively in 2000).

TABLE 2-3. Downtowns with Highest Shares of Different Household Types, 2000

Percent

Downtown	Nonfamily households[a]	Downtown	Family households	Downtown	Families without children	Downtown	Families with children	Downtown	Married-couple families with children	Downtown	Female headed households
Cincinnati	91.2	Lower Manhattan	49.2	Lower Manhattan	30.7	Columbus, GA	28.6	Lower Manhattan	14.7	Columbus, GA	22.0
Columbus, OH	86.1	Columbus, GA	47.7	Miami	25.7	Lafayette	21.1	San Antonio	11.1	Cleveland	17.2
Portland	85.5	San Antonio	42.2	Norfolk	25.4	Jackson	20.8	Lafayette	10.5	St. Louis	14.7
Shreveport	83.6	Miami	40.9	San Antonio	22.7	Cleveland	19.8	Mesa	10.3	Jackson	12.7
Seattle	82.8	Lafayette	38.8	Chicago	22.0	San Antonio	19.5	Los Angeles	9.8	Atlanta	12.3
Milwaukee	81.5	Mesa	38.3	Memphis	21.7	Lower Manhattan	18.5	Dallas	8.2	Detroit	11.0
Minneapolis	81.3	Jackson	37.1	Mesa	20.2	St. Louis	18.3	Miami	6.9	Chattanooga	10.9
San Diego	80.4	Chattanooga	36.8	Denver	20.2	Mesa	18.1	Midtown Manhattan	6.8	Lafayette	8.5
Des Moines	79.5	Detroit	32.7	Midtown Manhattan	19.7	Chattanooga	17.3	Jackson	6.1	Washington, DC	8.1
Denver	79.4	Orlando	32.1	Chattanooga	19.5	Detroit	16.8	Indianapolis	5.7	Pittsburgh	7.4

a. Nonfamily households include single people living alone and unrelated individuals living together.
Source: Author's analysis of decennial census data.

Homeownership rates across the sample downtowns in 2000 swung from a high of 41 percent in Chicago to a low of just 1 percent in Cincinnati (table 2-4). Lafayette, Louisiana (36 percent), Austin (35 percent), and Miami (34 percent) also were among those downtowns boasting a large relative share of homeowners in 2000, while St. Louis (3 percent), Cleveland (3 percent), and San Francisco (7 percent) were among those at the bottom. Of the ten downtowns with the highest rates, Chicago and Philadelphia had by far the greatest numbers of homeowners, at 18,181 and 15,608 respectively; half of the group (Lafayette, Denver, Austin, Norfolk, and Charlotte) had approximately 1,000 or fewer owners. Five of the ten downtowns with the lowest homeownership rates had less than 200 homeowners in 2000, with Cincinnati posting just fifteen.

While downtowns like Lafayette, Philadelphia, and Baltimore have historically had relatively high homeownership rates, several downtowns saw their rates skyrocket over the thirty years, increasing their share of homeowners considerably. The homeownership rate in Chicago, for example, was only 4 percent in 1970, but the number of homeowners shot up 1,583 percent over the next three decades. The number of homeowners in Denver grew 5,240 percent during this period (albeit from a very small base), pushing their share of all downtown households from 1 percent to 35 percent. Conversely, St. Louis and Cincinnati saw their already low homeownership rates decline over the thirty years, losing both a large number of housing units and a substantial share of their small cadre of homeowners.

Downtowns Became More Racially and Ethnically Diverse

Burgeoning numbers of Hispanic and Asian residents moved to the nation's downtowns over the past two decades, causing downtown racial composition to shift.[19] In 1980 the combined population of the forty-five downtowns was 57 percent non-Hispanic white and 24 percent black, with Hispanics (11 percent), Asians (7 percent), and other groups (1 percent) making up the remaining 19 percent. Over the next two decades, however, the number of whites and blacks living downtown remained relatively flat, while the number of Hispanics and Asians grew substantially. During the 1980s, the overall number of whites declined approximately 5 percent, while the black population declined 1 percent. By contrast, the number of Hispanics and Asians increased 11 percent and 41 percent, respectively, over the decade. By the 1990s, whites began returning downtown, increasing their numbers by

19. 1980 was the first year in which the Census Bureau collected data on the Hispanic/Latino population; therefore this part of the analysis is restricted to the 1980 to 2000 period.

TABLE 2-4. Downtowns with Highest and Lowest Homeownership Rates, 2000

Rank	Downtown	Occupied housing units	Owner-occupied housing units (number and percent)
1	Chicago	44,638	18,181 (40.7)
2	Lafayette	979	349 (35.6)
3	Denver	3,009	1,068 (35.5)
4	Austin	1,811	636 (35.1)
5	Miami	9,388	3,217 (34.3)
6	Philadelphia	47,075	15,608 (33.2)
7	Norfolk	949	294 (31.0)
8	Charlotte	3,224	973 (30.2)
9	Baltimore	16,277	4,392 (27.0)
10	Indianapolis	7,141	1,922 (26.9)
36	Milwaukee	8,305	884 (10.6)
37	Columbus, OH	3,578	341 (9.5)
38	Detroit	17,155	1,570 (9.2)
39	Albuquerque	352	30 (8.5)
40	Los Angeles	15,045	1,171 (7.8)
41	San Francisco	24,349	1,605 (6.6)
42	Shreveport	183	9 (4.9)
43	Cleveland	3,818	111 (2.9)
44	St. Louis	4,184	120 (2.9)
45	Cincinnati	1,512	15 (1.0)

Source: Author's analysis of decennial census data.

5 percent over the decade, while the black population remained steady. However, growth for Hispanic (13 percent) and Asian (39 percent) downtowners still significantly outpaced that for whites and blacks during the decade.

Given these fluctuations, by 2000 the sample downtowns were more racially and ethnically diverse than twenty years earlier. They were still majority white, but the white share of the population had fallen to 52 percent. The proportion of black residents living downtown (21 percent) had declined as well, while the share of Asians (12 percent) and Hispanics (12 percent) increased. The sample downtowns were more racially and ethnically diverse than their suburbs, which were still 71 percent white in 2000, but less diverse than their surrounding cities, which had fewer white residents (40 percent) but higher proportions of blacks (26 percent) and Hispanics (24 percent) (figure 2-2).

The racial and ethnic makeup of the individual downtowns in the sample differs considerably, with several geographic patterns emerging (table 2-5). Northeastern downtowns, on average, had the largest shares of white residents in 2000, although the five downtowns with the highest shares of white residents—including Boise, Idaho (88 percent), Salt Lake City (77 percent), and Colorado Springs (76 percent)—were located in the West. However, of

FIGURE 2-2. **Racial and Ethnic Composition of Downtowns, Cities, and Suburbs, 2000**

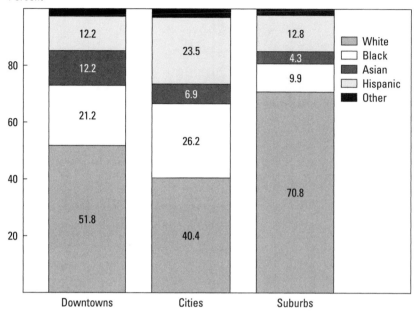

Source: Author's analysis of decennial census data.

the nineteen downtowns located in these two regions, only Lower Manhattan saw its share of white residents actually increase (albeit only slightly) over the two decades. By contrast, several Southern cities—such as Memphis, Dallas, and Charlotte—saw a surge in the proportion of white residents living downtown as the share of black residents fell.

With the exception of Pittsburgh, all ten of the downtowns with the highest percentages of black residents in 2000 were located in the South and Midwest, including Atlanta (75 percent), St. Louis (74 percent), and Detroit (70 percent). The Northeast and West had the highest shares of Asian residents downtown, particularly in Lower Manhattan and San Francisco, both of which have large "Chinatown" communities.

The downtowns with the largest percentages of Hispanic residents were located predominantly in the West and South. A majority of downtowners in San Antonio (74 percent) and Los Angeles (51 percent) were Hispanic, for example, while this group constituted just under half of the downtown population of Miami (49 percent) and Albuquerque (47 percent). Still, the

TABLE 2-5. Downtowns with Highest and Lowest Shares of Racial and Ethnic Groups, 2000

Highest white share	Percent	Highest black share	Percent	Highest Hispanic share	Percent	Highest Asian share	Percent
Boise	87.9	Atlanta	75.2	San Antonio	74.0	Lower Manhattan	41.8
Salt Lake City	76.7	St. Louis	74.3	Los Angeles	50.6	San Francisco	32.9
Colorado Springs	75.9	Detroit	70.3	Miami	49.4	Los Angeles	16.8
Portland	74.8	Columbus, GA	67.6	Albuquerque	46.8	Boston	14.3
Denver	74.4	Jackson	66.6	Dallas	38.7	Seattle	14.0
Philadelphia	73.3	Cleveland	62.6	Mesa	31.8	Midtown Manhattan	13.0
Midtown Manhattan	72.6	Pittsburgh	54.2	Phoenix	29.8	Washington, DC	8.9
Boston	71.8	Charlotte	52.7	San Diego	24.3	Chicago	8.4
Des Moines	70.8	Memphis	50.4	Austin	18.4	Portland	8.2
Milwaukee	69.2	Chattanooga	47.5	Washington, DC	13.3	Philadelphia	8.0

Lowest white share	Percent	Lowest black share	Percent	Lowest Hispanic share	Percent	Lowest Asian share	Percent
Jackson	30.4	Albuquerque	7.6	Chattanooga	2.3	Mesa	1.3
Washington, DC	29.9	Portland	6.4	Baltimore	2.3	Atlanta	1.2
Columbus, GA	29.0	Colorado Springs	5.5	Memphis	1.7	Charlotte	1.1
Cleveland	27.7	Denver	5.4	Shreveport	1.6	St. Louis	1.1
Miami	24.1	Lower Manhattan	4.8	Charlotte	1.5	Albuquerque	1.0
St. Louis	21.5	Boston	4.5	Norfolk	1.5	Jackson	0.6
Atlanta	17.9	Midtown Manhattan	4.2	Columbus, GA	1.5	San Antonio	0.6
Detroit	16.9	Salt Lake City	3.7	St. Louis	1.4	Lafayette	0.5
San Antonio	15.8	Mesa	3.1	Jackson	1.2	Columbus, GA	0.3
Los Angeles	12.6	Boise	1.5	Pittsburgh	1.1	Shreveport	0.0

Source: Author's analysis of decennial census data.

majority of Southern downtowns in the sample continue to have very small, though in most cases growing, Hispanic populations. Similarly, while nearly all Northeastern and Midwestern downtowns saw their Hispanic populations increase, only Washington, D.C., and Lower Manhattan had shares greater than 10 percent.

Downtowns Boasted High Shares of Young Adults and College-Educated Residents

Over the past decade, the popular image of the young, hip downtowner has become more prevalent—and perhaps rightly so. A look at the changing downtown age profile shows that this crowd has indeed moved in. In 1970, the twenty-five- to thirty-four-year-old group made up 13 percent of all downtowners, while today it makes up 24 percent, reflecting a 90 percent increase in its numbers over thirty years. The vast majority of that growth occurred between 1970 and 1990, before slowing considerably during the last decade (figure 2-3).

Young adults were not the only ones flocking downtown, however. In 1970, forty-five- to sixty-four-year-olds were the single largest age group living downtown. While their numbers dropped over the next two decades, during the 1990s they began to grow again, so that by 2000 this group constituted 21 percent of the downtown population, second in size only to the twenty-five- to thirty-four-year olds. As the baby boomers continue to age, even more of this group, most likely "empty-nesters," may be living downtown.

Between 1970 and 2000, other population dynamics shifted as well. Thirty years ago, children and elderly people together accounted for more than one-third (36 percent) of the downtowners in the sample. But from 1970 to 2000, the under-eighteen population declined by 42 percent and the number of residents over the age of sixty-five declined by 26 percent, so that by 2000 only 23 percent of the downtown population was made up of the youngest and oldest cohorts. At the same time, the sample downtowns also witnessed a 61 percent increase in the number of thirty-five- to forty-four-year-olds over the three decades, with their numbers jumping substantially during the 1980s. This group made up 16 percent of the population in 2000, up from 11 percent thirty years earlier. Notably, the percentage of eighteen- to twenty-four-year-olds downtown remained relatively unchanged during this period, hovering between 15 and 16 percent.

The 2000 demographic profile of the sample downtowns was quite distinct from that of their cities and suburbs, particularly among the groups under the age of thirty-five. The twenty-five- to thirty-four-year-olds and the eighteen- to twenty-four-year-olds were present in much higher proportions

FIGURE 2-3. Downtown Population Age Structure, 1970–2000

Proportion of population (percent)

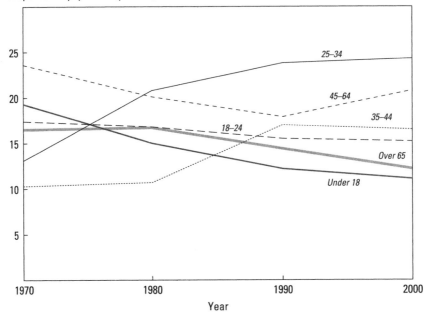

in downtowns (24 percent and 15 percent, respectively) than in their cities (18 percent and 11 percent) and suburbs (14 percent and 9 percent). And while children under eighteen were the largest single cohort in the sample's cities and suburbs (25 percent and 27 percent, respectively), they represented only 11 percent of the downtown population.

While this analysis of age distribution provides an overall sense of who was living downtown, it hides the numerical force of different groups in individual cities (table 2-6). Albuquerque, Dallas, and Philadelphia had the greatest share of twenty-five- to thirty-four-year-olds, although all of those in the top ten boasted shares between 27 and 31 percent. From 1990 to 2000, Seattle (up 134 percent), San Francisco (up 39 percent), and Chicago (up 28 percent) saw the greatest percentage gains in this coveted group. Chattanooga, St. Louis, and Columbus, Georgia, had the lowest shares of twenty-five- to thirty-four-year-olds (around 15 percent each), but, along with Jackson, they were among the top four downtowns in their share of children under eighteen. In fact, children made up nearly one-quarter of the population in both downtown Columbus and St. Louis. By contrast, children constituted a very small share (2 percent) of the downtown population in both Denver and Cincinnati.

TABLE 2-6. Downtowns with Highest Shares of Selected Age Groups, 2000

Downtown	Under 18 (percent)	Downtown	25 to 34 (percent)	Downtown	45 to 64 (percent)
Columbus, GA	25.9	Albuquerque	31.4	Charlotte	31.7
St. Louis	24.9	Dallas	30.9	San Diego	26.0
Jackson	18.7	Philadelphia	30.4	San Francisco	25.9
Chattanooga	17.9	Boston	29.0	Cincinnati	25.7
Detroit	17.8	Memphis	28.8	Seattle	25.6
Norfolk	17.8	Chicago	28.7	New Orleans	25.0
Los Angeles	17.6	Norfolk	28.4	Portland	24.8
Atlanta	17.6	Midtown Manhattan	28.0	Midtown Manhattan	24.6
Dallas	17.5	Charlotte	27.5	Chicago	23.4
Cleveland	17.4	Milwaukee	26.7	Lower Manhattan	22.7

As the share of young adults living downtown has increased, so too has residents' level of education. In 1970, 55 percent of the population in the sample downtowns had not finished high school and only 14 percent had four-year college degrees. Those rates were comparable to rates in the cities, but at the time the suburbs had a much lower share of residents without a high school diploma (38 percent).

While over the years national educational attainment has improved, the achievement levels for downtown populations have grown faster, especially with regard to college and advanced degrees. In 2000, 44 percent of downtowners had a bachelor's degree or higher, well above the rates for the nation (24 percent) and for the sample cities (27 percent) and suburbs (31 percent) (figure 2-4). Improvement occurred at the other end of the scale as well. The share of downtowners with no high school education shrank to 22 percent, and cities (25 percent) and suburbs (16 percent) showed similar improvements. The national share of those not completing high school in 2000 was 20 percent.

Educational levels in 2000 were highest in the Northeastern downtowns, where more than half (56 percent) of residents had a college degree or higher. This region contains three of the four downtowns with the highest attainment rates: Midtown Manhattan (72 percent), Philadelphia (67 percent), and Boston (64 percent). Rates in the Midwest (45 percent) also were higher than the sample average, with Chicago (68 percent) ranking second among all the sample cities. Philadelphia (36 percent), Chicago (33 percent), and Midtown Manhattan (33 percent) also had the highest percentage of residents with graduate and professional degrees (table 2-7).

On average, college attainment rates in the West (28 percent) and the South (28 percent) were substantially lower than rates in the Northeast and Midwest in 2000. But several Sun Belt downtowns may soon be catching up.

FIGURE 2-4. Share of Adults with a Bachelor's Degree, Downtowns, Cities, and Suburbs, 1970–2000

Proportion of adults age 25+ (percent)

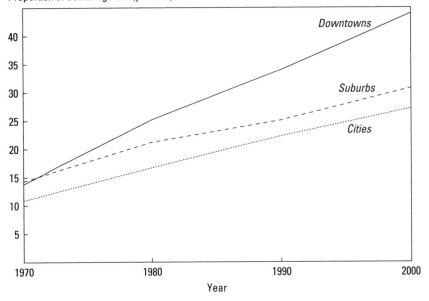

Source: Author's analysis of decennial census data.

TABLE 2-7. Downtowns with Highest and Lowest Shares of Adults with a College Degree

Rank	Downtown	Adults (25+) with college degree (percent)
1	Midtown Manhattan	71.5
2	Chicago	67.6
3	Philadelphia	66.7
4	Boston	63.6
5	Denver	48.5
6	Milwaukee	46.2
7	Austin	46.2
8	Baltimore	45.7
9	Minneapolis	43.0
10	Memphis	41.8
36	Des Moines	16.5
37	Albuquerque	16.0
38	St. Louis	15.9
39	Jackson	15.8
40	Los Angeles	15.3
41	Phoenix	15.1
42	Mesa	15.0
43	Columbus, GA	9.9
44	San Antonio	8.3
45	Shreveport	6.8

Source: Author's analysis of decennial census data.

Charlotte and Memphis, for example, both saw quadruple-digit gains in the share of their population with college degrees over the thirty-year period, while San Diego, Atlanta, and Denver each saw jumps of more than 500 percent. Still, while downtowns such as Denver (48 percent), Austin (46 percent), and Memphis (42 percent) boasted high college attainment rates in 2000, eight of the ten downtowns with the highest rates of residents with no high school degree (one-third of residents or more) also were located in the West and South. Topping this list were San Antonio; Columbus, Georgia; and Los Angeles, where nearly half the population of each downtown does not have a high school diploma.

Downtowns Contained Both Poor and Affluent Households

An important gauge of a downtown's relative success is how its median household income compares with that of its surrounding area. Analysis of the tracts with the highest and the lowest median incomes in each downtown reveals that the picture is quite mixed (table 2-8).[20] On the high end of the scale, for example, twenty-four of the forty-five sample downtowns had at least one tract whose household median income surpassed the city median, while nineteen downtowns had at least one tract whose median income was higher than that of the metropolitan area as a whole. Two downtowns—Midtown Manhattan and Dallas—had tracts with median incomes that exceeded metropolitan medians by more than 300 percent; Lower Manhattan, Miami, and New Orleans had tracts with median incomes that were well over 200 percent of their metropolitan medians. Of all downtown census tracts in the sample, the tract with the highest median income ($200,001) was located in Dallas, followed by Midtown Manhattan ($188,697) and Lower Manhattan ($113,332).

At the other end of the scale, thirty-six downtowns had at least one tract whose median income was at least 50 percent lower than the city median, and thirty-eight downtowns had at least one tract whose median income was at least 50 percent lower than the metropolitan median. A few downtowns housed only lower-income residents. The downtowns of Boise, Des Moines, and Lexington, Kentucky, for example, constituted only one census tract, in which median household income was less than half that of the city and the metropolitan area. In twenty-one downtowns, median income in the tracts with the highest and the lowest median incomes lagged behind medians in

20. By way of reference, in 2000 the median income for all U.S. households was $41,994; for metropolitan areas, $44,755; and for central city households, $36,964. In the sample, metropolitan median incomes ranged from $63,297 (San Francisco) to $23,483 (Miami) and city median incomes from $55,221 (San Francisco) to $25,928 (Cleveland).

TABLE 2-8. Median Household Income in Downtowns, Cities, and Metropolitan Areas, 2000

Region	Median income, lowest tract (dollars)	Median income, highest tract (dollars)	Metropolitan median income (dollars)	City median income (dollars)	Median income, lowest tract as share of metropolitan median (percent)	Median income, highest tract as share of metropolitan median (percent)	Median income, lowest tract as share of city median (percent)	Median income, highest tract as share of city median (percent)
Northeast								
Baltimore	12,857	77,340	49,938	30,078	25.7	154.9	42.7	257.1
Boston	12,165	81,804	55,183	39,629	22.0	148.2	30.7	206.4
Lower Manhattan	20,344	113,332	41,053	38,293	49.6	276.1	53.1	296.0
Midtown Manhattan	15,947	188,697	41,053	38,293	38.8	459.6	41.6	492.8
Philadelphia	8,349	87,027	47,536	30,746	17.6	183.1	27.2	283.1
Pittsburgh	13,449	70,125	37,467	28,588	35.9	187.2	47.0	245.3
Washington, DC	9,589	64,167	62,216	40,127	15.4	103.1	23.9	159.9
South								
Atlanta	8,469	42,906	51,948	34,770	16.3	82.6	24.4	123.4
Austin	27,768	45,063	48,950	42,689	56.7	92.1	65.0	105.6
Charlotte	9,494	36,711	46,119	46,975	20.6	79.6	20.2	78.2
Chattanooga	9,672	31,853	37,411	32,006	25.9	85.1	30.2	99.5
Columbus, GA	9,307	28,241	34,512	34,798	27.0	81.8	26.7	81.2
Dallas	6,250	200,001	48,364	37,628	12.9	413.5	16.6	531.5
Jackson	14,883	20,757	38,887	30,414	38.3	53.4	48.9	68.2
Lafayette	21,000	21,000	30,998	35,996	67.7	67.7	58.3	58.3
Lexington	17,060	17,060	39,357	39,813	43.3	43.3	42.9	42.9
Memphis	7,446	51,786	40,201	32,285	18.5	128.8	23.1	160.4
Miami	7,595	61,807	23,483	35,966	32.3	263.2	21.1	171.8
New Orleans	9,727	79,625	35,317	27,133	27.5	225.5	35.8	293.5

Norfolk	46,081	46,081	42,448	31,815	108.6	108.6	144.8	144.8
Orlando	9,800	45,375	41,871	35,732	23.4	108.4	27.4	127.0
San Antonio	12,781	18,929	39,140	36,214	32.7	48.4	35.3	52.3
Shreveport	19,911	19,911	32,558	30,526	61.2	61.2	65.2	65.2
Midwest								
Chicago	4,602	97,940	51,680	38,625	8.9	189.5	11.9	253.6
Cincinnati	17,721	35,278	44,248	29,493	40.0	79.7	60.1	119.6
Cleveland	6,336	50,568	42,089	25,928	15.1	120.1	24.4	195.0
Columbus, OH	16,636	29,864	44,782	37,897	37.1	66.7	43.9	78.8
Des Moines	16,875	16,875	46,651	38,408	36.2	36.2	43.9	43.9
Detroit	8,317	50,388	49,175	29,526	16.9	102.5	28.2	170.7
Indianapolis	12,154	33,650	45,548	40,051	26.7	73.9	30.3	84.0
Milwaukee	11,202	53,125	45,901	32,216	24.4	115.7	34.8	164.9
Minneapolis	17,230	55,556	54,304	37,974	31.7	102.3	45.4	146.3
St. Louis	6,875	34,826	61,807	26,196	11.1	56.3	26.2	132.9
West								
Albuquerque	27,333	27,333	39,088	38,272	69.9	69.9	71.4	71.4
Boise	19,513	19,513	42,570	42,432	45.8	45.8	46.0	46.0
Colorado Springs	14,700	26,770	46,844	45,081	31.4	57.1	32.6	59.4
Denver	30,607	33,750	51,191	39,500	59.8	65.9	77.5	85.4
Los Angeles	6,250	25,721	42,189	36,687	14.8	61.0	17.0	70.1
Mesa	23,702	23,702	44,752	42,817	53.0	53.0	55.4	55.4
Phoenix	12,353	24,688	44,752	41,207	27.6	55.2	30.0	55.9
Portland	8,179	45,779	47,077	40,146	17.4	97.2	20.4	114.0
Salt Lake City	16,978	28,125	48,594	36,944	34.9	57.9	46.0	76.1
San Diego	11,535	44,810	47,067	45,733	24.5	95.2	25.2	98.0
San Francisco	12,054	77,922	63,297	55,221	19.0	123.1	21.8	141.1
Seattle	13,057	38,361	52,804	45,736	24.7	72.6	28.5	83.9

their respective cities and region. These downtowns, primarily in the South and West, included Denver, Seattle, San Antonio, and Chattanooga.

Regional variation persists in measures of median income, as in measures of other demographic characteristics. The downtowns of the Northeast overall had the most affluent residents relative to those in their surrounding area, as each of the seven downtowns had at least one tract in which the median household income surpassed that of both the city and the metropolitan area. That was true for half of the downtowns in the Midwest, 38 percent of downtowns in the South, and just San Francisco in the West. Northeastern and Midwestern downtowns also had very poor tracts, however: none of lowest-median-income tracts in downtowns in the Midwest—and only one in the Northeast (in Lower Manhattan)—reached even 50 percent of metropolitan median income.

Population and Demographic Variation Suggests a Five-Part Downtown Typology

A closer look at the trends described above reveals that while individual downtowns had very different growth, demographic, and income profiles, they generally fell into one of five major categories, as distinguished by the number of households and growth rates: fully developed downtowns; emerging downtowns; downtowns on the edge of take-off; slow-growing downtowns; and declining downtowns (table 2-9). These typologies are dynamic, however—individual downtown classifications will surely change over time, especially for those places where downtown growth has accelerated since 2000.

The *fully developed downtowns* were relatively large (averaging 43,623 households) and densely settled (averaging twenty-three households per acre). In fact, while there were only five of this type—Boston, Midtown Manhattan, Lower Manhattan, Chicago, and Philadelphia—they contained almost half of the nation's downtown households. These downtowns sustained positive household growth in all three decades from 1970 to 2000; overall their number of households increased 38 percent during this period, exceeding growth in their city (up 2 percent) and suburbs (up 34 percent). Concentrated in major job centers with significant amenities, these downtowns attracted a very highly educated populace—on average, 61 percent of downtowners in these cities had college degrees. They also were relatively affluent—the median income in 58 percent of their tracts exceeded the median income of their respective metropolitan areas—and they had the highest rates of home-ownership (29 percent) of the sample.

Another quarter of downtown householders resided in *emerging downtowns*, which were located primarily in the South and West. These down-

TABLE 2-9. Downtown Typology

Fully developed downtowns	Emerging downtowns	Downtowns on the edge of takeoff	Slow-growing downtowns	Declining downtowns
Boston	Atlanta	Chattanooga	Albuquerque	Cincinnati
Chicago	Baltimore	Dallas	Austin	Columbus, GA
Lower Manhattan	Charlotte	Miami	Boise	Des Moines
Midtown Manhattan	Cleveland	Milwaukee	Colorado Springs	Detroit
Philadelphia	Denver	Washington, DC	Columbus, OH	Jackson
	Los Angeles		Indianapolis	Lexington
	Memphis		Lafayette	Mesa
	New Orleans		Phoenix	Minneapolis
	Norfolk		Pittsburgh	Orlando
	Portland		Salt Lake City	San Antonio
	San Diego			Shreveport
	San Francisco			St. Louis
	Seattle			

Source: Author's analysis.

towns were much smaller (averaging 8,500 households) and far less dense (five households per acre) than the fully developed downtowns. Their lower household growth rate (26 percent) between 1970 and 2000 reflects their volatility over the three decades: on average, these downtowns experienced a 5 percent decline in their number of households in the 1970s, almost no growth (0.7 percent) in the 1980s, and a very rapid increase (32 percent) in the 1990s, during which their growth actually outpaced that of their city and suburbs. Although they grew significantly, these downtowns had lower rates of homeownership (15 percent) and educational attainment (32 percent of residents had a college degree) than both fully developed downtowns and downtowns on the edge of take-off, and they were much less affluent (only 13 percent of their tracts had a median income exceeding that of the metropolitan area). Still, the emerging downtowns show promise of becoming fully developed downtowns if their high household growth continues. Atlanta, Baltimore, Norfolk, Portland, and San Diego are representative of the thirteen downtowns in this group.

The five *downtowns on the edge of take-off*—Chattanooga, Dallas, Miami, Milwaukee, and Washington, D.C.—were larger (averaging 9,500 households) than the emerging downtowns, although they were slightly less dense (four households per acre). (Washington, D.C., with more than 12,000 households and ten households per acre, led the group.) These downtowns experienced far greater losses in their number of households between 1970 and 1990 (−21 percent in the 1970s and −11 in the 1980s) than the emerging downtowns, but they made a considerable comeback in the 1990s, with household growth rates averaging 25 percent. Their growth significantly outpaced growth in their respective cities, which saw only a 4 percent increase in households over the decade. These downtowns had both higher rates of homeownership (19 percent) and educational attainment (37 percent with bachelor's degrees) than the emerging downtowns, and they also were relatively more affluent—the median income in 21 percent of their tracts was higher than that of their respective metropolitan areas.

Slow-growing downtowns, the majority of which were in the South and West, were the smallest (averaging 2,600 households) and least dense (two households per acre) of the entire sample. These downtowns experienced 9 percent growth in households in the 1990s, but they had suffered a substantial loss of households during the previous two decades. In fact, they saw an average 30 percent drop in their number of households between 1970 and 2000, while household growth in their respective cities (up 87 percent) and suburbs (up 181 percent) increased significantly. As a group, these downtowns had lower average educational attainment rates (25 percent of residents had bachelor's degrees) and were less affluent (only 4 percent of their tracts had a median income higher than that of their respective metropolitan areas) than downtowns in the categories listed above. Albuquerque, Austin, Salt Lake City, and Phoenix are representative of the ten downtowns in this group.

Finally, the *declining downtowns* were located primarily in the Midwest and South. They had an average of 5,300 households and were low density (three households per acre). These downtowns lost households in each of the last three decades, sustaining declines of 17 percent in the 1970s, 9 percent in the 1980s, and 13 percent in the 1990s. By 2000 they had just 65 percent of the number of households they had in 1970. By sharp contrast, their cities and suburbs saw their number of households jump 19 percent and 131 percent, respectively, over the thirty years. Several of these downtowns, including Minneapolis, Orlando, and St. Louis, have experienced increases in downtown households since 2000, but they all have miles to go to catch up to the other types of downtowns. On average, only 24 percent of their residents held bachelor's degrees, the lowest percentage of all the groups, and these downtowns were not very affluent when compared with their surrounding area—just 5 percent of their tracts had a median income above that of their metropolitan area.

DISCUSSION

This report examines downtown residential patterns from 1970 to 2000, describing who was living downtown then and how trends have changed over three decades. Awareness of these trends can help local public and private sector leaders better tailor development plans for their own downtown and the residents who call it home. As they consider future plans for downtown residential development, local leaders might note three areas of policy concern that emerge from this analysis: development climate, reliance on rental housing, and density choices.

Development Climate

As this study shows, downtown residential development takes a long time, it happens in specific places, and it does not occur by accident, although that topic is not covered in detail in this analysis. Among the sample, the most successful places—the fully developed downtowns—had sustained housing unit increases for two or three decades. Furthermore, those downtowns had attributes conducive to urban life—including a critical mass of jobs, amenities, and interesting physical features or architecture—that attracted increasing numbers of households, especially singles and childless families. A development strategy that includes adding such attributes or supplementing those that already exist could enhance the attractiveness of downtowns to selected population groups.

Reliance on Rental Housing

Despite the doubling of homeownership rates between 1970 and 2000, downtown housing was overwhelmingly rental—even Chicago's downtown ownership rate of 41 percent, the highest in the sample, pales in comparison with national suburban homeownership rates of 77 percent.[21] The current reliance on such a limited choice of dwelling units may be worrisome because it can threaten population stability. As the predominant twenty-five- to thirty-four-year-olds age or decide to leave the rental market, they have few options downtown, forcing them to look elsewhere for permanent homes. That in turn can foster a high number of transients, who often have limited interest in their communities, make few home improvements, and generally have little stake in the future of places that they consider temporary stopping points. Furthermore, depending on a narrowly defined population cohort and tailoring housing to satisfy its tastes can restrict the transferability of downtown dwellings to other groups in the future. As the emerging twenty-five- to thirty-four-year-old cohort is smaller than the current one, it may become increasingly difficult to fill the growing inventory of rental housing.

Density Choices

Density matters. In general, the evidence suggests that there is a relationship between density and the ability to attract downtown residents. While a city

21. U.S Census Bureau (2005).

with a substantial amount of vacant or underutilized land might be tempted to allow low-density residential construction in order to encourage any investment at all, that would likely be a mistake. Producing low-density suburban models in urban locations squanders the market advantages of centrally located real estate that many downtown dwellers value—namely, easy access to jobs, walkability, and an urban quality of life—and limits a downtown's ability to support the very services, facilities, and amenities that give it its urban character.[22] In addition, low-density development underutilizes existing infrastructure, including streets, water, parks, and transit systems.

CONCLUSION

While this study used available census data to focus on the decades from 1970 to 2000, more recent evidence indicates that in the past five years the impetus for downtown residential living has continued and is broadening. For example, Philadelphia, a fully developed downtown with 78,349 residents in 2000, documented a 12 percent increase, to 88,000, in 2005. Other cities have experienced similar rises. San Diego, an emerging downtown, anticipates adding 9,000 housing units between 2000 and 2005; Washington, D.C., a downtown on the edge of take-off, reports almost 3,000 new housing units already built or under construction since 2002; and even St. Louis, a declining downtown, estimates an increase of 1,300 units built or in the planning stages since 2000.[23] Furthermore, observers are seeing comparable increases in smaller cities. For example, the *Charlotte Observer* reported a 67 percent increase in its "Uptown" (Charlotte's name for its downtown) population in the past five years.[24]

Overall, the increase in households in the vast majority of the sample downtowns—whether a long-term trend or a recent boon—demonstrates an upswing in downtown living. This chapter reveals other positive trends as well, including a rise in homeownership rates, more racial and ethnic diversity, a surge in higher educational attainment, and the dramatic growth in specific age cohorts. But it also shows that not all downtowns are the same, despite popular conceptions. Understanding who lives in individual downtowns is of paramount importance in informing the kinds of housing and investment strategies needed to ensure that downtowns reach their potential to become vibrant, healthy places to live and work.

22. For information on how cities can create "walkable" downtowns, see Leinberger (2005).

23. Berger (2005); www.downtowndc.org; www.downtownsandiego.org; www.downtownstlouis.org/web/living.jsp.

24. Kerry Hall, "Uptown Visionary Talks Future," *Charlotte Observer*, August 17, 2005.

REFERENCES

Berger, Gideon. 2005. "Condos and Cubicles: Can Center City Sustain Its Housing Boom Despite a Declining Office Market?" Unpublished paper, Department of City and Regional Planning, University of Pennsylvania.

Birch, Eugenie L. 2002. "Having a Longer View on Downtown Living." *Journal of the American Planning Association* 68 (1): 5–21.

Brookings Institution and Fannie Mae Foundation. 1998. "A Rise in Downtown Living." Brookings.

Downtown Preservation Council. 2003. "The Boundaries of Downtown: A Study of 48 Major U.S. Cities" (www.downtownresearch.com/index.htm [October 28, 2005]).

Florida, Richard. 2002. *The Rise of the Creative Class and How It Is Transforming Work, Leisure, Community, and Everyday Life.* New York: Basic Books.

Fogelson, Robert. 2001. *Downtown: Its Rise and Fall, 1880–1950.* Yale University Press.

Friedan, Bernard, and Lynne B. Sagalyn. 1989. *Downtown Inc.: How America Rebuilds Cities.* MIT Press.

Fulton, William. 2004. "Living the Niche Life." *Governing,* August.

Gans, Herbert. 1982. *The Urban Villagers.* New York: Free Press.

Garvin, Alexander. 2001. *The American City: What Works, What Doesn't.* New York: John Wiley and Sons.

Gratz, Roberta, and Norman Mintz. 1998. *Cities Back from the Edge.* New York: John Wiley and Sons.

Hartman, Chester. 1993. *City for Sale.* University of California Press.

Isenberg, Alison. 2004. *Downtown America: A History of the Place and the People Who Made It.* University of Chicago Press.

Jacobs, Jane. 1961. *The Death and Life of Great American Cities.* New York: Random House.

Landry, Charles. 2000. *The Creative City: A Toolkit for Urban Innovators.* London: Earthscan.

Lang, Robert E. 2003. *Edgeless Cities: Exploring the Elusive Metropolis.* Brookings.

Leinberger, Christopher. 2005. "Turning Around Downtown: Twelve Steps to Revitalization." Brookings.

Murphy, Raymond E. 1972. *The Central Business District.* New York: Aldine-Atherton.

Redstone, Louis G. 1976. *The New Downtowns: Rebuilding Business Districts.* New York: McGraw Hill.

Sohmer, Rebecca R., and Robert E. Lang. 2003. "Downtown Rebound." In *Redefining Urban and Suburban America: Evidence from Census 2000,* vol. 1, edited by Bruce Katz and Robert Lang. Brookings.

U.S. Census Bureau. "Housing Vacancies and Homeownership: First Quarter, 2005." Department of Commerce.

3

Growth Counties: Home to America's New Suburban Metropolis

ROBERT E. LANG AND
MEGHAN ZIMMERMAN GOUGH

When asked "Why do you rob banks?" famed bank robber Willy Sutton responded, "Because that's where the money is." In that spirit, this chapter examines the development of "growth counties," because that's where the growth is. During the second half of the twentieth century, the decentralization of economic and residential life, not the revival of core cities and central downtowns, remained the dominant growth pattern in the United States. Suburbs across the country have boomed, as has the Sun Belt, which includes much of the South and West. Most of this growth is occurring in large metropolitan areas, especially in what this chapter identifies as U.S. "growth counties."

Growth counties are places that grew at double-digit rates in every decade from 1950 to 2000 and are found in the nation's fifty largest metropolitan areas.[1] Using this definition, we identified 124 growth counties in the United States.

Growth counties represent the new "suburban" metropolis, but many contain what the census defines as "principal cities."[2] Some of these cities are quite large (for example, Houston, Las Vegas, and San José). This is not a contradiction, however, because most "cities" in growth counties—even the large ones—are essentially suburban in nature. For example, during the

The authors acknowledge Patrick Simmons and Dawn Dhavale for their contributions.

1. Throughout this book, the metropolitan areas identified refer to the metropolitan statistical area (MSA) and consolidated metropolitan statistical area (CMSA) concepts in use at the time of Census 2000.

2. For a full explanation of census definitions see Frey and others (2004).

61

1990s, Houston's core lost population, yet the population of the city—one of the largest in terms of land area—increased by over 250,000.[3] In addition, Houston has been so aggressive with annexation that it contains 93.4 percent of its region's office space, most of which is found in office parks many miles outside downtown.[4]

It is important to understand growth counties because they are "where the action is" for studying development trends. The descriptive statistics used here provide an overview of growth since 1950. Looking at the overall size and pace of growth offers a kind of insight that differs from what would be found, for example, in a multivariate analysis.

METHODOLOGY

As noted above, growth counties are metropolitan counties that had double-digit growth rates in every decade from 1950 to 2000. We chose that period because it covers the post–World War II era, when most suburbs boomed. Almost all growth counties easily exceeded a 10 percent growth rate in every decade after 1950. But the minimum growth rate indicates a consistent, compounding growth in these places.

Growth counties are located in the fifty largest metropolitan areas. They may be divided into three subtypes: MEGA (Massively Enlarged, Growth Accelerated) counties, mid-metro counties, and fringe counties.

—*MEGA Counties.* In addition to meeting the broader criteria for growth counties, MEGA counties have populations over 800,000 and lie at or near the core of the region. The 800,000 threshold ranks MEGA counties among the largest counties in the United States. They are so large that they could stand as major metropolitan areas on their own. In fact, as of 2000, the smallest MEGA county would rank fifty-eighth in population among metropolitan areas. The smallest MEGA county would rank twelfth among U.S. cities, and it is larger than such famous city-county integrated places as Indianapolis and Jacksonville, Florida. The 800,000 threshold for MEGA counties balances the number of growth counties found in each respective subcategory (MEGA, mid-metro, fringe).[5]

—*Mid-Metro Counties.* Mid-metro counties are growth counties with between 200,000 and 800,000 residents. The lower bound doubles the size

---

3. The city of Houston is over 574 square miles. Berube and Forman (2002).
4. Lang (2000).
5. The threshold results in nearly two dozen cases, whereas a 1,000,000-person minimum would have produced just over a dozen MEGA counties.

of a census-defined large city (100,000 residents).[6] Mid-metro counties are larger than many big cities but smaller than MEGA counties. As with MEGA counties, the population range for mid-metro counties also provides a natural break in the population distribution, which enables growth counties to be cleanly separated into three reasonably sized and distinct subcategories.

—*Fringe Counties.* Fringe counties exhibit fast growth at the edges of metropolitan areas. They are, roughly speaking, "exurban" counties, added to their respective metropolitan areas after 1971. Fringe counties contain fewer than 200,000 people, and they often represent the newest growth in their regions. The maximum population threshold represented many leading exurban counties, such as Loudoun County, Virginia, and Douglas County, Colorado, which still had fewer than 200,000 residents in 2000. The fact that these counties were added to their metropolitan areas after 1971 reflects the two decades of post-war growth that helped spread the metropolis past its original suburban boundaries into remote rural counties. The Bureau of the Budget (now the Office of Management and Budget [OMB]) made significant adjustments to metropolitan definitions in the early 1970s to include these counties. Before their inclusion in the metropolis, the population boom in many fringe counties gave the impression that the United States was experiencing a "rural renaissance," when in reality this growth was concentrated at the edge of extended metropolitan areas.[7]

FINDINGS

Overall, we defined twenty-three MEGA counties, fifty-four mid-metro counties, and forty-seven fringe counties in the United States. MEGA counties are concentrated in California, Texas, and Florida.[8] Mid-metro counties, on the other hand, are distributed throughout the country, in both high-growth and slower-growing areas. Fringe counties are found mostly in the East, especially around Washington, D.C., and Atlanta. As the following findings suggest, significant contrasts separate MEGA counties, which are more urban in character, and fringe counties, which are more classically suburban (table 3-1).

6. The Census Bureau treats cities with over 100,000 residents somewhat differently from less populous ones by providing more detailed data, thereby making them the subject of much research.

7. Johnson and Beale (1994).

8. By 2010, according to the Census Population Projections Program, these will be the three largest states in the United States as Florida overtakes New York.

T A B L E   3 - 1 . **Overview of Metropolitan Growth Counties**

Attribute	MEGA Counties	Mid-Metro Counties	Fringe Counties	United States
Population range	Above 800,000	200,000 to 800,000	Below 200,000	
Total counties	23	54	47	3,141
No. of metro areas	17	26	26	276
Total population (2000)	37,000,000	20,800,000	4,700,000	281,400,000
Location in metro area	Near the core	Middle to edge	At the fringe	
U.S. distribution	Mostly in sunbelt	National	Mostly in East	
Tag line	New metro centers	Metro growth engines	Suburbs of suburbs	
What's unique?	High-tech centers	In slow-growth metros	Added to metro since 1971	
Example	Clark (NV)	Lake (IL)	Loudoun (VA)	

Source: Metropolitan Institute at Virginia Tech analysis of Census 2000 data.

Growth Counties Represented More than One-Third of the Nation's Growth over the Last Fifty Years

Although growth counties constituted just 124 of the nation's 3,141 counties, they accounted for 38.5 percent of total U.S. population growth from 1950 to 2000. Their combined population grew from 12 million in 1950 to 62 million in 2000 (see table 3A-1 in appendix).

In just the 1990s, growth counties added 12 million residents, a 26 percent increase (table 3-2). Given that the nation grew by 13 percent in the same period, growth counties gained new people at twice the U.S. rate. By 2000, one in five Americans lived in a growth county.

A metropolitan-level summary shows that growth counties are found in twenty-seven states and forty-one metropolitan areas. Only nine of the fifty largest metropolitan areas (Cleveland, Pittsburgh, Buffalo, Memphis, Indianapolis, Providence, Hartford, Rochester, and Louisville) did not have a growth county. All of these metropolitan areas, except Memphis, are located in the Northeast or Midwest, and it is likely they do not contain growth counties because of their slow regional growth. Note, however, that even some slow-growing metropolitan areas, such as St. Louis, have a county (or two) that qualifies as a growth county. In areas such as these, redistribution—or thinning—of population is occurring as the core declines and the edge grows.[9] The South has the most growth counties, including many "smaller" (but still top fifty) metropolitan areas.

Comparing growth counties with their metropolitan areas highlights their massive contribution to growth in the nation's largest regions. These counties cumulatively accounted for under half of total population in their respective metropolitan areas (39 percent) but represented almost two-thirds of their areas' overall growth in the 1990s (64 percent). Consider the Washington,

9. Fulton and others (2001).

T A B L E   3 - 2 .   Growth County Metropolitan Summary

Metro area	Growth counties in metro area	Population				Growth county share of (percent)	
		1990 metro area	1990 growth county	1990–2000 metro area increase	1990–2000 growth county increase	Metro population	Metro growth 1990–2000
Atlanta, GA	11	2,959,950	1,918,115	1,152,248	830,224	64.8	72.1
Austin, TX	2	846,227	642,021	403,536	267,848	75.9	66.4
Boston, MA	2	5,455,403	581,918	363,697	196,408	10.7	54.0
Charlotte, NC	1	1,162,093	511,433	337,200	184,021	44.0	54.6
Chicago, IL	5	8,239,820	2,156,109	917,720	558,870	26.2	60.9
Cincinnati, OH	1	1,817,571	291,479	161,631	41,328	16.0	25.6
Columbus, OH	1	1,345,450	103,461	194,707	19,298	7.7	9.9
Dallas, TX	4	4,037,282	3,393,603	1,184,519	831,302	84.1	70.2
Denver, CO	4	1,980,140	1,115,671	601,366	366,406	56.3	60.9
Detroit, MI	1	5,187,171	115,645	269,257	41,306	2.2	15.3
Grand Rapids, MI	2	937,891	278,277	150,623	65,702	29.7	43.6
Greensboro, NC	2	1,050,304	233,223	201,205	44,477	22.2	22.1
Houston, TX	4	3,731,131	3,452,726	938,440	794,229	92.5	84.6
Jacksonville, FL	2	906,727	149,927	193,764	48,550	16.5	25.1
Kansas City, MO	1	1,582,875	355,054	193,187	96,032	22.4	49.7
Las Vegas, NV	2	852,737	759,240	710,545	649,010	89.0	91.3
Los Angeles, CA	4	14,531,529	5,668,365	1,842,116	1,185,942	39.0	64.4
Miami, FL	2	3,192,582	3,192,582	683,798	683,798	100.0	100.0
Milwaukee, WI	1	1,607,183	95,328	82,389	22,165	5.9	26.9
Minneapolis, MN	7	2,538,834	862,721	429,972	279,672	34.0	65.0
Nashville, TN	1	985,026	118,570	246,285	63,453	12.0	25.8
New Orleans, LA	1	1,285,270	42,437	52,456	5,635	3.3	10.7
New York City, NY	4	19,549,649	979,569	1,650,216	138,869	5.0	8.4
Norfolk, VA	2	1,443,244	64,990	126,297	17,892	4.5	14.2
Oklahoma City, OK	1	958,839	174,253	124,507	33,763	18.2	27.1
Orlando, IL	4	1,224,852	1,224,852	419,709	419,709	100.0	100.0
Philadelphia, PA	3	5,892,937	1,147,652	295,526	138,157	19.5	46.7
Phoenix, AZ	1	2,238,480	2,122,101	1,013,396	950,048	94.8	93.7
Portland, OR	3	1,793,476	818,887	471,747	249,680	45.7	52.9
Raleigh, NC	3	855,545	699,066	332,396	270,321	81.7	81.3
Richmond, VA	3	865,640	243,654	130,872	54,485	28.1	41.6
Sacramento, CA	3	1,481,102	1,340,010	315,755	288,187	90.5	91.3
Salt Lake City, UT	2	1,072,227	913,897	261,687	223,484	85.2	85.4
San Antonio, TX	2	1,324,749	1,237,226	267,634	233,726	93.4	87.3
San Diego, CA	1	2,498,016	2,498,016	315,817	315,817	100.0	100.0
San Francisco, CA	6	6,253,311	3,370,451	786,051	493,987	53.9	62.8
Seattle, WA	5	2,970,328	1,463,009	584,432	354,717	49.3	60.7
St. Louis, MO	2	2,492,525	232,441	111,082	75,967	64.8	68.4
Tampa, FL	3	2,067,959	1,216,300	328,038	258,215	75.9	78.7
Washington, DC	14	6,727,050	3,157,242	881,020	665,837	10.7	75.6
West Palm Beach, FL	1	863,518	863,518	267,666	267,666	100.0	100.0
Mega counties total	23	61,182,572	29,957,244	11,537,447	7,079,914	50.9	61.4
Mid-metro counties total	54	103,179,959	16,500,473	14,965,757	4,290,493	17.6	28.7
Fringe counties total	47	73,776,146	3,347,322	11,806,374	1,310,233	5.4	11.1
Total	**124**	**128,806,643**	**49,805,039**	**19,994,509**	**12,680,640**	**26.2**	**63.6**

Source: Metropolitan Institute at Virginia Tech analysis of decennial census data.

D.C., metropolitan area. The region contains fourteen growth counties representing all three types: two MEGA counties (Montgomery County, Maryland, and Fairfax County, Virginia), four mid-metro counties (Anne Arundel County, Harford County, and Howard County, Maryland, and Prince William County, Virginia), and eight fringe counties (Charles County, Maryland; Calvert County, Maryland; Culpeper County, Virginia; Frederick County, Maryland; Loudoun County, Virginia; Queen Anne's County, Maryland; Spotsylvania County, Virginia; and Stafford County, Virginia.). Recent growth in these counties exemplified the national trend: the fourteen counties together accounted for less than half of the metropolitan area's population (47 percent), but for over 75 percent of the metropolitan area's growth from 1990 to 2000.

MEGA Counties Are Concentrated in the Sun Belt

MEGA counties have shown enormous population growth in the nation's largest regions since 1950. MEGA counties are large suburban counties outside the nation's largest cities, such as Chicago, Washington, D.C., Los Angeles, and San Francisco, and core urban counties in fast-growth metropolitan areas, such as Dallas, Houston, Phoenix, and Las Vegas.

Waves of decentralized growth since 1950—both from cities to suburbs and from the nation's older Northeast and Midwest industrial cores to the Sun Belt—have fed MEGA county growth. In 2000, these counties were home to over one in eight Americans. MEGA counties are now perhaps as important to the nation's commerce and culture as large cities. In many ways, MEGA counties are now the "new metropolitan heartlands." The twenty-three MEGA counties range in size from Harris County, Texas (which includes Houston), with 3.4 million people, to Travis County, Texas (which includes Austin), with slightly more than 800,000 people (see table 3A-1 in appendix). The average MEGA county contains over 1.6 million people.

MEGA counties are found mostly in the booming regions of the Sun Belt, particularly in the region's three biggest growth states since 1950— California, Texas, and Florida. California contains seven MEGA counties; Texas and Florida each have five. The Northeast and Midwest together have only one MEGA county: DuPage County, Illinois, west of Chicago.

As the nation's new metropolitan centers, MEGA counties are home to a remarkable number of the most important U.S. tourist areas, high-tech corridors, and business centers. Both Disneyland (Orange County, California) and Disney World (Orange County, Florida) are in MEGA counties, as is the Las Vegas Strip (Clark County, Nevada). They also feature the retirement and golfing areas of South Florida (Palm Beach, Broward, and Miami-Dade counties) and Central Arizona (Maricopa County).

MEGA counties contain the Silicon Valley of California (Santa Clara County), the Silicon Prairie of Texas (Travis County), and the Silicon Dominion of Virginia (Fairfax County). In addition, many of the biggest office centers in the nation found outside of a central business district are in MEGA counties.[10] These include Post Oak (Harris County, Texas), South Coast (Orange County, California), and Tysons Corner (Fairfax County, Virginia.).[11] Each of these centers ranks among the nation's twenty-five largest downtowns.[12] In addition, the big downtowns of Dallas (Dallas County), Houston (Harris County), San José (Santa Clara County), Phoenix (Maricopa County), Miami (Miami-Dade County), and Austin (Travis County) are found within MEGA counties.

Clark County, Nevada, experienced the fastest growth among this group between 1950 and 2000 (2,749 percent). The county's population grew from fewer than 50,000 people in 1950 to 1.4 million by 2000. The population of two additional counties (Broward County, Florida, and Orange County, California) jumped by more than 1,000 percent. Interestingly, two Orange counties (California and Florida) turn up as MEGA counties, indicating the role that mild climates played in facilitating metropolitan growth over the past half-century.[13] Another fast-growing MEGA county, Fairfax County, Virginia, expanded nearly tenfold since 1950 and is now the largest juris-diction in the Washington, D.C., area. In absolute terms, Maricopa County, Arizona, added the most people (2.7 million) between 1950 and 2000 among the MEGA counties. Harris County, Texas, followed close behind, gaining over 2.5 million new residents during the same period.

Twenty-one of the twenty-three MEGA counties exceeded the national growth rate during the 1990s (San Diego and Santa Clara counties in California were the exceptions). As a whole, the counties grew almost twice as fast as the nation (24 versus 13 percent) and represented 22 percent of the nation's total growth. Although MEGA counties remain fast-growing places, they are maturing as well. For example, Orange County, California, grew by 226 percent during the 1950s but just 18 percent in the 1990s. Because the county is now so large, however, it added nearly the same number of people in the 1990s as it did in the 1950s. Despite its growth slowdown, the county is now roughly as large as the city of Chicago, and it is growing much faster.

10. Lang (2003).
11. Many MEGA counties contain "edge cities," which are large concentrations of office and retail space. Garreau (1991).
12. Lang (2003).
13. Glaeser and Shapiro (2003).

MEGA counties are found in seventeen different metropolitan areas. These counties account for half the population of their respective regions (51 percent) but represent most of their regions' overall growth (61 percent). The Los Angeles metropolitan area exemplifies these trends: its three MEGA counties (Orange, Riverside, and San Bernardino) contain just over a third of the region's population but contributed 60 percent of its growth last decade.

The demographic profile of MEGA counties illustrates that these places are often far more racially diverse than the nation as a whole (see table 3A-2 in appendix). Just over half of all MEGA county residents are non-Hispanic whites (56 percent), compared to roughly seven in ten Americans overall. Miami-Dade County has the most diverse population of all the MEGA counties (21 percent non-Hispanic white), whereas Salt Lake County, Utah, is the least diverse (81 percent non-Hispanic white). The fact that MEGA counties are more diverse than the nation as a whole partly reflects their concentration in the South and West.

These suburban counties are also more "urban" in terms of homeownership, as the percentage of MEGA county residents owning their homes falls just under the national average. The same holds for households living in detached single-family housing units, owning three or more vehicles, and paying more than 35 percent of their income in rent. However, regional differences mark these overall demographic distinctions. For example, South Florida's large retirement population distinguishes its MEGA counties from the average on these measures, whereas suburban MEGA counties, such DuPage County, Illinois, have more "traditional" families (married couples with children at home) and more homeowners.

Mid-Metro Counties Doubled Their Share of U.S. Population Since 1950

The most numerous of the three growth county types, the fifty-four mid-metro counties, are found throughout the nation—from New England to Florida and from Southern California to the Pacific Northwest. The term "mid-metro county" refers to the fact that these places often lie at the mid-point of their regions geographically and that they lie midway in character between the MEGA and fringe counties.

Since 1950, the fastest population growth in the nation occurred in the Sunbelt. Most of this growth was in the form of low-density, "leap-frog" development, with mix-and-match subdivisions; low-slung, glass-cube office parks; big-box retail centers; and endless shopping strips. This characterization also describes most development in mid-metro counties. Mid-metro

counties typically contain "edgeless cities," a form of sprawling office development that never reaches the density or cohesiveness of edge cities. Edgeless
cities feature mostly isolated office buildings at varying densities over vast
swaths of metropolitan space.[14]

Mid-metro counties are widespread, located in twenty-one states and
twenty-seven metropolitan areas. They exist in a mix of metropolitan areas,
including high-growth regions, such as Atlanta, Los Angeles, and Orlando, and
slow-growing ones, such as St. Louis, Cincinnati, and Philadelphia.[15] Many
regions have multiple mid-metro counties: Atlanta, Chicago, Seattle, and
Washington, D.C., each have four, and Denver, Minneapolis, Philadelphia,
and Portland each have three.

Although older metropolitan areas have traditional high-density cores
and rings of older, pedestrian-oriented suburbs, they also feature the more
recent, sprawling growth often found in mid-metro counties. In a way, the
mid-metro counties of places such as Minneapolis and Boston are those
regions' "Sun Belts." They are the growth engines in many of these older
regions, accounting for a majority of population growth despite often containing just a fraction of total metropolitan population.

The fifty-four mid-metro counties range in population from Ventura
County in Southern California (750,000) to Washington County, east of
St. Paul, Minnesota (200,000) and have an average population of 385,000.
Similarly, the share of metropolitan growth and total population represented
by mid-metro counties varies considerably. St. Charles County, Missouri, in
suburban St. Louis, accounted for almost two-thirds of its region's growth
in the 1990s but contained only 10 percent of the region's residents. Johnson
County, Kansas, outside Kansas City, accounted for half of its metropolitan
area's growth but represented only 22 percent of its total population in 1990.

Conversely, mid-metro counties in the South's I-85 corridor region,
stretching from Raleigh, North Carolina, southwest to Atlanta, Georgia,
exhibited roughly equal shares of population growth and total population
share. In all cases, these mid-metro counties represented half or more of
their region's population increase.

The presence of mid-metro counties in so many of the nation's largest
metropolitan areas indicates that rapid population growth, to at least some
extent, affects most regions. In slower-growing metropolitan areas, such as
St. Louis, Kansas City, and Cincinnati, population growth is mostly concentrated in a single mid-metro county. Thus the edge of slow-growing regions

---

14. Lang (2003).
15. Some fast-growing regions—notably Phoenix and Las Vegas—lacked mid-metro counties because their main metropolitan county was too large and their other counties too small.

may come to resemble fast-developing metropolitan areas. The historian Sam Bass Warner Jr. observed that places that experience simultaneous growth come to resemble each other because they reflect the same market fashions and feasibilities.[16]

To better understand Warner's observation, consider mid-metro counties in the Atlanta and Chicago metropolitan areas. Comparisons often focus on the differences between the regions—Atlanta is a fast-growing Sunbelt boomtown that grew by nearly 40 percent in the 1990s, whereas Chicago is an older Midwest metropolis that grew by only 11 percent. Despite being located in two different types of metropolitan areas, two of their mid-metro counties—Cobb outside of Atlanta, and Lake outside of Chicago—nonetheless share similar growth patterns and demographic profiles (table 3-3). The two counties have similar populations, land areas, and densities. In terms of demographics, Cobb seems to be a bit more urban in profile than Lake, but there are no stark differences. Even their growth rates in the 1990s are comparable, with Cobb and Lake gaining by 36 and 25 percent respectively. The similar nature of these counties implies that they face a comparable set of policy challenges related to growth. Indeed, interviews with government officials in fourteen mid-metro counties revealed that most were concerned with financing and building adequate infrastructure to accommodate rapid growth.[17] Lake is like a lost Atlanta county that has ventured north.

Demographically, mid-metro counties fall somewhere between MEGA counties and fringe counties (see table 3A-2 in appendix). In general, mid-metro counties are slightly more racially diverse than the national average, but individually they include areas of high and low diversity. For example, the population in Rockingham County, New Hampshire, is 96 percent non-Hispanic white, whereas DeKalb County, Georgia, is only 32 percent non-Hispanic white. In contrast to MEGA counties, their average home-ownership rate exceeds the national average by more than 5 percent. The percentage of households with married couples with children under eighteen years, the percentage living in single-family detached homes, and the percentage with three or more vehicles all exceed averages for both MEGA counties and the nation as a whole.

Fringe Counties Are the Fastest-Growing and the Least Diverse Type of County

Fringe counties—fast-growing counties with fewer than 200,000 residents that have been added to metropolitan areas since 1965—are updated ver-

---

16. Warner (1972).
17. Atkins, Wolman, and Jordan (2002).

T A B L E   3 - 3 .   Comparison of Lake County, IL, and Cobb County, GA

Characteristic	Lake County, IL	Cobb County, GA	Average, all mid-metro counties
Total population	644,356	607,751	385,018
Land area (square miles)	448	340	714
Population per square mile	1,438	1,788	699
Percent non-Hispanic white	73	69	76
Percent married couples with children	35	28	28
Homeownership rate	78	68	72
Percent single-family detached units	69	66	66
Mean travel time (minutes)	30.1	31.3	27.4
Percent of households with 3+ vehicles	18	20	20
Percent population growth, 1990s	25	36	27

Source: Metropolitan Institute at Virginia Tech analysis of decennial census data.

sions of 1960s "sitcom suburbs."[18] These forty-seven counties are less diverse and have more "married with children" families and a larger proportion of homeowners than other growth counties.

Most fringe counties lie at the metropolitan edge. Unlike other growth counties, they are mostly bedroom suburbs and generally do not contain large concentrations of commerce. Traditional suburbs retreated to fringe counties over the past few decades, whereas other parts of the region, including many mature suburbs, grew more diverse and crowded. Fringe county suburbs are also overwhelmingly Republican. In over 90 percent of fringe counties, a majority of voters cast their ballots for George W. Bush in the 2000 and 2004 presidential elections. Fringe counties may actually be mid-metro counties in formation. Commercial development in mid-metro counties fuels the emergence of fringe counties, thereby promoting even more population growth farther from the regional core. They are "suburbs of suburbs" that in the future could spawn even more distant suburbs.

Fringe counties have a wide spectrum of populations. The smallest is New Kent County, outside Richmond, Virginia, which had just 13,462 people in 2000. The largest is Frederick County, Maryland, northwest of Washington, D.C., and home to 195,000 residents (thus just missing the cutoff for mid-metro county designation). Fringe counties are found in twenty-six different metropolitan areas, including high-growth regions such as Atlanta, Denver, and Las Vegas as well as the slow-growing areas of Milwaukee, Detroit, and Minneapolis.

Although found across the United States, fringe counties are concentrated in two Eastern regions, Washington, D.C., and Atlanta. The eight

18. Hayden (2003).

fringe counties found in Virginia and Maryland are fueled by continued settlement around the periphery of greater Washington, D.C. The Atlanta region, containing seven fringe counties, lacks natural geographic boundaries to curb its growth; thus its limits are defined only by demand. From 1990 to 2000, five of Atlanta's seven fringe counties exceeded metropolitan Atlanta's total growth rate (39 percent). Both Forsyth and Henry counties grew by over 100 percent.

The Southwest, which is the fastest-growing part of the United States, contained only two fringe counties in 2000—Douglas, outside of Denver, and Nye, outside of Las Vegas. The Southwest is noticeably underrepresented in fringe counties because its counties are too large to qualify. Most of their regional growth is represented in one or two counties. By contrast, many Northeastern counties do not qualify because they are not growing fast enough. In total, thirty-nine fringe counties lie in the East, whereas only eight are found in the West.

Douglas County, located south of Denver, led the fringe counties in numeric growth, adding over 172,000 new residents between 1950 and 2000. It also experienced the greatest percentage growth over that period (nearly 5,000 percent). Douglas began the post-war era as a "frontier" county, containing fewer than six people per square mile.[19] By 2000, it was the fastest-growing county in the nation, and it is now firmly in the new metropolitan frontier along the booming Front Range of the Rockies. In response to the 2000 census figures, Colorado's *Rocky Mountain News* touted Douglas as the nation's richest county, with a median household income of $82,929.[20] Just 2.1 percent of its residents lived below the poverty line.

The demographic profile of fringe counties shows them to be more traditionally suburban in their makeup (see table 3A-2 in appendix). Two fringe counties, St. Croix, Wisconsin, and Washington, Minnesota, illustrate this trend dramatically, each with a 97 percent white population. Osceola County, Florida, contains the most diverse population, at 60 percent non-Hispanic white. The proportion of households that are married couples with children in Douglas County, Colorado—42 percent—is almost twice the national average (23.5 percent). Interestingly, almost half have three or more vehicles. The homeownership rate and percentage of single-family detached homes in fringe counties exceed the national average. Only 11 percent of the residents in New Kent and Powhatan counties (outside Richmond, Virginia) rent, and fully 94 percent of Powhatan homes are single-family detached units.

19. Lang, Popper, and Popper (1997).
20. Michele Ames, "Douglas Richest County in Nation," *Rocky Mountain News,* June 4, 2002.

DISCUSSION

A half-century of sustained growth has transformed the U.S. metropolis, and growth counties led the change. Although many growth counties contain principal cities (especially MEGA counties), most of their overall growth is suburban. In fact, in part because of growth in these counties, half the nation now lives in the suburbs.[21] This typology points metropolitan and suburban leaders toward their peers in different areas of the United States, where they might draw lessons on how to deal with the specific challenges they confront.

MEGA Counties

For decades, three main forces drove MEGA county growth: abundant land, new (often federally financed) infrastructure, and new home climate-control technologies. In 1950, MEGA counties (even the ones with "big" cities) were wide-open spaces. The Federal Interstate Highway System would soon make these spaces accessible. Inventions in home climate control allowed people to live in large numbers in formerly inhospitable climates in the Sun Belt, from the arid Southwest to the humid Southeast.[22] Immigrants from around the nation and the world began to flock to these regions.

People still flock to the Sun Belt, but MEGA counties are increasingly not the places in which native-born Americans settle. Some MEGA counties are not even keeping pace with surrounding metropolitan growth. They are running out of land—from Southern California, where "sprawl hits a wall," to South Florida, where efforts to preserve the Everglades have shut down new subdivisions.[23] Federal and state funds to support their growth are also drying up. Because MEGA counties are so built up, they lose resources to new growth at the edge of the region.[24]

Thus the major policy implications for MEGA counties concern the sustainability of future growth. Development in these counties after 1950 was often rapid and poorly planned. As a result, they now face a number of unresolved growth issues. MEGA counties—even those without traditional big cities—must accept that they are urbanizing and manage that urbanization accordingly. Suburban counties, such as Fairfax (Virginia), Montgomery (Maryland), and DuPage (Illinois), are waking up to the fact that they too

21. Lang, Blakely, and Gough (forthcoming).
22. Fishman (2000).
23. University of Southern California and Brookings Institution Center on Urban and Metropolitan Policy (2001).
24. Orfield (2002).

are now large cities. Although they maintain a mostly suburban look, these counties must plan for the new diversity of people, places, and incomes characteristic of urban places. Were it not for immigration, some MEGA counties would have already stopped gaining population altogether.

MEGA counties typically have abundant resources. Because most edge cities are located in MEGA counties, they are often loaded with ratable development, such as office parks, creating high fiscal capacity to fund local schools.[25] But MEGA counties have an accompanying share of problems to address—for example, schools with growing foreign-born populations, overwhelmed county hospitals, older housing stock, and traffic congestion. They have traditionally grown horizontally, but now many will—and must—grow vertically. These places will provide the venue for new urban design and so-called "smart growth" policies. Within their borders, MEGA counties can both boom and decline, which means balancing growth across the county will be more difficult than in the past.

The median age of MEGA counties' housing stock now approaches twenty-five years.[26] In some of these areas, large immigrant families are moving into old bungalows and tract houses that are too small to accommodate them.[27] At the same time, affluent households are increasingly tearing down smaller homes and replacing them with "monster houses," creating tensions between neighbors.[28] In addition, many less affluent older areas are being retrofitted as gated communities because of increasing security concerns.[29]

These trends add up to a complicated development picture in MEGA counties such as Fairfax County, Virginia. Like California, Fairfax's growth is almost entirely due to immigration and the high birth rates of immigrant families. Part of the county is mature, stable suburbs. Another area is older but booming as larger immigrant families replace smaller households. Yet another part of the county is still developing, with new homes mostly attracting traditional "married with children" households. In sum, Fairfax is simultaneously mature and stable, redeveloping rapidly, and still developing. Orange County, California, faces a similar situation: the north is booming with immigrants, the center is stable and mature, and the south is still developing. Creating public policies that address these different conditions is challenging to say the least.

25. Lang (2003).
26. Metropolitan Institute at Virginia Tech analysis of Census 2000 data.
27. Simmons (2005).
28. Lang and Danielsen (2002).
29. Blakely and Snyder (1997); Lang and Danielsen (1997); Sanchez, Lang, and Dhavale (2005).

Mid-Metro Counties

Although not as mature and large in scale as MEGA counties, many mid-metro counties will soon face a future when they too must assume a different growth model. In some regions, the exurbs just beyond the mid-metro counties are now offering competition as a newer suburban alternative. It is fascinating how quickly "newness" can fade in the suburbs. The booming places of the 1980s and even the 1990s are at risk of being usurped by exurbs where growth is just starting to take off. The once hot town of Schaumburg, Illinois, in Kane County, outside Chicago, which saw its office market soar in the 1980s, stopped growing in 1990 as development moved further west to its exurbs.[30]

The real challenge for the mid-metro counties is that they must decide what they want to be when they grow up. Many are filling up with big-box retail centers as households flood in, demanding convenient access to everyday goods and services. But as mid-metro counties urbanize, they must decide if they want to retain their residential character or evolve into more diverse job centers, forcing a broader vision of future growth and development.

Fringe Counties

The major policy implications for fringe counties concern managing the repercussions of recent growth. These counties are relatively new to their region and therefore should expect sustained or increased growth over future decades. As people search for more open space and cheaper housing, county growth will continue to push farther out to the metropolitan fringe.

Fringe counties face an increasingly public request for growth management policies and programs. In fact, the nation's most visible struggles over population growth and development take place in fringe counties. Many battles revolve around preservation of farmland and open space, loss of wildlife habitat, and air and water pollution resulting from increased development.[31]

The biggest immediate challenge for fringe counties is meeting the demand for increased services. Fringe counties currently have difficulty keeping up with the fast pace of their growth. Providing public services and infrastructure for new residential development on the fringe area is costly. Residents are concerned with crowded schools, transportation infrastructure, and other public services. Development concerns relate directly to the impact on taxpayers. In response to new development, residents of these fast-growing counties experience rising tax burdens. Lack of a substantial commercial real estate base means that these places often lack the fiscal capacity for growth,

30. Lang (2003).
31. Gough (2003).

and yet they continue to grow. As the nation's population grows, the public battles over issues related to growth will become even more complex.

CONCLUSION

During the second half of the twentieth century, the nation's settlement pattern shifted strongly toward decentralized growth. Suburbs across the United States boomed, as did the Sunbelt, which includes much of the South and West. Most of this growth occurred in large metropolitan areas, especially in the growth counties discussed here.

But as this chapter makes clear, despite the fact that suburbia dominates growth, suburbs themselves are remarkably diverse.[32] The 124 growth counties represent a range of suburban and urban places—from old city centers and first generation post-war suburbs in the MEGA counties to the newest exurbs in the fringe counties. Growth counties also indicate that a variety of places continue to gain population. The MEGA counties rely on both new foreign-born residents and a high rate of natural increase to fuel their growth, whereas fringe counties have high rates of domestic in-migration. Mid-metro counties often exhibit all these components of growth.

In the end, the three growth county subtypes face different challenges and opportunities. As such, it is incumbent upon policymakers at all levels to recognize and understand these differences and to deal with the myriad issues that they raise in that context.

In addition to establishing baseline data for future metropolitan growth analyses, it is hoped that this chapter will pave the way for better "peer county" analysis, so that best practices can be shared among similar kinds of places.[33] At the moment, the National Association of Counties, in Washington, D.C., has a caucus made up of the 100 largest urban counties in the United States. But the reality is that large urban counties, such as Maricopa, Arizona (which contains Phoenix), and New York (with Manhattan) may not have that much in common other than that they are large. The growth county analysis adds another dimension to the mix, including development trends. Maricopa may be better served by partnering with places that are both fast-growing and large. This chapter illustrates the fact that growth since 1950 has disproportionably affected a relatively small number of counties and that these places should now look to their peers for ideas on how to confront the challenges that fast development often brings.

32. Mikelbank (2004).

33. Arthur C. Nelson at Virginia Tech uses the growth county typology to frame a study for the U.S. Department of Housing and Urban Development looking at environmental regulation and housing affordability. He argues that growth counties will have the most development pressure and will therefore be the most likely to have extensive environmental regulation.

TABLE 3A-1. Growth Counties by State and Metropolitan Area

Growth counties	State	Metro area	1950 population	2000 population	Change, 1950–2000 Number	Percent	Growth county type
Maricopa	AZ	Phoenix	331,770	3,072,149	2,740,379	826	MEGA
Orange	CA	Los Angeles	216,224	2,846,289	2,630,065	1216	MEGA
Riverside	CA	Los Angeles	170,046	1,545,387	1,375,341	809	MEGA
San Bernardino	CA	Los Angeles	281,642	1,709,434	1,427,792	507	MEGA
Ventura	CA	Los Angeles	114,647	753,197	638,550	557	Mid-Metro
El Dorado	CA	Sacramento	16,207	156,299	140,092	864	Fringe
Placer	CA	Sacramento	41,649	248,399	206,750	496	Mid-Metro
Sacramento	CA	Sacramento	277,140	1,223,499	946,359	342	MEGA
San Diego	CA	San Diego	556,808	2,813,833	2,257,025	405	MEGA
Contra Costa	CA	San Francisco	298,984	948,816	649,832	217	MEGA
Napa	CA	San Francisco	46,603	124,279	77,676	167	Fringe
Santa Clara	CA	San Francisco	290,547	1,682,585	1,392,038	479	MEGA
Santa Cruz	CA	San Francisco	66,534	255,602	189,068	284	Mid-Metro
Solano	CA	San Francisco	104,833	394,542	289,709	276	Mid-Metro
Sonoma	CA	San Francisco	103,405	458,614	355,209	344	Mid-Metro
Arapahoe	CO	Denver	52,125	487,967	435,842	836	Mid-Metro
Boulder	CO	Denver	48,296	291,288	242,992	503	Mid-Metro
Douglas	CO	Denver	3,507	175,766	172,259	4912	Fringe
Jefferson	CO	Denver	55,687	527,056	471,369	847	Mid-Metro
Clay	FL	Jacksonville	14,323	140,814	126,491	883	Fringe
Nassau	FL	Jacksonville	12,811	57,663	44,852	350	Fringe
Broward	FL	Miami	83,933	1,623,018	1,539,085	1834	MEGA
Miami-Dade	FL	Miami	495,084	2,253,362	1,758,278	355	MEGA
Lake	FL	Orlando	36,340	210,528	174,188	479	Mid-Metro
Orange	FL	Orlando	114,950	896,344	781,394	680	MEGA
Osceola	FL	Orlando	11,406	172,493	161,087	1412	Fringe
Seminole	FL	Orlando	26,883	365,196	338,313	1259	Mid-Metro
Hernando	FL	Tampa	6,693	130,802	124,109	1854	Fringe
Hillsborough	FL	Tampa	249,894	998,948	749,054	300	MEGA
Pasco	FL	Tampa	20,529	344,765	324,236	1579	Mid-Metro
Palm Beach	FL	West Palm Beach	114,688	1,131,184	1,016,496	886	MEGA
Barrow	GA	Atlanta	13,115	46,144	33,029	252	Fringe
Cherokee	GA	Atlanta	20,750	141,903	121,153	584	Fringe
Clayton	GA	Atlanta	22,872	236,517	213,645	934	Mid-Metro
Cobb	GA	Atlanta	61,830	607,751	545,921	883	Mid-Metro
DeKalb	GA	Atlanta	136,395	665,865	529,470	388	Mid-Metro
Douglas	GA	Atlanta	12,173	92,174	80,001	657	Fringe
Forsyth	GA	Atlanta	11,005	98,407	87,402	794	Fringe
Gwinnett	GA	Atlanta	32,320	588,448	556,128	1721	Mid-Metro
Henry	GA	Atlanta	15,857	119,341	103,484	653	Fringe
Paulding	GA	Atlanta	11,752	81,678	69,926	595	Fringe
Rockdale	GA	Atlanta	8,464	70,111	61,647	728	Fringe
DuPage	IL	Chicago	154,599	904,161	749,562	485	MEGA
Kane	IL	Chicago	150,388	404,119	253,731	169	Mid-Metro
Lake	IL	Chicago	179,097	644,356	465,259	260	Mid-Metro
McHenry	IL	Chicago	50,656	260,077	209,421	413	Mid-Metro
Will	IL	Chicago	134,336	502,266	367,930	274	Mid-Metro
Johnson	KS	Kansas City	62,783	451,086	388,303	619	Mid-Metro
St. Charles Parish	LA	New Orleans	13,363	48,072	34,709	260	Fringe
Anne Arundel	MD	Washington	117,392	489,656	372,264	317	Mid-Metro
Calvert	MD	Washington	12,100	74,563	62,463	516	Fringe

(continued)

TABLE 3A-1. Growth Counties by State and Metropolitan Area (*continued*)

Growth counties	State	Metro area	1950 population	2000 population	Change, 1950–2000 Number	Change, 1950–2000 Percent	Growth county type
Charles	MD	Washington	23,415	120,546	97,131	415	Fringe
Frederick	MD	Washington	62,287	195,277	132,990	214	Fringe
Harford	MD	Washington	51,782	218,590	166,808	322	Mid-Metro
Howard	MD	Washington	23,119	247,842	224,723	972	Mid-Metro
Montgomery	MD	Washington	164,401	873,341	708,940	431	MEGA
Queen Anne's	MD	Washington	14,579	40,563	25,984	178	Fringe
Livingston	MI	Detroit	26,725	156,951	130,226	487	Fringe
Allegan	MI	Grand Rapids	47,493	105,665	58,172	123	Fringe
Ottawa	MI	Grand Rapids	73,751	238,314	164,563	223	Mid-Metro
Anoka	MN	Minneapolis	35,579	298,084	262,505	738	Mid-Metro
Carver	MN	Minneapolis	18,155	70,205	52,050	287	Fringe
Dakota	MN	Minneapolis	49,019	355,904	306,885	626	Mid-Metro
Scott	MN	Minneapolis	16,486	89,498	73,012	443	Fringe
Sherburne	MN	Minneapolis	10,661	64,417	53,756	504	Fringe
Washington	MN	Minneapolis	34,544	201,130	166,586	482	Mid-Metro
St. Charles	MO	St. Louis	29,834	283,883	254,049	852	Mid-Metro
Warren	MO	St. Louis	7,666	24,525	16,859	220	Fringe
Mecklenburg	NC	Charlotte	197,052	695,454	498,402	253	Mid-Metro
Davidson	NC	Greensboro	62,244	147,246	85,002	137	Fringe
Randolph	NC	Greensboro	50,804	130,454	79,650	157	Fringe
Durham	NC	Raleigh	101,639	223,314	121,675	120	Mid-Metro
Orange	NC	Raleigh	34,435	118,227	83,792	243	Fringe
Wake	NC	Raleigh	136,450	627,846	491,396	360	Mid-Metro
Hillsborough	NH	Boston	156,987	380,841	223,854	143	Mid-Metro
Rockingham	NH	Boston	70,059	277,359	207,300	296	Mid-Metro
Hunterdon	NJ	New York City	42,736	121,989	79,253	185	Fringe
Ocean	NJ	New York City	56,622	510,916	454,294	802	Mid-Metro
Sussex	NJ	New York City	34,423	144,166	109,743	319	Fringe
Gloucester	NJ	Philadelphia	91,727	254,673	162,946	178	Mid-Metro
Clark	NV	Las Vegas	48,289	1,375,765	1,327,476	2749	MEGA
Nye	NV	Las Vegas	3,101	32,485	29,384	948	Fringe
Orange	NY	New York City	152,255	341,367	189,112	124	Mid-Metro
Butler	OH	Cincinnati	147,203	332,807	185,604	126	Mid-Metro
Fairfield	OH	Columbus	52,130	122,759	70,629	136	Fringe
Cleveland	OK	Oklahoma City	41,443	208,016	166,573	402	Mid-Metro
Clackamas	OR	Portland	86,716	338,391	251,675	290	Mid-Metro
Marion	OR	Portland	101,401	284,834	183,433	181	Mid-Metro
Washington	OR	Portland	61,269	445,342	384,073	627	Mid-Metro
Bucks	PA	Philadelphia	144,620	597,635	453,015	313	Mid-Metro
Chester	PA	Philadelphia	159,141	433,501	274,360	172	Mid-Metro
Rutherford	TN	Nashville	40,696	182,023	141,327	347	Fringe
Hays	TX	Austin	17,840	97,589	79,749	447	Fringe
Travis	TX	Austin	160,980	812,280	651,300	405	MEGA
Dallas	TX	Dallas	614,799	2,218,899	1,604,100	261	MEGA
Denton	TX	Dallas	41,365	432,976	391,611	947	Mid-Metro
Johnson	TX	Dallas	31,390	126,811	95,421	304	Fringe
Tarrant	TX	Dallas	361,253	1,446,219	1,084,966	300	MEGA
Brazoria	TX	Houston	46,549	241,767	195,218	419	Mid-Metro
Fort Bend	TX	Houston	31,056	354,452	323,396	1041	Mid-Metro
Galveston	TX	Houston	113,066	250,158	137,092	121	Mid-Metro

(*continued*)

TABLE 3A-1. Growth Counties by State and Metropolitan Area (*continued*)

Growth counties	State	Metro area	1950 population	2000 population	Change, 1950–2000		Growth county type
					Number	Percent	
Harris	TX	Houston	806,701	3,400,578	2,593,877	322	MEGA
Bexar	TX	San Antonio	500,460	1,392,931	892,471	178	MEGA
Comal	TX	San Antonio	16,357	78,021	61,664	377	Fringe
Davis	UT	Salt Lake	30,867	238,994	208,127	674	Mid-Metro
Salt Lake	UT	Salt Lake City	274,895	898,387	623,492	227	MEGA
Gloucester	VA	Norfolk	10,343	34,780	24,437	236	Fringe
James City	VA	Norfolk	6,317	48,102	41,785	662	Fringe
Henrico	VA	Richmond	57,340	262,300	204,960	357	Mid-Metro
New Kent	VA	Richmond	3,995	13,462	9,467	237	Fringe
Powhatan	VA	Richmond	5,556	22,377	16,821	303	Fringe
Culpeper	VA	Washington	13,242	34,262	21,020	159	Fringe
Fairfax	VA	Washington	98,557	969,749	871,192	884	MEGA
Loudoun	VA	Washington	21,147	169,599	148,452	702	Fringe
Prince William	VA	Washington	22,612	280,813	258,201	1142	Mid-Metro
Spotsylvania	VA	Washington	11,920	90,395	78,475	658	Fringe
Stafford	VA	Washington	11,902	92,446	80,544	677	Fringe
Island	WA	Seattle	11,079	71,558	60,479	546	Fringe
Kitsap	WA	Seattle	75,724	231,969	156,245	206	Mid-Metro
Pierce	WA	Seattle	275,876	700,820	424,944	154	Mid-Metro
Snohomish	WA	Seattle	111,580	606,024	494,444	443	Mid-Metro
Thurston	WA	Seattle	44,884	207,355	162,471	362	Mid-Metro
Washington	WI	Milwaukee	33,902	117,493	83,591	247	Fringe
St. Croix	WI	Minneapolis	25,905	63,155	37,250	144	Fringe
Total MEGA (23)			6,666,644	37,037,158	30,370,514	456	
Total Mid-Metro (54)			4,472,128	20,790,966	16,318,838	365	
Total Fringe (47)			999,060	4,657,555	3,658,495	366	
Total (124)			12,137,832	62,485,679	50,347,847	415	

Source: Metropolitan Institute at Virginia Tech analysis of decennial census data.

TABLE 3A-2. Growth County Demographic Profile

Percent, except as indicated

Variable	National average	MEGA Counties			Mid-Metro Counties			Fringe Counties		
	Average	Average	High	Low	Average	High	Low	Average	High	Low
Non-Hispanic white	69.1	55.7	Salt Lake, UT 80.9	Miami-Dade, FL 20.7	76.5	Rockingham, NH 96.1	DeKalb, GA 32.2	84.2	St. Croix, WI 97.4	Osceola, FL 59.6
Married couples with children	23.5	25.4	Salt Lake, UT; DuPage, IL 32.0	Palm Beach, FL 18.0	28.1	Davis, UT 41.7	Pasco & Lake, FL 16.7	29.9	Douglas, GA 41.6	Hernando, FL 15.4
Homeownership rate	66.2	63.4	DuPage, IL 76.4	Travis, TX 51.4	71.6	Washington, MN 85.7	Durham, NC 54.3	78.9	Powhatan, VA 88.8	Orange, NC 57.6
Single-family detached housing units	60.3	56.0	San Bernardino, CA 69.2	Broward, FL 40.9	65.8	Fort Bend, TX 82.3	Howard, MD 53.8	73.7	Powhatan, VA 94.2	Nye, NV 38.8
Mean travel time (minutes)	25.5	27.4	Contra Costa, CA 34.4	Salt Lake, UT 22.5	27.4	VA 36.9	Prince William, Ottawa, MI 19.4	30.5	Calvert, MD 39.8	Orange, NC 22.0
Households with 3+ vehicles	17.1	16.3	Santa Clara, CA 24.4	Palm Beach, FL 9.6	20.3	Davis, UT 29.9	Pasco, FL 11.0	25.2	Douglas, CO 46.6	Hernando, FL 12.0
Renters who are cost burdened (>35 income)	31.9	32.5	Miami-Dade, FL 42.0	Fairfax, VA 23.9	29.8	Ocean, NJ 40.1	Johnson, KS 23.1	28.5	Hays, TX 44.3	Washington, WI 20.3
Percent Homeowners who are Cost-Burdened	15.9	18.8	Miami-Dade, FL 28.4	Tarrant, TX 13.2	15.8	Santa Cruz, CA 26.1	St. Charles, MO 10.0	15.0	Douglas, GA 38.0	Douglas, CO 5.5

Source: Metropolitan Institute at Virginia Tech analysis of Census 2000 data.

REFERENCES

Atkins, Patricia S., Hal Wolman, and Jessica Jordan. 2002. "Edge Counties Struggle with Impacts of Rapid Growth." *Housing Facts and Findings* 4 (3): 1, 6–7.

Berube, Alan, and Benjamin Forman. 2002. "Living on the Edge: Decentralization within Cities in the 1990s." Brookings.

Blakely, Edward J., and Mary Gail Snyder. 1997. *Fortress America: Gated Communities in the United States.* Brookings and Lincoln Institute of Land Policy.

Fishman, Robert. 2000. "The American Metropolis at Century's End: Past and Future Influences." *Housing Policy Debate* 11 (1): 199–213.

Frey, William, and others. 2004. "Tracking Metropolitan America into the 21st Century: A Field Guide to the New Metropolitan and Micropolitan Definitions." Brookings.

Fulton, William, and others. 2001. "Who Sprawls the Most: How Growth Patterns Differ across the U.S." Brookings.

Garreau, Joel. 1991. *Edge City: Life on the New Frontier.* New York: Doubleday.

Glaeser, Ed, and Jesse Shapiro. 2003. "City Growth: Which Places Grew and Why." In *Redefining Urban and Suburban America: Evidence from Census 2000,* vol. 1, edited by Bruce Katz and Robert E. Lang. Brookings.

Gough, Meghan Zimmerman. 2003. "Country Ain't Country No More: A Typology of the Nation's Fast-Growing Peripheral Counties." Master's thesis, Metropolitan Institute at Virginia Tech, Virginia Polytechnic State University.

Hayden, Dolores. 2003. *Building Suburbia: Green Fields and Urban Growth, 1820–2000.* New York: Pantheon Books.

Johnson, Kenneth, and Calvin Beale. 1994. "The Recent Revival of Widespread Population Growth in Nonmetropolitan Areas of the United States." *Rural Sociology* 59: 655–67.

Lang, Robert E. 2000. "Office Sprawl: The Evolving Geography of Business." Brookings.

———. 2003. *Edgeless Cities: Exploring the Elusive Metropolis.* Brookings.

Lang, Robert E., Edward J. Blakely, and Meghan Zimmerman Gough. Forthcoming. "Keys to the New Metropolis: America's Big, Fast-Growing Counties," *Journal of the American Planning Association.*

Lang, Robert E., and Karen A. Danielsen. 1997. "Gated Communities in America: Walling the World Out." *Housing Policy Debate* 8 (4): 867–99.

———. 2002. "Monster Homes." *Planning* (May): 45–50.

Lang, Robert E., Deborah Epstein Popper, and Frank J. Popper. 1997. "Is There Still a Frontier? The 1890 Census and the Modern West." *Journal of Rural Studies* 13 (4): 377–86.

Mikelbank, Brian A. 2004. "A Typology of Suburban Places." *Housing Policy Debate* 15 (4): 935–64.

Orfield, Myron. 2002. *American Metropolitics.* Brookings.

Sanchez, Thomas W., Robert E. Lang, and Dawn Dhavale. 2005. "Security versus Status? A First Look at the Census's Gated Community Data." *Journal of Planning Education and Research* 24 (3): 289–91.

Simmons, Patrick A. 2005. "Patterns and Trends in Overcrowded Housing." In *Redefining Urban and Suburban America: Evidence from Census 2000,* vol. 2, edited by Alan Berube, Bruce Katz, and Robert E. Lang. Brookings.

University of Southern California and Brookings Institution Center on Urban and Metropolitan Policy. 2001. "Sprawl Hits the Wall: Confronting the Realities of Metropolitan Los Angeles."

Warner, Sam Bass, Jr. 1972. *The Urban Wilderness.* New York: Harper & Row.

Are the Boomburbs Still Booming?

4

ROBERT E. LANG

Previous research using Census 2000 data documented the rise of a new type of large, fast-growing suburb known as the "boomburb."[1] In recent years, many of the top boomburbs have outgrown their traditional and better-known big-city peers.

This chapter updates boomburb growth trends using recently released 2000–03 population estimates. The analysis reveals that most boomburbs continue to top the list of the nation's fastest-growing cities. As a group, boomburbs now have a total population exceeding that of the Chicago metropolitan area, the nation's third-largest region after New York and Los Angeles. Several individual boomburbs continue to ascend to the ranks of the nation's largest cities. Although most boomburbs have maintained blistering growth rates, a few have been built out as far as they can go and have added residents more slowly in the early years of the twenty-first century than in the 1990s. Two mature, minority-dominated boomburbs saw sharply lower growth rates, as did two Bay Area boomburbs that have more or less gone "bust" after the dot.com bubble burst.

METHODOLOGY

Lang and Simmons (2003) defined "boomburg" as an incorporated place with more than 100,000 residents that is *not* the largest city in its metropolitan area and that has maintained a double-digit population growth rate in

1. Lang and Simmons (2003). The author thanks Rebecca Sohmer of the Brookings Institution for suggesting the term "boomburb."

recent decades.[2] They developed the boomburb concept to provide a contrast with more traditional big cities, having observed that since 1950 most fast-growing cities have really been overgrown suburbs. The boomburb analysis thus formalizes the classification of these places into a family of cities that share a similar size, growth rate, and infrastructure.

Boomburbs typically do not resemble traditional central cities or, for that matter, older satellite cities, such as Long Beach, California, and Jersey City, New Jersey. Although boomburbs have many urban elements, such as apartment buildings, retail centers, entertainment venues, and large offices, they typically do not develop in a traditional urban pattern. For example, boomburbs usually lack a dense business core. Boomburbs are thus distinct from traditional cities—not so much in terms of their function, but in terms of their low density and loose spatial configuration. Boomburbs are urban in fact, but not in feel.

As of April 2003, the United States contained fifty-three boomburbs. The population in four of them topped 300,000, and in fifteen it surpassed 200,000 (table 4-1). All boomburbs grew quickly over the past several decades, with some areas experiencing explosive growth. For example, Irving, Texas, outside Dallas, grew by a spectacular 7,211 percent between 1950 and 2000. Henderson, Nevada, and Chandler, Arizona, also posted startling gains, growing by 4,714 percent and 4,548 percent, respectively.

Although boomburbs are found throughout the nation, most are located in the Southwest. By contrast, in the Northeast and Midwest no big region except Chicago has a single boomburb. Even most large and rapidly growing Sun Belt metropolitan areas east of the Mississippi, such as Atlanta, lack boomburbs. Thus a region can boom and still end up without boomburbs.

Just nine (17 percent) of the boomburbs lie outside the Southwestern states, which stretch from Texas to California. Los Angeles, Dallas, and Phoenix alone contain thirty-two (60 percent) of the nation's boomburbs. The Southeast, except for South Florida, contains only a few boomburbs. Only one boomburb with more than 200,000 residents (Hialeah, Florida) can be found east of the Mississippi River.

Many boomburbs, especially in the West, are products of master-planned community developments, which need to form large water districts.[3] These communities gobble up unincorporated land as they grow. The land and its

2. Lang and Simmons (2003).
3. Even a relatively small metropolis such as Las Vegas, with its expansive master-planned communities and desert surroundings, contains two boomburbs. The Las Vegas metropolitan area also contains three large "Census Designated Places" with populations over 100,000. The boomburb analysis, however, does not include these areas because they are not incorporated municipalities (Lang and Dhavale 2003).

TABLE 4-1. Boomburb Population Change 2000–03

Rank[a]	Boomburb	State	Metro area	April 1, 2000, population[b]	July 1, 2003, population	Change 2000–03 Percent	Change 2000–03 Number
1	Gilbert	AZ	Phoenix	109,949	145,250	32.1	35,301
2	North Las Vegas	NV	Las Vegas	115,488	144,502	25.1	29,014
3	Henderson	NV	Las Vegas	175,406	214,852	22.5	39,446
4	Chandler	AZ	Phoenix	176,643	211,299	19.6	34,656
5	Irvine	CA	Los Angeles	143,072	170,561	19.2	27,489
6	Rancho Cucamonga	CA	Los Angeles	127,743	151,640	18.7	23,897
7	Fontana	CA	Los Angeles	128,937	151,903	17.8	22,966
8	Peoria	AZ	Phoenix	108,685	127,580	17.4	18,895
9	Chula Vista	CA	San Diego	173,553	199,060	14.7	25,507
10	Corona	CA	Los Angeles	125,251	142,454	13.7	17,203
11	Riverside	CA	Los Angeles	255,175	281,514	10.3	26,339
12	Moreno Valley	CA	Los Angeles	142,379	157,063	10.3	14,684
13	Plano	TX	Dallas	222,008	241,991	9.0	19,983
14	Mesa	AZ	Phoenix	397,776	432,376	8.7	34,600
15	Pembroke	FL	Miami	137,415	148,927	8.4	11,512
16	Coral Springs	FL	Miami	117,549	127,005	8.0	9,456
17	Santa Clarita	CA	Los Angeles	151,131	162,742	7.7	11,611
18	Scottsdale	AZ	Phoenix	202,596	217,989	7.6	15,393
19	Naperville	IL	Chicago	128,409	137,894	7.4	9,485
20	Grand Prairie	TX	Dallas	127,427	136,671	7.3	9,244
21	Arlington	TX	Dallas	332,969	355,007	6.6	22,038
22	Carrollton	TX	Dallas	109,578	116,714	6.5	7,136
23	Glendale	AZ	Phoenix	218,831	232,838	6.4	14,007
24	Oxnard	CA	Los Angeles	170,359	180,872	6.2	10,513
25	Thousand Oaks	CA	Los Angeles	117,005	124,192	6.1	7,187
26	Lancaster	CA	Los Angeles	118,718	125,896	6.0	7,178
27	Ontario	CA	Los Angeles	158,011	167,402	5.9	9,391
28	Chesapeake	VA	Norfolk	199,184	210,834	5.8	11,650
29	San Bernardino	CA	Los Angeles	185,237	195,357	5.5	10,120
30	Aurora	CO	Denver	275,923	290,418	5.3	14,495
31	Simi Valley	CA	Los Angeles	111,365	117,115	5.2	5,750
32	Salem	OR	Portland	136,991	142,914	4.3	5,923
33	Fullerton	CA	Los Angeles	126,003	131,249	4.2	5,246
34	Mesquite	TX	Dallas	124,523	129,270	3.8	4,747
35	Oceanside	CA	San Diego	161,029	167,082	3.8	6,053
36	Santa Rosa	CA	San Francisco	147,854	153,386	3.7	5,532
37	Orange	CA	Los Angeles	128,821	132,197	2.6	3,376
38	West Valley City	UT	Salt Lake City	108,896	111,687	2.6	2,791
39	Westminster	CO	Denver	100,998	103,391	2.4	2,393
40	Escondido	CA	San Diego	133,747	136,093	1.8	2,346
41	Irving	TX	Dallas	191,615	194,455	1.5	2,840
42	Santa Ana	CA	Los Angeles	337,977	342,510	1.3	4,533
43	Anaheim	CA	Los Angeles	328,071	332,361	1.3	4,290
44	Garland	TX	Dallas	215,794	218,027	1.0	2,233
45	Costa Mesa	CA	Los Angeles	108,756	109,563	0.7	807
46	Fremont	CA	San Francisco	203,413	204,525	0.5	1,112
47	Tempe	AZ	Phoenix	158,625	158,880	0.2	255
48	Hialeah	FL	Miami	226,419	226,401	0.0	−18
49	Bellevue	WA	Seattle	112,495	112,344	−0.1	−151
50	Clearwater	FL	Tampa	108,902	108,272	−0.6	−630
51	Lakewood	CO	Denver	144,137	142,474	−1.2	−1,663
52	Sunnyvale	CA	San Francisco	131,844	128,549	−2.5	−3,295
53	Daly City	CA	San Francisco	103,625	100,819	−2.7	−2,806
Total				8,804,307	9,406,367	6.8	602,060

Source: Author's tabulations of Census Bureau data.

a. Rank is based on percent population change, 2000–03.

b. April 1, 2000, population reflects adjustments to the Census 2000 population as a result of the Census 2000 Count Question Resolution program, updates from the Boundary and Annexation Survey, and geographic program revisions.

new residents are added to municipalities, turning small towns into boomburbs. In addition, the public lands in the West that surround big metropolitan areas are often transferred to developers in large blocks.[4] By contrast, master-planned community builders in the East typically assemble their land from mostly smaller, privately held parcels. Western water districts also play a role in promoting boomburbs. The West is mostly dry, and places seeking to grow must organize efforts to access water.[5] Large incorporated places are better positioned to grab a share of the water supply. This greater leverage provides an incentive for fragmented suburban areas to join large incorporated cities.

FINDINGS

Census Bureau sub-county population estimates for 2003 show that most boomburbs have continued to boom (table 4-1). In fact, boomburbs are the fastest-growing U.S. cities with populations over 100,000. From April 2000 to July 2003, five of the fastest-growing cities were boomburbs.[6] The four top-growth boomburbs are in the Phoenix and Las Vegas metropolitan areas. Five of the ten highest-growth boomburbs are in Southern California—four in the Los Angeles region and one in the San Diego metropolitan area.

Gilbert, Arizona (the fastest-gaining boomburb), grew 32 percent in just over three years. At that pace, Gilbert could easily more than double its population in a decade. The next eleven boomburbs following Gilbert all grew by more than 10 percent over the same period. More than a quarter of boomburbs (fifteen) each gained more than 15,000 residents.

Overall, the boomburb population jumped from 8.8 million to 9.4 million, a gain of more than a half million residents in just over three years. Together, boomburbs now have a slightly larger population than the Chicago metropolitan area (9.3 million people as of July 2003).[7]

4. Abbot (1993).
5. Lang (2002).
6. U.S. Census Bureau (2004c). The Census Bureau produces annual estimates for population change at the sub-county level based on the "Distributive Housing Unit Method," which uses building permits, mobile home shipments, and estimates of housing-unit loss to update the housing-unit change. The bureau developed a household population estimate by applying the occupancy rate and the average number of persons per household from the latest census to an estimate of the housing units. The estimates obtained from this method are controlled for by comparing them with the final county population estimate (U.S. Census Bureau 2004b).
7. Office of Management and Budget (2004).

Boomburbs Continue to Gain on Traditional Cities

From 2000 to 2003, population growth in the boomburbs significantly out-paced that in traditional cities of the same size. Non-boomburb cities with populations from 100,000 to 500,000 (the boomburb range) saw a 2.1 per-cent average growth rate for the period. By contrast, boomburbs had a 7.2 percent average growth rate. In addition, 36 percent of the non-boom-burbs (fifty-eight of the 161) lost residents, whereas only 11 percent of the boomburbs (six of the fifty-three) shrank.

In total, cities with populations between 100,000 and 500,000 gained 1,140,066 people from 2000 to 2003. The fifty-three boomburbs accounted for 602,060 new residents, whereas the 158 non-boomburbs added 538,006 new residents. Thus, although boomburbs represent only a quarter of U.S. cities with populations between 100,000 and 500,000, they accounted for more than half of the population growth of these cities. Lang and Simmons reported similar findings for the 1990s.[8] Boomburbs added about 2.1 mil-lion new residents in the 1990s, a gain of just over 200,000 each year. Based on boomburb performance from 2000 to 2003, the group is roughly on pace to match its population growth in the 1990s.

Since the 2000 census, the populations of many of the top boomburbs have jumped ahead of those of their traditional (and better known) big-city peers. Mesa, Arizona (432,376), is now bigger than Atlanta (423,019); Arlington, Texas (355,007), Santa Ana, California (342,510), and Anaheim, California (332,361), have passed St. Louis, Missouri (332,223); Aurora, Colorado (290,418), has overtaken Buffalo, New York (285,018); and Peoria, Arizona (127,580), has surged ahead of its namesake Peoria, Illinois (112,907).

Growth in Some Boomburbs Has Stalled

Although most boomburbs are on pace to grow at double-digit rates through 2010, growth in several is slowing or even declining. One reason for stalled population growth relates to development patterns. Most boom-burbs are "horizontal cities" that build out rather than up. Landlocked boomburbs, such as Tempe, Arizona (with a 0.2 percent growth rate from 2000 to 2003), have nowhere to go but up. Such landlocked boomburbs are at a crossroads: to keep growing they must change their land use patterns to accommodate higher-density development, though their original com-petitive advantage was their greenfield development opportunities.

8. Lang and Simmons (2003).

The infill market remains untested in most boomburbs. Many now have enough scale and economic assets to make them central to the region. Their mostly centerless form, however, does not offer infill housing consumers the type of dense urban environments they typically seek.[9] The future of built-out boomburbs may depend on the success of urban design movements—such as New Urbanism—in introducing more traditional, city-like development into the suburbs.

Growth is also slowing in the "New Brooklyns," boomburbs that are now, or are rapidly becoming, immigrant-dominated communities similar to the old Brooklyn. The foreign-born population shares of Hialeah, Florida, and the California cities of Santa Ana, Daly City, Sunnyvale, and Anaheim either match or exceed that of Brooklyn, New York (currently 38 percent foreign-born). Other examples of New Brooklyns include Pembroke Pines, Florida, Irving, Texas, and Aurora, Colorado, each of which has a foreign-born population share that greatly exceeds the national average of 11 percent.

The New Brooklyns tend to be older, denser, and built-out suburbs, factors that can limit population growth. As one commentator observes, "Although the New Brooklyns were once new settlements on the suburban frontier, they're getting old. Their housing, accordingly, is more attractive to immigrants looking for bargains and is less attractive to longtime [mostly native-born] Americans who can afford to move up."[10]

Some New Brooklyns can continue to gain population (if not quite boom) if their foreign-born population maintains a relatively high birth rate. These places have also seen resident turnover as large, young immigrant families replace older, empty-nester couples, a trend that fuels population growth. In time, however, as foreign-born populations age and assimilate, the New Brooklyns' growth should slow further.

A third reason some boomburbs are slowing down or even declining is the 2001–02 national recession and its reverberations through regional economies. Census 2000 gathered data at the peak of the last economic expansion, when employment and equity markets were at all-time highs. Many cities fared well in the decade leading up to that census. Even older industrial cities experienced their best decade-long population gains since the 1940s.[11]

9. Danielson, Lang, and Fulton (1999).
10. Hampson (2003).
11. Simmons and Lang (2003).

The latest estimates, however, hint at a potential reversal in some places. Traditional cities that were growing in the 1990s, such as Chicago and San Francisco, lost population from 2000 to 2003.[12] In places such as the Bay Area in Northern California, a region hit hard by the tech recession, boomburbs saw significant losses. For example, Sunnyvale, California, located in the heart of the Silicon Valley, lost 2.5 percent of its population between 2000 and 2003. The fastest-declining boomburb (with a 2.7 percent loss) was Daly City, just south of San Francisco. Sunnyvale and Daly City also happen to be New Brooklyns; their relative maturity, combined with the Bay Area's economic problems, turned them from 1990s boomburbs into this decade's "bustburbs."

Boomburb Housing Growth and Conditions Vary Widely

—*Homebuilding.* One of the primary businesses of a fast-growing boomburb is the building of the boomburb itself. A review of the websites of the largest national homebuilders—Centex Homes, D. R. Horton, Kaufman & Broad, Lennar, and Pulte Homes—reveals that all five are developing new boomburb residences.[13] Not surprisingly, these builders are most active in the exploding Phoenix and Las Vegas areas. Although harder to survey, smaller national and regional builders are also active in boomburb markets.

Data from the Census Bureau's Building Permits Survey provide a more complete picture of overall building activity.[14] In 2003, 67,117 new housing permits were issued in the boomburbs, with the greatest number of new permits issued in North Las Vegas and Henderson, Nevada, and Chandler, Arizona. Three-quarters of these permits were for single-family dwellings. Irvine and Riverside, California, issued the most multi-family permits of any boomburbs (1,742 and 1,329 permits, respectively). Given California's collapse in multi-family housing in the 1990s, these gains are especially impressive.[15]

—*Homeownership.* For all fifty-three boomburbs combined, the home-ownership rate is lower than for the nation as a whole (62.5 percent versus 66.2 percent). As with other area characteristics, however, the rate varies

---

12. U.S. Bureau of the Census (2004a).

13. Lennar's site was also searched. It listed fourteen pages of projects in Phoenix alone, but it was hard to determine from the website in which cities these developments were located.

14. See www.census.gov/const/www/permitsindex.html.

15. Myers and Park (2002).

widely across the areas, ranging from 85 percent in Gilbert, Arizona, to 37 percent in the New Brooklyn of Irving, Texas. Homeownership rates in several other New Brooklyns, including Sunnyvale and Santa Ana, California, are also relatively low (48 percent and 49 percent, respectively).

—*Overcrowding.* Interestingly, some boomburbs with relatively few housing starts still managed to grow significantly. Higher occupancy rates, especially in rental units, appear partly responsible for this growth. A housing unit is generally considered overcrowded if it has more than one occupant per room. By this standard, 21 percent of rental units in the boomburbs are overcrowded, compared with 11 percent of all rental units nationwide. Southern California boomburbs, in particular, have crowded rentals, with 35 percent of renters in such fast-growing boomburbs as Oxnard and Ontario living in overcrowded conditions. Some slower-growing New Brooklyns also appear to be squeezing more residents into existing housing. In Santa Ana, more than 60 percent of renters live in overcrowded housing, as do 40 percent of renters in Hialeah, Florida.

—*Age of Housing Stock.* The housing stock in most boomburbs is newer than in the nation as a whole. At the time of the 2000 census, one-third of the nation's housing stock was twenty years old or younger. By contrast, half the boomburb housing stock was built after 1980. Gilbert, Arizona, and Henderson, Nevada, have the newest homes, with roughly 90 percent of each city's housing stock built within the last 20 years.

—*Affordability.* Housing in the boomburbs is slightly less affordable than in the nation as a whole, especially for homeowners. Housing is widely considered unaffordable if a household spends more than 30 percent of its gross income on housing costs. By this definition, in 2000 the share of boomburb renters with affordability problems (44 percent) slightly exceeded the share of all U.S. renters with affordability problems (42 percent). The boomburb rental market was most affordable in the Texas boomburbs of Carrollton and Irving, where three in ten renters paid more than 30 percent of their monthly incomes for housing. In contrast, more than five in ten renters in both San Bernardino, California, and Hialeah, Florida, shoulder unaffordable housing costs.

Among owners, the gap between boomburb and national affordability rates was somewhat greater: 27 percent of boomburbs owners faced excessive housing costs, compared with 22 percent of all owners. As with rentals, the most affordable owner-occupied homes were located in the Texas boomburbs. In Mesquite, Arlington, and Irving, only 17 to 18 percent of owners had excessive housing costs in 2000. By contrast, nearly 40 percent of homeowners in Hialeah, Florida, paid more than 30 percent of their income on home payments.

CONCLUSION

For now, most boomburbs seem to be humming along. But many will probably experience relative population declines in the not-too-distant future. One problem could be that the West (where most boomburbs are found) is running out of water. Almost all of the current water sources—from Denver to Southern California—have been over-allocated.[16] Unless planners find ways to divert more water from agriculture or to tap new supplies, the West will likely face a crisis that could dampen its boomburb growth, in addition to the region's broader growth.

Even if the water supply problem is resolved, the current group of boomburbs will ultimately experience much slower population gains. No place can (or should) boom forever. Today's boomburbs are tomorrow's mature cities. But a whole new batch of boomburbs is already emerging. Consider Arizona's Central Valley: As Tempe's growth stalls, and Mesa's slows, places such as Apache Junction and Buckeye are just getting started.

REFERENCES

Abbott, Carl. 1993. *The Metropolitan Frontier: Cities in the Modern American West.* Tucson: University of Arizona Press.

Danielsen, Karen A., Robert E. Lang, and William Fulton. 1999. "Retracting Suburbia: Smart Growth and the Future of Housing." *Housing Policy Debate* 10 (3): 513–40.

Hampson, Rick. 2003. " 'New Brooklyns' Replace White Suburbs." *USA Today,* May 18, pp. A1, A2.

Lang, Robert E. 2002. "Open Space, Bounded Places: Do Western U.S. Cities Really Sprawl?" *Housing Policy Debate* 13 (4): 755–78.

Lang, Robert E., and Dawn Dhavale. 2003. "Reluctant Cities? Exploring Large Census Designated Places." Metropolitan Institute at Virginia Tech Census Note Series 03:01 (July).

Lang, Robert E., and Patrick A. Simmons. 2003. "Boomburbs: The Emergence of Large, Fast-Growing Suburban Cities." In *Redefining Urban and Suburban America: Evidence from Census 2000,* vol. 1, edited by Bruce Katz and Robert E. Lang. Brookings.

McKinnon, Shaun. 2003. "Water: Growing Demand, Dwindling Supply." *Arizona Republic,* July 6, p. A1.

Myers, Dowell, and Julie Park. 2002. *The Great California Housing Collapse.* Washington: Fannie Mae Foundation.

Office of Management and Budget. 2004. *Metropolitan Statistical Area Definitions.* OMB Bulletin No. 04–03, February 18. Washington.

16. McKinnon (2003).

Simmons, Patrick A., and Robert E. Lang. 2003. "The Urban Turnaround." In *Redefining Urban and Suburban America: Evidence from Census 2000,* vol. 1, edited by Bruce Katz and Robert E. Lang. Brookings.

U.S. Census Bureau. 2004a. Table 1: *Annual Estimates of the Population for Incorporated Places over 100,000* (SUB-EST2003–01). Released June 24, 2004. Washington: U.S. Department of Commerce.

————. 2004b. *Estimates and Projections Area Documentation: Subcounty Total Population Estimates.* Washington: U.S. Department of Commerce.

————. 2004c. "Arizona, Nevada and California Cities Show Fastest Growth, Census Bureau Says." Census Bureau Press Release CB04–101, June 24, 2004. Washington: U.S. Department of Commerce.

5

Living Together: A New Look at Racial and Ethnic Integration in Metropolitan Neighborhoods, 1990–2000

DAVID FASENFEST, JASON BOOZA, AND
KURT METZGER

Racial integration has served as a benchmark for social progress since racial equality entered the social policy agenda. The degree to which society accepts racial and ethnic diversity depends on the degree to which people of different races and ethnic groups live in harmony over time. Racial segregation signifies a host of inequalities within urban settings, and many argue that integration promotes greater economic and social equity, increased stability (through the preservation of housing stock and community values), and greater social harmony.[1]

Census 2000 confirms that, overall, the United States is becoming a more racially and ethnically diverse society. The 100 largest cities in the country are, in the aggregate, now majority nonwhite or Hispanic.[2] Suburbs have become much more diverse since 1990, and minorities now make up about 27 percent of suburban populations.[3] Segregation in metropolitan areas has declined, most strongly in rapidly growing regions, and as a result there are few entirely white census tracts.[4]

The authors thank Alan Berube, Audrey Singer and the staff of the Brookings Institution Center on Urban and Metropolitan Policy, and George Galster at Wayne State University for their useful comments and suggestions.

1. Discussions of racial segregation and integration invariably focus on urban populations, because most nonwhite people live in and around the nation's major urban centers.

2. Berube (2003).

3. Frey (2001). A portion of this increased diversity owes to the ability of Census 2000 respondents to select more than one race category, consistent with the increasingly "fluid" way in which people identify their racial/ethnic heritage. Singer (2002).

4. Glaeser and Vigdor (2001).

With these findings in mind, several questions arise about whether people of different races and ethnicities are truly "living together" in metropolitan America. To what degree do patterns of greater diversity and increased integration play out at the neighborhood level? Will those patterns persist in the long run? What is a "stable integrated neighborhood"? Should we promote neighborhood integration if it leads to increased residential change over time? Indeed, some research suggests that an increase in the prevalence of multi-ethnic neighborhoods does not necessarily imply stable integration. Denton and Massey find that in the 1970s, multigroup neighborhoods (those containing at least two racial/ethnic groups) tended to retain their mixed character over the decade, unless blacks made up one of the two groups. In those cases, the neighborhood tended to become predominantly black, perhaps signaling economic and social decline.[5]

In order to explore whether neighborhoods are truly integrated, one must first define "integrated neighborhood" in quantifiable terms. Because research on racial integration is still nascent compared with research on racial segregation, this topic has been debated widely only during the past decade. According to Smith, "We have only a limited understanding of the extent to which integrated places occur within the more general landscape" and therefore cannot anticipate when they will emerge and whether they will be stable.[6]

However, a growing body of literature aims to define and study neighborhood integration. Several recent studies have attempted to answer many of the theoretical and methodological questions regarding integrated neighborhoods.[7] These questions include the following: What is the appropriate spatial unit(s) of analysis? Should one apply a comparative or absolute approach to defining integration? How many racial groups should be included? How does one compare results across time and space? What statistical formula best measures integration? We do not attempt to answer these questions in this chapter, but rather aim to define integrated neighborhoods in a way that permits a first look at experiences and outcomes over the 1990s.

This chapter departs somewhat from previous studies by exploring integration beyond the typical white/black dichotomy. We develop a neighborhood typology that explores the affect of a growing Hispanic and, in some areas, Asian population on integration. Census 2000 offers an opportunity to revisit the definitions of integration empirically and so introduces greater texture to our understanding of changing racial and ethnic residential patterns over time. We believe our findings show that integration should be

5. Denton and Massey (1991).
6. Smith (1998).
7. Ellen (1998); Galster (1998); Maly (2000); Nyden and others (1998); Smith (1998).

understood in both racial and ethnic terms and that traditional arguments about residential integration in black-and-white terms alone are lacking.

The remainder of this report proceeds in several steps. In the next section we describe the data and the neighborhood typologies we employ to evaluate the changing racial and ethnic composition of the nation's ten largest metropolitan areas. The body of the chapter explores our key findings on the prevalence of integrated neighborhoods today, how the picture changed in the 1990s, and how trends differed across the ten metropolitan areas. We conclude by discussing the implications of these changes and highlight research that could further our understanding of the conditions that foster racial integration in communities.

METHODOLOGY

This chapter examines Census 2000 data for the ten largest metropolitan areas in the United States: Los Angeles, New York, Chicago, Philadelphia, Detroit, Washington, D.C., Houston, Atlanta, Dallas, and Boston.[8] These areas account for over 20 percent of the nation's metropolitan population and over 30 percent of its minority population. Thus, although our findings do not necessarily capture the true extent of racial integration nationally, they likely reflect the overall direction of change in metropolitan areas during the 1990s. Following other research, we consider census tracts to be proxies for neighborhoods. Although they are larger than most neighborhoods and their boundaries may change over time, census tracts are widely used in studies of racial integration and segregation. The chapter employs the term "community" synonymously with "neighborhood."

Data

The data used in this chapter derive from the race and ethnicity (Hispanic/Latino) questions from the decennial census, as reported in the Census Bureau's 1990 Summary Tape File 1 (STF1) and 2000 Summary File 1 (SF1). The analysis classifies as Hispanic those individuals who, regardless of their race, denote Spanish, Hispanic, or Latino ethnicity. Other categories—white, black, Asian/Pacific Islander, American Indian, and "other"—include non-Hispanic individuals who selected one of those categories. Meanwhile, the neighborhood typology excludes individuals who selected more than one race—an option available for the first time in Census 2000—as they

8. We use the metropolitan statistical area (MSA) and primary metropolitan statistical area (PMSA) concepts as defined by the Office of Management and Budget for Census 2000. We use a consistent set of census tracts for each metropolitan area in 1990 and 2000.

represent a small share of the overall population and are unlikely to affect our findings.[9] In sum, the bulk of the report focuses on white, black, Hispanic, and Asian populations.

Most metropolitan areas have undergone significant changes in racial and ethnic composition within their own borders, as whites and more affluent blacks left the central city for suburban communities in recent decades. But fast population increases among nonwhites account for broader changes in the overall racial and ethnic profile of metropolitan areas. As figure 5-1 demonstrates, the ten metropolitan areas grew by 12.6 percent overall in the 1990s; the gain was entirely attributable to growth in Asian, Hispanic, and black populations. Overall, the total number of whites living in these metropolitan areas fell by about 2.7 percent from its 1990 level.[10] Still, although the data suggest that some white out-migration occurred during the 1990s, whites continued to constitute over 50 percent of the combined population of the ten areas in 2000. Immigration—and the larger family sizes and birth rates among Hispanics—helped account for the increased prominence of nonblack minority populations.

Neighborhood Typology

Between decennial censuses, the Census Bureau modified some census tract definitions in response to changes in population or local requests. In order to measure neighborhood change and stability based on a consistent geography, Geographic Information Systems (GIS) were used to equate 1990 and 2000 census tract boundaries.[11] Census tracts with fewer than 500 persons were eliminated, as were those in which people living in group quarters (for example, in college dormitories, nursing homes, prisons) constituted at least half of the population. The resulting data set consists of 12,447 census tracts across the 10 metropolitan areas. Our methods follow those from similar inquiries on neighborhood change.[12]

9. When combined with the Hispanic/non-Hispanic classification, the race question generates 126 mutually exclusive race/ethnicity categories, compared to just ten categories in the 1990 census. When Hispanics are removed from the population classified as multi-race, the national rate of multi-race response is just 1.6 percent of the population. The comparable rate for our ten metropolitan areas is 1.9 percent. The 1990 census did not have a multi-racial category, thus complicating comparisons across the decade.

10. Some portion of this decrease may be attributable to individuals selecting more than one race in 2000 after classifying themselves as white in 1990, thereby excluding themselves from our analysis.

11. To ensure that this process did not unduly affect the 1990 data, we applied our methodology to both the original 1990 census tracts and the "realigned" 1990 tracts and found that the results were nearly identical.

12. Lee and Wood (1990); Ellen (1998).

FIGURE 5-1. **Population Change by Race/Ethnicity, Ten Largest Metropolitan Areas, 1990–2000**

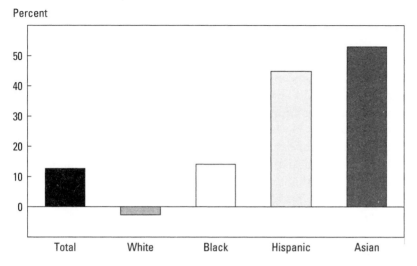

Source: Authors' calculations from 1990 and 2000 census data.

Previous research offers two approaches to defining neighborhood integration: absolute and comparative. The absolute approach defines integration with respect to a predetermined racial composition.[13] The comparative approach, by contrast, defines integration based on the demographic composition of the area within which the neighborhood is located. Both approaches have their proponents and their critics.[14]

From our perspective, the foremost problem with the comparative approach is that the metropolitan area in which a neighborhood is located may itself not be racially integrated. For example, a neighborhood in the Salt Lake City-Ogden, Utah, metropolitan statistical area (MSA) that is 1 percent black might be considered integrated because the MSA as a whole is 1 percent black. On the other hand, a neighborhood in the Mobile, Alabama, MSA that is 24 percent black might not be considered integrated because the MSA as a whole is 27 percent black.

13. For instance, researchers at the University of Wisconsin–Milwaukee recently studied the prevalence of census blocks in which at least 20 percent of the population is white and at least 20 percent black. They acknowledge that dealing with only two race groups constrains this measure, as well as traditional measures of segregation. Quinn and Pawasarat (2003).

14. Smith (1998) criticizes the absolute approach as being nonprecise, nongrounded, arbitrary, and atheoretical. However, Galster (1998) finds that the comparative approach also has its faults.

A second problem with the comparative approach concerns its limitations in comparing neighborhood integration across time, because the demographic compositions of metropolitan areas change across decades. A neighborhood defined as integrated in 1990 that did not change its residential makeup at all could lose this designation in 2000, due to racial and ethnic changes occurring elsewhere in the metropolitan area. Given these drawbacks, this chapter employs an absolute approach to defining integration, assuming that it should be based upon a nontrivial degree of racial diversity.[15]

The particular measure of integration employed here, meanwhile, reflects the nature of population change in the 1990s. This survey presumes that the increase of nonblack minorities in metropolitan areas, particularly during the 1990s, renders black/white measures of neighborhood integration insufficient. Therefore, this analysis employs a multi-ethnic neighborhood typology in order to recognize the growing role of Hispanics and Asians in neighborhood integration.[16] This typology categorizes neighborhoods in seven ways—three in which a single race is predominant and four that are racially mixed or integrated. In order to keep the number of descriptive categories manageable, all nonblack minorities (Asians, Hispanics, American Indians, Native Hawaiians and Pacific Islanders, and those indicating "other" race) have been assembled into an omnibus "other" category. With few exceptions, growth in this category reflects Hispanic population growth, though in some cases Asian growth proves an important factor.[17]

Following this approach, the chapter deems a neighborhood homogeneous if one group predominates within the overall racial/ethnic composition. Thus there are three types of homogeneous neighborhoods: predominantly white, predominantly black, and predominantly other-race (see box 5-1). If any minority group other than the predominant group represents more than 10 percent of the population in a neighborhood, the neighborhood is classified as mixed-race. The typology consists of four mixed-race or integrated neighborhoods: mixed white-and-other; mixed white-and-black; mixed black-and-other; and mixed multi-ethnic.

The different threshold levels for blacks and whites, such as those defining homogeneous status (at least 50 percent for blacks and 80 percent for whites), reflect the overall difference in the proportion of blacks and whites in the general population. The ten metropolitan areas contain roughly three

15. Galster (1998).
16. This "absolute" approach follows that of Ellen (1998).
17. Native Americans and persons of "other" races constitute less than 4 percent of our sample, and their presence does not affect the typology significantly in any of the ten metropolitan areas.

BOX 5-1. A NEIGHBORHOOD INTEGRATION TYPOLOGY

Homogeneous

Predominantly white: at least 80 percent white, and no minority group represents more than 10 percent of the population.

Predominantly black: at least 50 percent black, and no other minority group represents more than 10 percent of the population.

Predominantly other-race: at least 50 percent non-black minority, and no more than 10 percent black.

Mixed-race

Mixed white-and-other: between 10 percent and 50 percent of the population classified as other, and less than 10 percent black.

Mixed white-and-black: between 10 percent and 50 percent of the population black, and less than 10 percent classified as other.

Mixed black-and-other: at least 10 percent black, at least 10 percent classified as other, and no more than 40 percent white.

Mixed multi-ethnic: at least 10 percent black, at least 10 percent classified as other, and at least 40 percent white.

times as many whites as blacks, and none contains more blacks than whites (table 5-1). Los Angeles is the only metropolitan area in which whites do not represent at least a plurality of the population.

To provide context for our neighborhood typology analysis, consider each metropolitan area relative to the seven neighborhood categories. Two are homogeneous—Boston is predominantly white and Los Angeles is predominantly other-race (thanks to its large Hispanic and Asian populations). The other eight are mixed: Houston is mixed black-and-other; Philadelphia, Washington, D.C., Detroit, and Atlanta are mixed white-and-black regions; and New York, Dallas, and Chicago are mixed multi-ethnic metropolitan areas.

Neighborhood Racial/Ethnic Change

This chapter makes point-in-time comparisons by applying this typology to metropolitan neighborhoods in 1990 and 2000. Particular mixes of whites, blacks, Hispanics, and Asians define neighborhood types, but a neighborhood may have changed its type between 1990 to 2000 for a variety of reasons.

First, an influx of one or another group can shift a neighborhood's composition. This could indicate that the community is prospering and attracting

T A B L E   5 - 1 .   Population by Race/Ethnicity, Ten Largest Metropolitan Areas, 2000

Metro area	White		Black		Hispanic		Asian	
	Number	Percent	Number	Percent	Number	Percent	Number	Percent
Atlanta	2,445,308	60	1,162,877	29	267,465	7	132,960	3
Boston	2,708,501	80	217,908	6	198,322	6	161,405	5
Chicago	4,761,157	58	1,511,842	18	1,407,934	17	373,621	5
Dallas	1,963,564	56	516,927	15	806,440	23	140,752	4
Detroit	3,086,750	70	1,002,945	23	127,500	3	103,052	2
Houston	1,914,488	46	708,637	17	1,243,847	30	217,264	5
Los Angeles	2,926,479	31	887,775	9	4,222,646	45	1,134,524	12
New York	3,654,722	40	2,095,414	23	2,319,231	25	834,779	9
Philadelphia	3,540,107	70	985,615	20	252,360	5	168,598	3
Washington	2,736,529	56	1,253,817	26	429,597	9	327,164	7
Total	29,737,605	53	10,343,757	18	11,275,342	20	3,594,119	6

Source: Authors' calculations from Census 2000 data.

economically successful groups or that it is in decline and its housing stock has recently become more affordable and attractive to less well-off in-migrants.

Second, selective out-migration of a particular group can alter a neighborhood's racial/ethnic profile. The change may result from internal push factors (such as a perception of detrimental changes in its racial mix, leading to the typical "white flight" scenario) or external pull factors (rising incomes may make more expensive homes elsewhere affordable). The movement of Detroit's black professional class from the central city to nearby suburbs provides one example of push-and-pull factors operating simultaneously.

Third, changes may take place among a neighborhood's existing households—births, deaths, marriages, children leaving home, and elderly parents moving in with children—that alter the neighborhood's overall racial and ethnic character. Although it is beyond the scope of this study, examining demographic characteristics of the population across the decade may offer insights into which factors drive change in a particular neighborhood.

To illustrate the various ways in which neighborhoods may evolve from one type to another, we looked more closely at examples of stable and transitional locales within our case studies. Four examples from Chicago and Washington, D.C., demonstrate that both rising and declining populations can experience changing degrees of neighborhood integration (table 5-2).

Two of our example neighborhoods retained their type across the decade—Capitol Hill in Washington, D.C., and Hyde Park in Chicago. Capitol Hill's overall population remained steady, although it experienced increases in both white and Hispanic populations and a concomitant decline in its black population. Yet these changes did not alter its makeup enough to result in the neighborhood changing classification from mixed white-and-black. On the other hand, population dropped noticeably in Chicago's

TABLE 5-2. Racial/Ethnic Characteristics of Selected Neighborhoods, Washington, D.C., and Chicago, 1990–2000[a]

| Neighborhood | Year | Population | | | | Population share (percent) | | | Type |
		White	Black	Asian	Hispanic	White	Black	Other	
Capitol Hill, DC	1990	2,315	1,041	48	64	67	30	3	Mixed white-and-black
	2000	2,469	801	56	139	70	23	6	Mixed white-and-black
Southwest Waterfront, DC	1990	1,813	1,724	54	105	49	46	4	Mixed white-and-black
	2000	1,361	2,094	67	169	36	55	6	Predominantly black
Hyde Park, Chicago	1990	1,939	155	303	86	78	6	16	Mixed white-and-other
	2000	1,671	189	386	81	69	8	19	Mixed white-and-other
Logan Square, Chicago	1990	225	208	10	1,366	12	11	76	Mixed black-and-other
	2000	226	185	14	1,608	11	9	79	Predominantly other-race

Source: Authors' calculations from 1990 and 2000 census data.
a. Data represent one census tract within each of the named neighborhoods.

Hyde Park, thanks almost entirely to a decline in white population. That decline alone, though, was not sufficient to change the neighborhood's mixed white-and-other assignment.

Two other examples show that many neighborhoods made the transition from one type to another over the decade independent of their overall growth trend. The Southwest Waterfront neighborhood in Washington, D.C., for example, seems to have "tipped" from its prior mixed white-and-black status to a predominantly black one due to a precipitous decline in white population, coupled with growth in the black population. Total population in the neighborhood remained roughly the same, however. Alternatively, the population of Logan Square in Chicago changed little aside from a strong growth in Hispanics. That growth meant that blacks no longer made up more than 10 percent of the population, so that the neighborhood's classification changed from a mixed category to a homogeneous one.

As these examples demonstrate, the fact that a community changes designation does not necessarily imply that it has hit a "tipping point." Research on changes in the 1980s points to racial and/or ethnic stability in integrated neighborhoods as an important indicator of economic and social success. Yet stable neighborhoods may in fact experience population decline across the board, whereas transitional neighborhoods may simply reflect a new distribution of residents by racial and ethnic background. The goal here is to demonstrate that integration and neighborhood transformation take on various dimensions and should not be viewed solely as a matter of black versus white.

FINDINGS

Strong growth in Hispanic and Asian populations, steady growth in the black population, and a slight decline in the white population characterized the overall population trend in the ten largest metropolitan areas during the 1990s. These overarching changes accompanied a profound transformation in the racial and ethnic composition of metropolitan neighborhoods over the same period.

Predominantly White Neighborhoods Fell 30 Percent in the 1990s

Overall, mixed-race neighborhoods replaced homogeneous neighborhoods in large numbers. In 1990, over half (55 percent) of all communities in these ten metropolitan areas had a homogeneous classification—predominantly white, predominantly black, or predominantly other-race (figure 5-2). By 2000, that share fell to under half (48 percent) of all neighborhoods. Three distinct patterns lay beneath this shift.

FIGURE 5-2. Neighborhood Types, Ten Largest Metropolitan Areas, 1990–2000

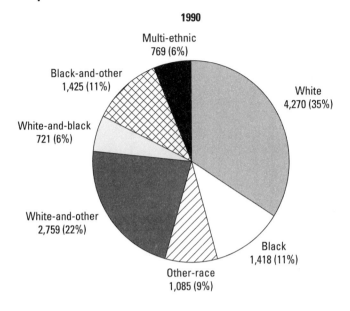

1990

Multi-ethnic
769 (6%)

Black-and-other
1,425 (11%)

White-and-black
721 (6%)

White-and-other
2,759 (22%)

White
4,270 (35%)

Black
1,418 (11%)

Other-race
1,085 (9%)

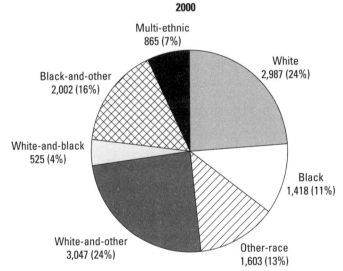

2000

Multi-ethnic
865 (7%)

Black-and-other
2,002 (16%)

White-and-black
525 (4%)

White-and-other
3,047 (24%)

White
2,987 (24%)

Black
1,418 (11%)

Other-race
1,603 (13%)

Source: Authors' calculations from 1990 and 2000 census data.

First, the number of predominantly white neighborhoods fell by 30 percent over the decade. Consequently, the share of all neighborhoods that were predominantly white dropped from 35 percent to 24 percent. Second, the growth of Hispanic (and to a lesser degree Asian) populations resulted in a large increase in predominantly other-race neighborhoods. Third, the number of predominantly black neighborhoods remained at the same level, about 11 percent of all neighborhoods. Thus the nation's homogeneous neighborhoods were more likely to be dominated by racial and ethnic minorities at the end of the decade than in 1990.

With the decline in homogeneous neighborhoods came an increase in mixed-race neighborhoods. Large increases in mixed white-and-other (up 10 percent) and mixed black-and-other (up 41 percent) neighborhoods countered the drop in predominantly white neighborhoods. Together, these two neighborhood types constituted 40 percent of all neighborhoods in 2000, reflecting the growing prominence of Hispanics and Asians in both white and black communities.

Interestingly, amid the growth in nonblack minority populations, the number of mixed multi-ethnic communities in the 10 metropolitan areas remained about the same—there were just ninety-six more neighborhoods overall (a 13 percent increase), representing 7 percent of the total, in 2000. Meanwhile, mixed white-and-black communities dwindled to just 4 percent of all neighborhoods. In this fashion, the growth of Hispanic and Asian populations apparently did not generate a substantial increase in truly multi-ethnic communities, but instead contributed to a growing number of neighborhoods in which *either* whites or blacks live alongside nonblack minority populations.

To be sure, sweeping judgments about neighborhood transitions from these aggregate data remain inappropriate. After all, much of the change in neighborhood classifications results from large increases in nonwhite—usually Hispanic—populations in each metropolitan area. It is worth noting, however, that the unchanged number of predominantly black communities may indicate that blacks did not move much during the 1990s and that few new arrivals of other races moved into predominantly black communities. Meanwhile, the small increase in mixed multi-ethnic neighborhoods, and the decline in mixed white-and-black communities, may signal that Hispanic and Asian populations tended to grow fastest in communities where they already predominated or were already integrated with another race group.[18]

---

18. Because the number of predominantly black communities stays fairly constant, we posit that the decline in the number of mixed white-and-black neighborhoods owes to growth in Hispanic or Asian population, not a decline in the white population.

Mixed-Race Neighborhoods Increased in Most Metropolitan Areas

The aggregate pattern across the ten metropolitan areas—a decline in homogeneous neighborhoods and a rise in mixed-race neighborhoods—reflected changes taking place in each of the areas during the 1990s. With the exception of Los Angeles, all of the metropolitan areas saw declines in the number of neighborhoods where one racial/ethnic group predominated and increases in the number of neighborhoods with two or more racial/ethnic groups present in significant numbers (see table 5A-1 in appendix for metropolitan-level statistics). The drop in homogeneous neighborhoods tracked large declines in the number of predominantly white communities in almost all of the metropolitan areas, even as predominantly Hispanic/Asian neighborhoods rose in nine out of ten.

Although the ten metropolitan areas all lost homogeneous neighborhoods, they diverged on the types of mixed-race neighborhoods that proliferated. Most of the growth in mixed communities in Dallas, Houston, New York, and Washington, D.C., came in the form of mixed black-and-other neighborhoods. Figure 5-3 shows that in the Washington area, these neighborhoods more than doubled in number over the decade, representing 13 percent of all metropolitan communities by 2000. Hispanic (and to a lesser degree Asian) populations grew sharply in all four of these metropolitan areas during the 1990s, and these data indicate that their numbers grew substantially in communities that were also home to blacks.

In another set of metropolitan areas—including Boston, Chicago, and Detroit—growth in mixed white-and-other neighborhoods drove the overall increase in mixed-race communities. Figure 5-3 shows that mixed white-and-other neighborhoods replaced predominantly white neighborhoods as the most common neighborhood type in the Chicago region by 2000. Other types of heterogeneous communities also increased in Chicago during the decade, but at a much slower rate than neighborhoods in which whites lived alongside Hispanics or Asians.[19]

The occurrence of predominantly black communities also changed in different ways among the ten metropolitan areas. Consistent with the aggregate pattern, changes at the metropolitan-area level in the number of these neighborhoods were not large. But as six metropolitan areas saw declines in this type of community, four (Atlanta, Chicago, Detroit, and Philadelphia) saw increases. These same four metropolitan areas also have the highest proportion of predominantly black communities among the ten analyzed here.

19. Atlanta and Philadelphia experienced similar increases in mixed white-and-other and mixed black-and-other neighborhoods.

FIGURE 5-3. Distribution of Neighborhoods by Type, Selected Metropolitan Areas, 1990–2000

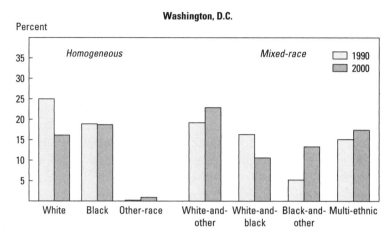

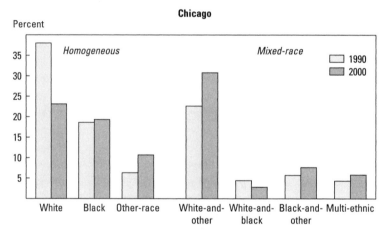

Source: Authors' calculations from 1990 and 2000 census data.

Growing Hispanic and Asian populations in these areas do not appear to have settled in black communities to the degree that they did in other places.[20]

Given these patterns of change, where did the different metropolitan areas end up in 2000? Houston, Dallas, New York, and Washington, D.C., exhibit the highest proportions of mixed-race communities. Increased neighborhood mixing between black and Hispanic/Asian populations

20. Not surprisingly, these four metropolitan areas rank higher on the index of dissimilarity between blacks and Hispanics than the other six. Logan (2003).

in these metropolitan areas in the 1990s apparently contributed to this outcome. Otherwise, Washington, D.C., and Dallas—and to a lesser extent Atlanta and Houston—boast the highest proportions of mixed multi-ethnic communities (though Houston experienced a decline over the decade). How these neighborhoods evolved in different metropolitan areas and how stable they may prove to be over time is examined below.

Whites and Blacks Lived in More Heterogeneous Neighborhoods; Hispanics and Asians Lived in More Homogeneous Neighborhoods

During the 1990s, the shifting profile of neighborhoods in the nation's largest metropolitan areas placed different racial/ethnic groups in closer proximity. Neighborhoods classified as mixed-race under our typology now account for more than half of all neighborhoods across the ten metropolitan areas. But how have these changes affected the type of neighborhood in which members of different races and ethnicities live? Did all groups live in more heterogeneous communities in 2000 than they did in 1990?

The shifting distribution of racial and ethnic groups among different neighborhood types owes primarily to the fact that these groups grew at different rates in the ten metropolitan areas during the 1990s. A decline in the proportion of whites living in predominantly white communities, for instance, does not indicate that whites relocated *en masse* to mixed-race neighborhoods over the decade. It does, however, reflect the growth of black and nonblack minority populations in previously homogeneous neighborhoods.

At any rate, both whites and blacks were much less likely to live in a neighborhood in which their group predominated in 2000 than in 1990. Figure 5-4 shows the percentage of each racial/ethnic group's members that lived in each of the neighborhood types in both years. Whites and blacks experience nearly mirror-image declines in the proportion of individuals living in homogeneous neighborhoods in the ten metropolitan areas. The drop in the proportion of whites living in predominantly white communities— from 52 percent to 41 percent—equated to a decline of nearly 3.8 million whites in such neighborhoods over the decade. The result was a much higher proportion—35 percent—living in mixed white-and-other communities in 2000, up from 27 percent in 1990. And although whites were more likely to live in a mixed white-and-black community in 1990 than a mixed multi-ethnic one, by 2000 greater numbers lived in multi-ethnic communities.

These findings suggest that growth in Hispanic and Asian populations brought about two distinct changes (among others) within our neighborhood typology. Thanks to growth in other-race residents, many predominantly

FIGURE 5-4. Distribution of Racial/Ethnic Groups by Neighborhood Type, Ten Largest Metropolitan Areas, 1990–2000

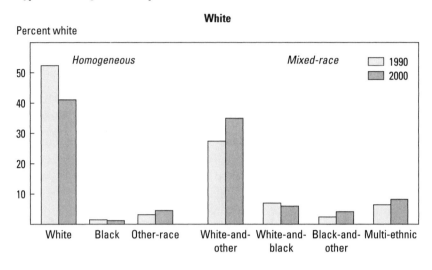

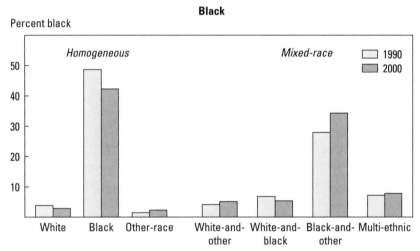

Source: Authors' calculations from 1990 and 2000 census data.

white communities appear to have become mixed white-and-other communities and many mixed white-and-black communities became mixed multi-ethnic.

For the black population, a similar pattern prevailed. About half of blacks lived in a predominantly black neighborhood in 1990, and fewer

F I G U R E 5 - 4 . **Distribution of Racial/Ethnic Groups by Neighborhood Type, Ten Largest Metropolitan Areas, 1990–2000 (*continued*)**

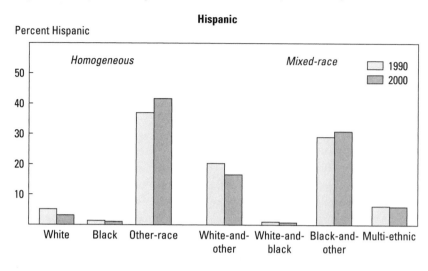

Hispanic

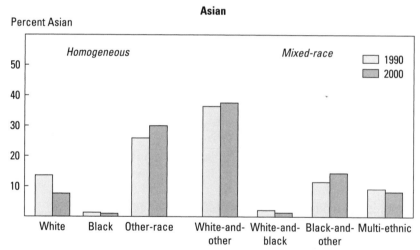

Asian

Source: Authors' calculations from 1990 and 2000 census data.

than 28 percent lived in mixed black-and-other neighborhoods. The pro-portions in each of these neighborhood types grew much closer by 2000 (42 percent and 35 percent, respectively), paralleling the trend for whites. Because the overall black population in the ten metropolitan areas grew by 13 percent over the 1990s, about the same number of blacks lived in predominantly black communities in 2000 as in 1990. But their numbers climbed by over 1 million in neighborhoods with mixed black and Hispanic or Asian populations.

Although the proportions of whites and blacks living in homogeneous communities declined, the exact opposite held for Hispanics and Asians. They are living in predominantly other-race neighborhoods in greater numbers and greater proportions, as shown in figure 5-4. In 2000, 42 percent of Hispanics and 30 percent of Asians lived in neighborhoods in which they made up at least 50 percent of the population (and blacks no more than 10 percent).

At the same time, two factors distinguish the residential locations of Hispanics from those of Asians. First, Hispanics are significantly more likely than Asians to live in a predominantly other-race neighborhood. The rate at which Hispanics live in this neighborhood type is about the same as the rate at which whites and blacks live in neighborhoods where they predominate (41–42 percent). This type of neighborhood is the most common location for Hispanics in the ten metropolitan areas, whereas the most common neighborhood type for Asians is a mixed white-and-other neighborhood. This suggests a higher level of integration among Asians and whites than among Hispanics and whites at the neighborhood level.

Second, as the share of Asians living in mixed white-and-other neighborhoods climbed slightly during the 1990s, that share declined for Hispanics. By 2000, Hispanics were about twice as likely as Asians to live in a mixed neighborhood with blacks (mixed black-and-other), whereas Asians were more than twice as likely as Hispanics to live in a mixed neighborhood with whites (mixed white-and-other). In sum, it seems that in neighborhoods where Hispanics live alongside another racial/ethnic group, that group is more often black, whereas for Asians it is more often white.

Most Multi-Ethnic and Mixed White/Black Neighborhoods Made the Transition in the 1990s

To most observers, "stability" implies growth, development, improved quality of life for residents, and, in general, a "good" to be achieved. Its opposite—"instability"—is fraught with images of decay and decline—boarded-up shops and abandoned cars—and an ever-downward spiral of economic despair for residents trapped in such neighborhoods. Viewed through a different lens, however, stability carries negative implications. For example, racially or economically segregated communities that remain stable by definition remain segregated. This section employs the term "stability" more simply. A "stable" community is one that did not undergo significant racial and ethnic change during the 1990s. A "transitioning" neighborhood, by contrast, changed and shifted its racial/ethnic classification during the decade.

With these considerations in mind, this section explores the varying degrees of stability and transition that each neighborhood type exhibited during the 1990s. To this end, table 5-3 presents a matrix showing, for each neighborhood type as of 1990, the proportion of its communities falling into each classification in 2000. Shaded cells in the matrix suggest the proportion of neighborhoods remaining in the same category throughout the decade, providing a sort of "stability rating" for each type. For instance, reading left to right, the matrix reveals that 68 percent of neighborhoods classified as predominantly white in 1990 were still predominantly white in 2000.

The rate at which different neighborhood types changed over the decade signals the widespread and significant growth in Hispanic and Asian populations that occurred in these ten metropolitan areas. Multi-ethnic neighborhoods were the least likely to retain their designation over the decade (see table 5-3). Only 41 percent of all mixed multi-ethnic neighborhoods in 1990 remained that way by 2000. The statistics indicate that growth in "other" groups (Hispanics and Asians), perhaps combined with some white population loss, tilted almost half of these neighborhoods toward mixed black-and-other status. By contrast, just 9 percent of multi-ethnic communities became mixed white-and-other neighborhoods. This distinction also reflects that white population dropped slightly in these ten metropolitan areas in the 1990s, whereas black population grew by 13 percent.[21]

Other neighborhood types proved more stable in their racial/ethnic profile. Mixed black-and-other neighborhoods were the least changed, with nine of ten retaining that designation over the decade.[22] Approximately seven in ten mixed white-and-other communities retained that character and generally became predominantly other-race neighborhoods when they changed (again reflecting the influence of growing Hispanic and Asian populations in all types of neighborhoods). Mixed white-and-black neighbor-

---

21. The likelihood that a particular neighborhood type makes the transition to another type also depends on how close neighborhoods were to threshold proportions for certain race/ethnic groups in 1990. The typical multi-ethnic neighborhood across the ten metropolitan areas in 1990 was 59 percent white, 20 percent black, 15 percent Hispanic, and 7 percent Asian. All else being equal, a multi-ethnic neighborhood would become mixed white-and-other if its black proportion fell below 10 percent, and it would become mixed black-and-other if its white proportion fell below 40 percent. Thus the former scenario represents a drop by half in the black population share of the typical multi-ethnic community (amid rising black population overall), whereas the second, more common, scenario represents a drop by one-third in the white population share (amid a slight drop in white population overall).

22. Of those that did change designation, most became predominantly other-race neighborhoods, perhaps reflecting a two-decade process of Hispanic population growth.

TABLE 5-3. Proportion of 1990 Neighborhoods by Type in 2000, Ten Largest Metropolitan Areas

| | Percentage in 2000 neighborhood type | | | | | | |
1990 neighborhood type	Predominantly white	Predominantly black	Predominantly other-race	Mixed white-and-other	Mixed white-and-black	Mixed black-and-other	Mixed multi-ethnic
Predominantly white	68.1	0.4	0.0	22.9	4.2	0.4	4.1
Predominantly black	0.1	88.3	0.0	0.0	0.4	11.0	0.3
Predominantly other-race	0.0	0.0	94.7	2.3	0.0	2.8	0.2
Mixed white-and-other	1.2	0.0	16.9	71.0	0.0	3.8	7.1
Mixed white-and-black	6.4	15.4	0.0	2.2	47.0	7.9	21.1
Mixed black-and-other	0.0	2.5	6.5	0.1	0.1	89.5	1.3
Mixed multi-ethnic	0.0	0.5	2.1	8.6	0.3	47.3	41.2

Source: Authors' calculations of 1990 and 2000 census data.

hoods, however, changed classification much more frequently. Fewer than half retained that mix over the decade. Most often, they became mixed multi-ethnic communities or predominantly black. The latter type of transition reflects the classic "tipping point" (such as occurred along the Southwest Waterfront in Washington, D.C.). At the same time, the fact that more of these neighborhoods became mixed multi-ethnic suggests that Hispanic and Asian growth during the 1990s did not inevitably lead to significant losses of white population.

What became of neighborhoods that were racially/ethnically homogeneous in 1990? Predominantly white neighborhoods made the transition to mixed status more often than any other type during the 1990s, as 23 percent developed into mixed white-and-other neighborhoods by 2000. Predominantly black and predominantly other-race communities experienced lower rates of racial/ethnic turnover than predominantly white communities. Specifically, predominantly black neighborhoods were only half as likely as predominantly white neighborhoods to absorb Hispanic/Asian population sufficient to change to mixed status. And predominantly other-race communities changed categories at less than half the rate (5.3 percent versus 11.7 percent) that predominantly black communities did.

It should be noted that these patterns also reflect whether neighborhood population increased or decreased. Neighborhoods with stable or declining population tended to retain their racial/ethnic profile over the decade; those with growing populations tended to change. For instance, predominantly black neighborhoods in which population rose changed categories more often (20 percent of the time) than those in which population declined. Predominantly other-race neighborhoods, in which increasing population

TABLE 5-4. Metropolitan Areas with Most and Least Stable Neighborhood Types, 1990–2000ᵃ

1990 neighborhood type	Most stable		Least stable	
	Metro area	Percent	Metro area	Percent
Predominantly white	Detroit	85.7	Dallas	40.3
Predominantly black	Detroit	98.1	Houston	51.8
Predominantly other-race	Boston; Detroit; Washington, DC	100.0	Philadelphia	60.0
Mixed white-and-other	Washington, DC	84.6	Atlanta	40.0
Mixed white-and-black	Philadelphia	62.5	Houston	14.3
Mixed black-and-other	Washington, DC	96.2	Atlanta	50.0
Mixed multi-ethnic	Washington, DC	60.8	Atlanta	19.0

Source: Authors' calculations from 1990 and 2000 census data.

a. Table reports percentage of neighborhoods of a given type in 1990 that remained the same type in 2000.

tended to reinforce already high proportions of Hispanics or Asians, were the only exception to this rule.

The relative stability of different neighborhood types varied among the 10 metropolitan areas, too. Table 5-4 shows, for each neighborhood type, the metropolitan areas where the highest and lowest proportions of neighborhoods retained the same designation across the decade. This display of the most and least stable neighborhoods reveals that the aggregate figures in table 5-3 mask some sharply contrasting trends. In general, 40 percentage points or more separate the least stable and most stable metropolitan area for each neighborhood category. Approximately six in seven predominantly white neighborhoods in the Detroit area remained that way, but the same held for fewer than half the predominantly white neighborhoods in the Dallas area. Detroit also showed significant stasis in its predominantly black communities, but changes occurred much more often in this type of community in areas that had booming Hispanic populations (for example, Houston).

The stability of mixed white-and-black neighborhoods also varied greatly among metropolitan areas. These neighborhoods displayed moderate stability in the Philadelphia area, but only one in seven mixed white-and-black communities in the Houston area in 1990 was still that way by 2000. A more robust 50 percent of white-and-black communities in Atlanta, Detroit, and Washington, D.C., maintained their profile. This may reflect the presence in each of these metropolitan areas of well-established black-and-white neighborhoods with above-average household incomes.[23]

23. Maps of neighborhood integration typologies for each of the ten metropolitan areas in 1990 and 2000 are available online at www.brookings.edu/metro/publications/20040428_fasenfest.htm.

In sum, the widespread growth of Hispanic and Asian populations strongly influenced the likelihood that different types of communities changed their racial and ethnic profile during the 1990s. That influence was amplified in predominantly white neighborhoods, relative to predominantly black neighborhoods. Truly multi-ethnic communities were the least stable in their makeup, but even as many made the transition to a somewhat less diverse makeup, new ones formed from previously white-and-black neighborhoods.

CONCLUSION

This report reveals that a striking new level of racial and ethnic mixing occurred in the nation's major metropolitan areas during the 1990s. Moreover, the survey offers a glimpse of the future. The ten large metropolitan areas assessed here exhibit the sort of demographic changes that increasingly are reshaping urban America and soon will occur on a much broader scale nationally. These early trends therefore offer an important opportunity to discuss what we mean by integration, how integrated communities will look in the future, and how we might create appropriate conditions for integration that lead to positive social outcomes in an increasingly diverse society.

To be sure, the findings here offer only limited insights as to how and why neighborhoods changed the way that they did. The task of predicting the nature of neighborhood change and assessing the factors that cause it, moreover, requires additional research. Meanwhile, the emergence of predominantly other-race—whether Asian or Hispanic—neighborhoods may not reflect segregation so much as the gravitation of immigrants to communities of common interest. With those caveats in mind, however, a few observations can be made about the meaning of the changes that have taken place in the nation's largest metropolitan areas—observations that may have broad relevance in other locales.

First, the overall changes show that both whites and blacks are increasingly living among people of other ethnicities, not just with each other. That means that national and local policies to foster the integration of blacks and whites alone may miss the mark. For example, programs that subsidize homeownership or home rental in mixed communities may fail to recognize progress if they define goals strictly in terms of the proportion of a community that is black or white. As we have seen, mixed white-and-black communities are in decline, but mixed communities of other forms are on the rise. At the same time, programs that provide financial support for disadvantaged black families, regardless of their eventual residential location, may be a better fit with unfolding realities. At any rate, this report

114

suggests that measurements of integration should consider whether populations live in truly multicultural communities, not just whether blacks and whites live in the same neighborhoods.

Second, it bears noting that the spread of integration has implications for the allocation of public resources. Abundant evidence documents that nonwhite families tend to include more and younger children. Thus increases in mixed-race neighborhoods point to shifting household composition and age distribution in these communities. As many cities have discovered, population shifts have caused some schools to become increasingly underutilized whereas others become increasingly overcrowded. Examining neighborhood integration levels, as well as the kinds of community composition that remain stable over time, can help inform educational policymakers on where to devote new resources and how to redirect existing ones.

A third insight is that, depending on the regional context, local community-level changes may indicate renewed economic vitality or portend economic struggle. Ethnic entrepreneurship has blossomed in many cities (for example, Korean green grocers in New York, Arab convenience store owners in Detroit), leading to new economic activity but at the same time exacerbating complaints about lack of access and opportunity for existing residents relative to new in-migrants. Understanding the forces driving these neighborhood transitions is critical if local and regional policymakers wish to support positive changes on one hand and blunt negative changes on the other.

A final observation: Over the past decade, nonwhite populations fueled continued growth in the nation's major metropolitan areas, contributing to a rise in mixed-race communities. So long as these communities remain economically vibrant and viable, this increased diversity should be welcomed as a stabilizing social influence. Prior research does find that as a community's relative share of whites declines, it can go into an economic tailspin. However, this was more likely to prove true at an earlier time, when an "invasion-succession" model of neighborhood change prevailed. Under that model, a decline in the share of residents who were white usually indicated an out-migration of economically better-off residents and an influx of poorer black residents. But such analyses were based on a white/nonwhite dichotomy. For that reason, they may not capture the more diverse economic profile of newer mixed-race communities, with increased Hispanic and Asian populations. Future research should examine whether the increase in mixed black-and-other neighborhoods might bode well for blacks and whether the decrease in mixed white-and-black neighborhoods might break the "traditional" cycle of economic decline for blacks living in transitional neighborhoods.

In closing, a careful review of how researchers and policymakers understand integration seems in order—as does more research on how integration occurs and how it affects the nation's metropolitan areas. The goal of improving the economic and social standing of the poorest (and most often black) segments of the nation's urban populations is still a pressing one, and the latest evidence should encourage us to reconsider the profile of stable integrated neighborhoods as well as our strategies to support them.

T A B L E 5 A - 1 . Proportion of Neighborhoods by Type, Ten Largest Metropolitan Areas, 1990–2000

Percent

Metro area	Year	Homogeneous			Mixed-race			
		White	Black	Other-race	White-and-other	White-and-black	Black-and-other	Multi-ethnic
Atlanta	1990	47.3	22.2	0.0	0.8	25.7	0.6	3.4
	2000	28.8	22.5	0.2	6.9	18.8	10.5	12.3
	Change	−18.5	0.3	0.2	6.1	−6.9	9.9	8.9
Boston	1990	71.9	1.4	0.7	14.1	1.7	5.2	4.9
	2000	55.7	0.6	1.7	26.3	0.6	8.4	6.8
	Change	−16.2	−0.8	1.0	12.2	−1.1	3.2	1.9
Chicago	1990	38.0	18.6	6.3	22.6	4.4	5.7	4.3
	2000	23.1	19.3	10.7	30.8	2.8	7.6	5.8
	Change	−14.9	0.7	4.4	8.2	−1.6	1.9	1.5
Dallas	1990	31.3	6.1	3.8	32.2	4.1	8.1	14.5
	2000	13.0	3.7	11.2	36.3	1.3	17.7	16.7
	Change	−18.3	−2.4	7.4	4.1	−2.8	9.6	2.2
Detroit	1990	68.3	21.3	0.1	2.0	6.1	0.9	1.4
	2000	58.9	23.6	0.6	6.7	5.9	2.2	2.0
	Change	−9.4	2.3	0.5	4.7	−0.2	1.3	0.6
Houston	1990	16.6	7.4	7.8	34.5	1.8	15.3	16.6
	2000	8.0	4.1	14.5	34.7	0.3	27.9	10.6
	Change	−8.6	−3.3	6.7	0.2	−1.5	12.6	−6.0
Los Angeles	1990	3.8	0.9	34.3	39.4	0.1	18.4	3.2
	2000	1.9	0.6	44.4	30.9	0.0	19.8	2.5
	Change	−1.9	−0.3	10.1	−8.5	−0.1	1.4	−0.7
New York	1990	18.2	9.5	7.7	30.4	0.5	27.1	6.5
	2000	9.4	8.9	12.6	31.4	0.3	32.4	4.9
	Change	−8.8	−0.6	4.9	1.0	−0.2	5.3	−1.6
Philadelphia	1990	65.5	11.5	0.4	2.5	13.7	3.7	2.7
	2000	55.0	12.7	0.2	6.5	12.3	6.8	6.4
	Change	−10.5	1.2	−0.2	4.0	−1.4	3.1	3.7
Washington, DC	1990	25.0	18.9	0.2	19.2	16.3	5.2	15.1
	2000	16.1	18.7	0.9	22.9	10.6	13.3	17.4
	Change	−8.9	−0.2	0.7	3.7	−5.7	8.1	2.3

Source: Authors' calculations from 1990 and 2000 census data.

REFERENCES

Berube, Alan. 2003. "Racial and Ethnic Change in the Nation's Largest Cities." In *Redefining Urban and Suburban America: Evidence from Census 2000*, vol. 1, edited by Bruce Katz and Robert E. Lang. Brookings.

Denton, Nancy, and Douglas Massey. 1991. "Patterns of Neighborhood Transition in a Multiethnic World: U.S. Metropolitan Areas, 1970–1980." *Demography* 28 (1): 41–63.

Ellen, Ingrid Gould. 1998. "Stable Racial Integration in the Contemporary United States: An Empirical Overview." *Journal of Urban Affairs* 20 (1): 27–42.

Frey, William. 2001. "Melting Pot Suburbs: A Census 2000 Study of Suburban Diversity." Brookings.

Galster, George. 1998. "A Stock/Flow Model of Defining Racially Integrated Neighborhoods." *Journal of Urban Affairs* 20 (1): 43–51.

Glaeser, Edward L., and Jacob Vigdor. 2001. "Racial Segregation in the 2000 Census: Promising News." Brookings.

Lee, Barrett A., and P. Wood. 1990. "The Fate of Residential Integration in American Cities: Evidence for Racially Mixed Neighborhoods, 1970–1980." *Journal of Urban Affairs* 12 (4): 425–36.

Logan, John. 2003. "Ethnic Diversity Grows, Neighborhood Integration Lags." In *Redefining Urban and Suburban America: Evidence from Census 2000*, vol. 1, edited by Bruce Katz and Robert E. Lang. Brookings.

Maly, Michael T. 2000. "The Neighborhood Diversity Index: A Complementary Measure of Racial Residential Settlement." *Journal of Urban Affairs* 22 (1): 37–47.

Nyden, Phillip, and others. 1998. "Neighborhood Racial and Ethnic Diversity in U.S. Cities." *Cityscape* 4 (2): 1–17.

Quinn, Lois M., and John Pawasarat. 2003. "Racial Integration in Urban America: A Block-Level Analysis of African American and White Housing Patterns." University of Wisconsin–Milwaukee Employment and Training Institute.

Singer, Audrey. 2002. "America's Diversity at the Beginning of the Twenty-First Century: Reflections from Census 2000." Brookings.

Smith, Richard A. 1998. "Discovering Stable Racial Integration." *Journal of Urban Affairs* 20 (1): 1–5.

6

Modest Progress: The Narrowing Spatial Mismatch between Blacks and Jobs in the 1990s

STEVEN RAPHAEL AND MICHAEL A. STOLL

Duncan the latter half of the twentieth century, changes in the location of employment opportunities within metropolitan areas increased the physical distance between predominantly black residential areas and important employment centers.[1] Although black residential locations have remained fairly centralized and concentrated in older urban neighborhoods, employment has continuously decentralized toward suburbs and exurbs. Many social scientists argue that this "spatial mismatch" between black residential locations and employment opportunities at least partly explains the stubbornly inferior labor market outcomes experienced by African Americans.[2] The difficulties of reverse commuting in many metropolitan areas, coupled with the fact that a high proportion of blacks do not own cars,[3] may render inaccessible many jobs for which black workers are suited.[4]

1. We use the terms "black" and "African American" interchangeably.

2. For recent and extensive reviews of the empirical research on the spatial mismatch hypothesis see Ihlanfeldt and Sjoquist (1998) and Pugh (1998).

3. See Raphael and Stoll (2001) for an analysis of the affect of racial differences in car ownership rates on racial labor market inequality. In 1995, 24 percent of black households had no car, compared to 5 percent of white households and 12 percent of Latino households.

4. There is an extensive literature on why and how space matters in employment. It establishes that the time and monetary costs of travel and information limit the distances workers are willing or able to commute to get to work, especially for low-skill or young workers. Public transit increases the time cost of travel, as does how far workers must commute to employment opportunities. Purchasing and maintaining a car, as well as paying for gas and insurance, increases the monetary cost of travel. Furthermore, distance from employment opportunities raises the costs of getting information about these jobs. As any of these costs rise, workers will be less willing to travel an additional mile. See Stoll (1999) and Holzer, Ihlanfeldt, and Sjoquist (1994).

At the same time, several developments during the 1990s suggest that the geographic isolation of minority communities from employment opportunities may have lessened. The economic boom in the late 1990s brought tremendous economic and employment growth—so much so that the hemorrhaging of central city employment centers that characterized the previous four decades slowed and, in some cases, reversed.[5] With talk of the revival of central cities, many middle- and upper-income households began to repopulate older urban neighborhoods, bringing in consumer dollars and businesses that cater to the middle and upper class. With this revival came talk of the "competitive advantage of the inner city," in which poor, distressed, and predominantly minority urban neighborhoods were seen as strategic areas for capital investment because of their underserved retail markets and geographic proximity to central business districts, among other factors.[6] In fact, in some instances, the development and repopulation of these neighborhoods proceeded to the point where many observers of urban affairs increasingly turned their attention to the potentially negative consequences of gentrification.[7]

Together, these trends suggest that employment may have moved closer to black residential locations during the 1990s. Moreover, several economic trends indicate that black residential mobility may have increased. First, in large part because of the economic boom, black unemployment rates dropped to record lows during the decade, a development that is likely to have increased housing demand among black households.[8] Second, black homeownership rates also increased, a development that likely indicates greater black representation in suburban communities.[9] These factors are largely consistent with reports that residential segregation of African Americans and whites declined by modest amounts in the United States over the 1990s.[10]

Thus central city job growth, coupled with black residential mobility, may have ensured that African Americans' spatial proximity to jobs improved in

5. See U.S. Department of Housing and Urban Development (2000) for evidence on central city and suburban employment growth during the 1990s.

6. See Porter (1995) for a thorough discussion of this argument and the entire volume 24 of *Review of Black Political Economy* (1995) for critics of this approach to inner-city development.

7. For research on the affect of gentrification on the poor, see Vigdor (2002).

8. In 1999, the black unemployment rate was 8 percent. Although this was nearly double the national unemployment rate, the annual rate of 8 percent is the lowest recorded for black unemployment rates since the Bureau of Labor Statistics began to collect separate unemployment figures for African Americans in 1972. See table B-42 in *Economic Report of the President* (2001).

9. Between 1994 and 2001, the black homeownership rate increased by 13 percent, from 42.3 percent in 1994 to 47.7 percent in 2001. U.S. Census Bureau (2002). See also Frey (2001).

10. For direct evidence on this question see Logan (2003); for indirect evidence see Glaeser and Vigdor (2003).

the 1990s. The magnitude of this improvement, however, has yet to be quantified. In this chapter, we assess the extent to which the geographic mismatch between blacks and jobs changed during the 1990s. Using data from the 1990 and 2000 decennial censuses, along with Census Bureau data on the geographic location of employment opportunities, we constructed measures of the degree of geographic imbalance between people and jobs within the nation's 316 metropolitan areas. We used these measures to assess how the U.S. urban landscape has changed along this dimension and to compare the experience of African Americans to that of other racial and ethnic groups. We focused particular attention on the twenty metropolitan areas in the United States with the largest black populations, which together contain a majority of the nation's African American population.

Our analysis of these data provide new evidence that although African Americans remain the racial/ethnic group most segregated from jobs, this segregation declined by modest amounts during the 1990s. Moreover, we find that these marginal improvements are driven entirely by the residential movement of blacks within metropolitan areas. Despite the impression of urban revitalization in many U.S. cities, we find that the overall patterns of job growth in the 1990s were biased toward aggravating the large spatial imbalance between blacks and employment opportunities.

METHODOLOGY

We measured the spatial imbalance between jobs and residential locations using the "index of dissimilarity." The dissimilarity index has been employed in the past to measure the extent of residential segregation of members of different racial and ethnic groups within a given metropolitan area. Our analysis treats *jobs* as one population of interest and measures the degree of separation at the metropolitan level between the physical locations of those jobs and the locations of members of a particular racial/ethnic group.

We adopted the dissimilarity index to describe the imbalance between residential and employment distributions for each of the 300-plus metropolitan areas in the United States.[11] The dissimilarity index ranges from 0 to 100, with higher values indicating a greater geographic mismatch between populations and jobs being described, and a given index value describing the imbalance for an entire metropolitan area. Hence the index value for blacks and retail jobs in Chicago describes the extent to which the neighborhoods that blacks

11. Our universe of metropolitan areas includes metropolitan statistical areas (MSAs) and primary metropolitan statistical areas (PMSAs) as defined by the U.S. Office of Management and Budget for Census 2000.

reside in are different from the geographic locations of retail jobs for the nine-county Chicago metropolitan area. Although this measure does not capture the actual distance that individual workers travel to reach their jobs, it does allow us to make useful comparisons between groups in the degree to which workers are co-located with employment opportunities.

The actual numerical value of the dissimilarity index has a convenient interpretation. In this analysis, the index can be interpreted as the percentage of either jobs or people that would have to be relocated to different neighborhoods to completely eliminate any geographic imbalance. For example, the 1990 index value describing the imbalance between the residential distribution of blacks and the spatial distribution of total employment in Chicago is 73.7. This indicates that in 1990, 73.7 percent of blacks residing in Chicago would have had to relocate within the metropolitan area to be spatially distributed in perfect proportion with the spatial distribution of employment opportunities.[12] A hypothetical index of zero, on the other hand, would indicate that black residences were distributed in exactly the same proportions as jobs throughout the metropolitan area and that no relocation would be necessary to achieve spatial balance.

In this fashion, we calculated dissimilarity indexes for all metropolitan areas for the years 1990 and 2000. In other words, we presented jobs-people mismatch indexes for four population groups: whites, blacks, Asians, and Hispanics. Moreover, we measured geographic mismatch relative to two measures of employment—total employment and retail employment—for each population group. Indexes based on total employment provide an overall measure of the imbalance between people and jobs. Indexes based on retail employment provide estimates of the geographic imbalance between our four racial/ethnic groups and relatively low-skill jobs because a large fraction of retail jobs require relatively little education or training.[13] To calculate the indexes, we used data on total population measured at the ZIP code level from the 1990 and 2000 Census of Population and Housing and

12. As noted, a mismatch index based on the dissimilarity measure does not actually measure the physical distance between the average member of a given population and jobs. The index measures the imbalance across geographic sub-units of the metropolitan area (for example, ZIP codes or census tracts) between members of the population and jobs. To take an extreme example, suppose that all black residents resided in one ZIP code of a city, but all jobs were located in a different ZIP code. Whether these two ZIP codes are one or twenty miles apart will not influence the dissimilarity measure. In both instances, the dissimilarity index will be equal to 100. Nonetheless, as a summary measure, the dissimilarity index does allow comparison of geographic areas over time as well as comparisons across geographic areas. For mismatch measures that take into account distance between populations and jobs, see Raphael (1998).

13. In 2001 the U.S. Bureau of Labor Statistics estimated that retail trade accounted for 18 percent of all jobs.

employment data from the 1992 Economic Census and 1994 and 1999 ZIP Code Business Patterns files. A technical discussion of the dissimilarity index along with a detailed discussion of our data sources is presented in the technical appendix.

One caveat to the interpretation of these measures is in order. In this chapter, we do not examine variation in black proximity to employment opportunities by differences in socioeconomic status among blacks. To the extent that any improvements we observe are driven by the residential mobility of upper-income black households, spatial proximity to employment for poor blacks, those arguably most affected by spatial isolation from employment, may not have improved at all. We do, however, provide evidence suggesting that black households across the socioeconomic spectrum may have shared in the overall trends on spatial mismatch in the 1990s.

FINDINGS

Trends over the latter part of the last century served to increase the physical separation between minority households—particularly African Americans—and jobs. Our analysis of spatial mismatch in the final decade of the century confirms that blacks remained at a significant disadvantage in proximity to jobs relative to other racial/ethnic groups.

Spatial Isolation from Jobs Was Highest for Blacks

Figure 6-1 presents average values for our measures of geographic mismatch in 2000—the dissimilarity indexes for total employment and retail employment—by race and ethnicity. These averages are weighted by the metropolitan area population counts for the racial/ethnic group being described by the index.[14]

The most striking pattern observed in figure 6-1 is that clear racial/ethnic differences persisted in the degree of mismatch between people and jobs. In 2000, the index values indicate that more than 50 percent of blacks would have had to relocate to achieve an even distribution of blacks relative to jobs. The comparable figures for whites are 20 to 24 percentage points lower. The degree of geographic mismatch from employment opportunities experienced by Asians and Hispanics lies between the values for whites and

14. Weighting the calculation of the average will place more weight on metropolitan areas with large populations. For example, New York, Chicago, and Atlanta will all receive relatively large weights in the calculation of the black mismatch measures, given the relatively large black populations of these cities. The weighting permits us to interpret the patterns in figures 6-1 and 6-2 as the average degree of mismatch experienced by the typical member of each group.

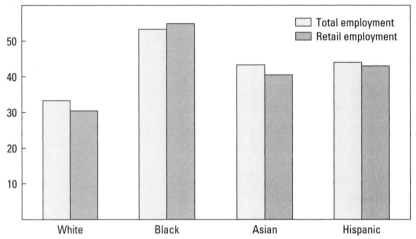

FIGURE 6-1. Spatial Mismatch between People and Employment, by Race/Ethnicity, Metropolitan Areas, 2000

Spatial mismatch index

Source: Authors' calculations using data from 1990 and 2000 censuses; 1992 Economic Census; and 1994/1999 ZIP Code Business Patterns.

blacks. The values for the Asian mismatch indexes are from 10 to 15 percentage points lower than those for blacks, while the index values for Hispanics are 9 to 12 percentage points lower. Interestingly, for all racial and ethnic groups, the degree of mismatch calculated using retail employment is comparable to the degree of mismatch calculated using total employment, suggesting that minorities are perhaps no more isolated from low-skilled jobs than they are from employment generally.[15]

Looking behind the aggregate national values, table 6-1 presents total employment and retail employment index values for blacks and whites for the twenty metropolitan areas with the largest black populations.[16] (Table 6A-1

15. In tabulations not reported here, we also calculated the mismatch indexes using the number of retail establishments as the measure of employment opportunities rather than the number of retail jobs. For blacks, Asians, and Hispanics, the mismatch indexes using retail establishments were nearly identical to the mismatch indexes calculated with retail employment. For whites, however, the retail establishment indexes were nearly 10 points lower than the retail employment indexes. This pattern indicates that there is an abundance of small retail establishments in white ZIP codes relative to predominantly black, Asian, or Hispanic ZIP codes. These figures are available from the authors upon request.

16. The cumulative black populations of these metropolitan areas accounted for nearly 52 percent of the black population residing in metropolitan areas in 2000.

T A B L E   6 - 1 .   Spatial Mismatch between Blacks and Whites and Total and Retail Employment in the Twenty Metropolitan Areas with the Largest Black Populations, 1990–2000

Percent

Metro area	Total employment				Retail employment			
	Blacks		Whites		Blacks		Whites	
	2000	Change, 1990–2000	2000	Change, 1990–2000	2000	Change, 1990–2000	2000	Change, 1990–2000
Atlanta	53.9	−3.2	39.6	1.0	52.4	−6.2	30.5	−2.4
Baltimore	51.9	−4.1	37.1	3.1	55.9	−1.0	31.0	2.3
Charlotte	34.5	−6.2	35.4	0.2	34.0	−12.8	31.9	−2.9
Chicago	69.5	−4.2	34.5	1.7	70.3	−4.1	27.7	−0.3
Cleveland	62.0	−2.5	31.0	0.0	64.6	−2.0	26.0	−0.3
Dallas	56.5	−1.2	40.4	0.4	51.9	−0.8	31.4	0.2
Detroit	71.4	−4.2	36.5	1.6	76.8	−2.6	30.1	3.7
Ft. Lauderdale	46.9	−4.0	30.0	4.0	47.1	−6.2	21.8	0.9
Houston	56.5	−2.0	39.6	1.2	54.2	−2.9	29.6	−1.4
Los Angeles–Long Beach	61.6	−3.2	37.3	2.8	61.2	−4.6	27.9	0.1
Memphis	46.7	−7.3	42.1	3.2	45.2	−8.7	38.3	5.3
Miami	64.7	2.5	35.8	1.9	62.0	1.9	28.6	3.7
New Orleans	49.9	1.5	39.6	1.0	49.9	1.1	33.7	−1.7
New York	70.3	0.4	44.4	−2.7	68.5	−2.0	34.4	−1.4
Newark, NJ	65.2	−3.0	33.6	2.4	67.0	−2.1	29.5	−0.2
Norfolk	36.2	0.3	37.1	3.4	41.3	−2.1	37.0	6.0
Oakland	55.4	−1.4	36.9	1.4	55.3	−5.4	31.0	2.6
Philadelphia	64.2	−4.3	34.4	−0.3	67.1	−4.7	28.5	−0.9
St. Louis	62.6	−2.3	38.4	2.3	66.7	−0.8	28.8	−0.4
Washington, DC	55.5	−2.9	42.3	2.0	52.6	−3.6	35.8	1.1

Source: Authors' calculations using data from 1990 and 2000 censuses; 1992 Economic Census; and 1994/1999 ZIP Code Business Patterns.

in the appendix presents comparable figures for the same twenty metropolitan areas for Hispanics and Asians.) The uniformity is striking: in eighteen of these areas, blacks contended with a much higher degree of spatial mismatch than whites in 2000. For instance, the separation between blacks and jobs in Chicago and Cleveland was roughly double that experienced by whites. The sole exceptions are the Charlotte and Norfolk metropolitan areas, where the index values for whites and blacks were nearly identical.

The Spatial Mismatch Gap between Blacks and Whites Narrowed in the 1990s

As with residential segregation, spatial mismatch between blacks and jobs declined in the 1990s, but the changes were modest in scale. The total employment mismatch index for blacks dropped by 3.2 percentage points between

1990 and 2000, whereas the retail employment index declined by 3.8 percentage points—both statistically significant changes (figure 6-2). For Hispanics, there was no significant decline in the geographic imbalance between residence and total employment opportunities, but the retail employment mismatch index did decline by a statistically significant 2.5 percentage points. For whites and Asians, there were small changes in the average mismatch values, none large enough to be statistically significant. Overall, slight improvements in mismatch conditions for blacks in the 1990s, combined with no measurable change for whites, served to narrow the difference in average mismatch between these groups by approximately 13 percent.

The average trend documented in figure 6-2 is also evident when we examine the indexes for specific metropolitan areas. Table 6-1 shows that the improvements experienced by blacks in the aggregate occurred in nearly all of the metropolitan areas displayed in the table. Of the twenty metropolitan areas with the largest black populations, eighteen experienced declines in spatial mismatch between black residences and total employment, whereas sixteen experienced declines in mismatch between black residences and retail employment. For whites, Asians, and Hispanics, fewer areas saw mismatch measures decline, and the changes in the indexes were generally smaller. Indeed, among the twenty metropolitan areas examined in table 6-1, only New York exhibited a significant decrease in spatial mismatch between whites and total employment in the 1990s.

At the same time, black spatial mismatch within metropolitan areas appears to vary by where the metropolitan area is located and the relative size of the black population there. Table 6-2, which presents mismatch indexes by region and black share of the population, reveals these patterns:[17]

—Blacks residing in metropolitan areas in the Northeast and Midwest were the most physically isolated from employment opportunities, and blacks residing in the South were the least isolated. Although average mismatch indexes declined in all areas, the declines were smallest in the Northeast. Midwestern metropolitan areas, which had exhibited the highest average degree of mismatch between blacks and jobs in 1990, experienced a comparatively large decline in overall mismatch during the decade.

17. Concerning the percentage of the metropolitan area that is black, we first ranked the 300-plus MSAs/PMSAs by percent of black population and then separately identified the 25 percent of PMSAs with the lowest values of this variable, the lower-middle quarter, the upper-middle quarter, and the quarter with the highest proportion of black residents. In these calculations, the average values are weighted by the black population counts for each metropolitan area within the substratum defined in the table.

FIGURE 6-2. Changes in Spatial Mismatch, by Race/Ethnicity, Metropolitan Areas, 1990–2000[a]

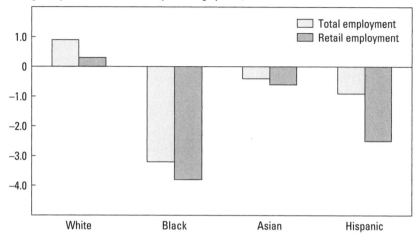

Change in spatial mismatch index (percentage points)

Source: Authors' calculations using data from 1990 and 2000 censuses; 1992 Economic Census; and 1994/1999 ZIP Code Business Patterns.

a. Both results for blacks and retail employment result for Hispanics are statistically significant.

TABLE 6-2. Spatial Mismatch between Blacks and Total and Retail Employment, by Region and Black Share of Metro Area Population, 1990–2000

Percent

	Total employment		Retail employment	
	2000	*Change, 1990–2000*	*2000*	*Change, 1990–2000*
Region				
Northeast	62.9	−1.9	65.0	−2.8
Midwest	62.5	−4.7	65.9	−4.0
South	45.4	−2.9	46.7	−3.2
West	51.9	−4.3	51.0	−5.2
Black share of metro population[a]				
Bottom quarter	31.8	−4.7	35.9	−2.5
Lower-middle quarter	48.2	−4.3	50.5	−4.6
Upper-middle quarter	52.7	−3.8	55.4	−5.0
Top quarter	54.5	−2.8	55.6	−3.3

Source: Authors' calculations using data from 1990 and 2000 censuses; 1992 Economic Census; and 1994/1999 ZIP Code Business Patterns.

a. Black population shares in the bottom quarter range from 0 to 2.2 percent; in the lower-middle quarter, from 2.3 to 6.9 percent; in the upper-middle quarter, from 6.9 to 15.4 percent; and in the top quarter, from 15.4 percent up.

—The level of mismatch between blacks and jobs proved most severe in metropolitan areas where a relatively large percentage of the population is black. As the black population share increased, the degree to which black residences were physically separated from jobs also increased. The gap in the blacks/jobs mismatch index between metropolitan areas with high black representation (more than 15 percent) and low black representation (2 percent or less) was more than 20 percentage points. In addition, metropolitan areas with a smaller black population share exhibited larger declines in spatial mismatch between blacks and total employment in the 1990s.

These patterns raise several questions about how regional differences in growth dynamics and racial composition affect the geographic imbalance between black residences and employment opportunities. The next section explores whether metropolitan-area differences in residential segregation may explain differences in the spatial mismatch facing black households.

Metropolitan Areas with Greater Segregation Exhibited Greater Mismatch between Blacks and Jobs

The patterns in tables 6-1 and 6-2 indicate a fair degree of variation across metropolitan areas in the extent to which blacks are isolated from employment opportunities. Further analysis suggests that much of this cross-area variation can be explained by the degree of housing segregation of blacks and whites in each of the 316 metropolitan areas. Moreover, it turns out that changes in the degree of black/white residential segregation played a role in changing regional mismatch conditions during the 1990s.[18]

First, the data indicate a strong positive relationship between spatial mismatch for blacks and black/white segregation. Figure 6-3 presents a visual representation of this relationship for all metropolitan areas in 2000.[19] Each point on the scatter plot represents a single metropolitan area, with its black/white residential segregation index on the horizontal axis and its blacks/total employment mismatch index on the vertical axis. Clearly, as residential segregation of blacks and whites increases, the physical separation of blacks from total employment also increases. Examples at the extremes illustrate

18. To show this, we append data on black/white dissimilarity indexes for 1990 and 2000 to our data series measuring the degree of mismatch between blacks and jobs. Like the mismatch indexes, the dissimilarity index between blacks and whites is interpreted as the proportion of blacks (or whites) that would have to relocate to yield perfectly even distributions of black and white households across the neighborhoods of a given metropolitan area. Data on black/white dissimilarity for 1990 and 2000 come from the Lewis Mumford Center for Comparative Urban and Regional Research website. These data are available at http://mumford1.dyndns.org/cen2000/data.html.

19. We omit the scatterplot using the blacks/retail employment indexes because these are nearly identical to the scatterplots presented for the total-employment mismatch indexes.

FIGURE 6-3. Blacks/Jobs Mismatch versus Black/White Residential Segregation, Metropolitan Areas, 2000

Blacks/total jobs mismatch index (percent)

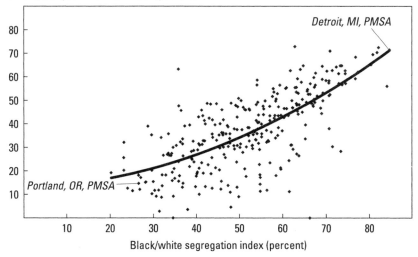

Black/white segregation index (percent)

Source: Authors' calculations using data from 1990 and 2000 censuses; 1992 Economic Census; and 1994/1999 ZIP Code Business Patterns.

this point. In the Portland, Oregon, metropolitan area, only 26 percent of the black population would have needed to relocate in 2000 to achieve an even distribution of blacks and whites across neighborhoods. There, the mismatch index between blacks and jobs was just 19 percent. In the Detroit metropolitan area, 85 percent of the black population would have had to relocate in 2000 to achieve an even black-white residential distribution, and the mismatch index for blacks and total employment was 71 percent.

Moreover, our analysis finds that nearly 50 percent of the variation in the mismatch index across metropolitan areas in 2000 can be explained by the degree of black/white residential segregation. These results go a long way in explaining the findings in tables 6-1 and 6-2, which document lower mismatch indexes for blacks in the South and in areas with smaller black populations. Historically, racial residential segregation has been relatively low in both of these types of metropolitan areas.[20] For instance, in Southern metropolitan areas with a lower degree of spatial mismatch for blacks—such as Charlotte, North Carolina, and Norfolk, Virginia—black/white segregation indexes are 20 to 30 percentage points lower than in Midwestern

20. Logan (2003); Glaeser and Vigdor (2003).

metropolitan areas, such as Chicago and Cleveland, where blacks are more isolated from employment. Hence, the figures imply that a direct cost of black/white segregation is the physical isolation of blacks from employment opportunities. This is not surprising, considering that our mismatch indexes indicate that jobs and white residential locations tend to be co-located (as can be seen by the low mismatch values for whites in figure 6-1 and table 6-1).

To assess whether changes in the degree of black/white residential segregation were related to declines in mismatch between blacks and jobs, figure 6-4 presents a similar scatterplot of the changes in these two indexes during the 1990s. As can be seen, changes in mismatch conditions are positively associated with changes in residential segregation. Again, to use examples from the extremes, as residential segregation of blacks and whites declined by 16 to 17 percentage points in the Minneapolis-St. Paul and Pittsburgh metropolitan areas, the mismatch index for blacks declined by 11 percentage points. On the other hand, segregation climbed by 11 percentage points in the Mansfield, Ohio, metropolitan area, and the mismatch between blacks and jobs increased by 17 percentage points.

Overall, the relationship displayed in figure 6-4 suggests that the general trend of decreasing black-white segregation in metropolitan areas in the 1990s contributed to a modest decline in spatial mismatch between blacks and jobs over the decade. Nonetheless, although the positive relationship shown is highly statistically significant, only 10 percent of the variation in the mismatch index can be explained by the change in black/white housing segregation. The implication is that other factors besides changing residential segregation clearly contributed to the changing imbalance between black residences and employment in the 1990s.

Of course, our results cannot confirm that lower-income black households saw an across-the-board decline in their spatial isolation from job opportunities, because our analysis does not take into account the socioeconomic status of black households across metropolitan areas. Nonetheless, the fact that the vast majority of metropolitan areas saw declines in spatial mismatch, together with the association between declining mismatch and declines in black/white housing segregation, strongly suggests that the benefits of narrowing spatial mismatch in the 1990s were not confined to upper-income black households alone.

Residential Movement of Black Households Accounted for the Decline in Spatial Mismatch

The decline in the degree of spatial isolation experienced by blacks could have been the result of several forces. One possible explanation is that blacks were

FIGURE 6-4. Change in Blacks/Jobs Mismatch versus Change in Black/White Residential Segregation, Metropolitan Areas, 1990–2000

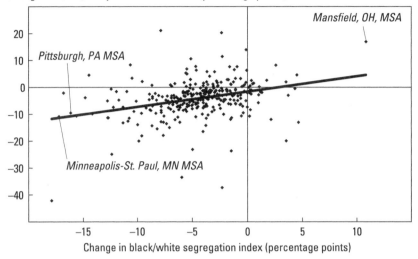

Source: Authors' calculations of data from 1990 and 2000 censuses; 1992 Economic Census; and 1994/1999 ZIP Code Business Patterns.

increasingly choosing to live in metropolitan areas with low levels of spatial isolation between blacks and jobs. If that were the case, even in the absence of any metropolitan-level improvement in these indexes, black migration between metropolitan areas would lower the average value (because migration patterns would increase the weight placed on low-mismatch areas).

Alternatively, the improvements observed during the 1990s may have been driven entirely by changes in job location occurring *within* metropolitan areas. It may be the case that the decentralization of employment, a long-term trend in U.S. cities extending back to at least World War II, reversed during the 1990s. In this scenario, the decline in urban crime, the gentrification of older urban neighborhoods, and federal, state, and local urban development policies geared toward encouraging job growth in central cities may all have improved the balance between where blacks live and where jobs are located.

Another possible contributor is black residential mobility within metropolitan areas. To the extent that black households suburbanized during the 1990s or, more generally, tended to move where the jobs are, such movement would cause improvements in the mismatch indexes that we measured. In fact, the observed relationship between declines in the extent of mismatch and declines in black/white housing segregation documented in the previous section suggests that black residential mobility was an important factor.[21]

We assessed the causes of the modest improvements in the mismatch indexes for blacks and Hispanics documented above, first considering whether the observed improvements were driven by between-area migration or within-area improvements. We then analyzed whether the improvements occurring within metropolitan areas were driven by a more favorable geographic pattern of employment growth or by the residential mobility of black households. (A detailed description of the methodology we used to conduct this part of the analysis can be found in the technical appendix.)

Improvement Occurred within Metropolitan Areas

Our first finding is that the modest overall decline in spatial mismatch between blacks and jobs in the 1990s was driven not by the relocation of the black population to metropolitan areas with lower degrees of spatial mismatch but by actual reductions within metropolitan areas in the physical isolation of black residences from employment locations. Figure 6-5 presents the results of these decompositions for the indexes that changed by a statistically significant degree in the 1990s—retail employment for Hispanics and both total employment and retail employment for blacks.

In figure 6-5, each bar represents the total contribution, in percentage points, of either the within-metropolitan-area or the between-metropolitan-area trend to the total decline in the spatial mismatch measure indicated. For instance, 2.8 percentage points of the overall 3.2 percentage point decrease in the mismatch between blacks and total employment was driven by improvements *within* metropolitan areas. By contrast, the movement of black households *between* metropolitan areas contributed only 0.4 percentage points to the overall 3.2 percentage point decline.

Figure 6-5 demonstrates that the lion's share of the improvement in the jobs-people mismatch for blacks and Hispanics resulted from changes within metropolitan areas. This finding is not surprising given the visible declines in these indexes for blacks presented in table 6-1. Conversely, it seems that little inter-area migration was driven by the desire of black or Hispanic households to reside in metropolitan areas with lower spatial isolation from jobs.

---

21. Note that both the gentrification of urban neighborhoods and black residential mobility are likely to reduce the degree of black/white housing segregation as well as the degree of mismatch between blacks and jobs. In light of this fact, the findings in the previous section regarding the association between changing mismatch conditions and changing black/white segregation do not allow us to discriminate among these alternative explanations.

FIGURE 6-5. Causes of Decline in Spatial Mismatch for Blacks and Hispanics, Metropolitan Areas, 1990 to 2000

Decline in mismatch index (percentage points)

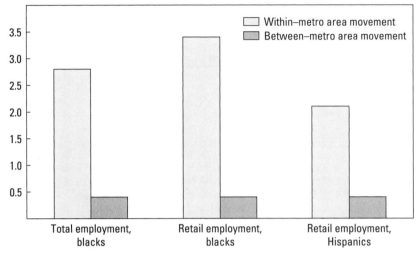

Source: Authors' calculations using data from 1990 and 2000 censuses; 1992 Economic Census; and 1994/1999 ZIP Code Business Patterns.

Residential Mobility Drove the Decline in Spatial Mismatch

We now turn to the question of whether the large within-area improvement was caused by black and Hispanic residential mobility or by changes in the geography of job growth. To address this question, we computed two hypothetical indexes that, when compared to the actual values for 1990 and 2000, allowed us to discern the forces driving the within-area reductions in mismatch. Both indexes, along with actual values for 1990 and 2000, are displayed in table 6-3.

—The first hypothetical mismatch measure uses 1990 population data and 2000 employment data. It can be interpreted as measuring the imbalance between people and jobs that would have resulted if the black population had not moved during the 1990s but employment distributions had undergone their actual change over the course of the decade.

—Our second hypothetical mismatch measure uses 2000 population data and 1990 employment data. It can be interpreted as the level of spatial imbalance between jobs and people that would have resulted had the geographical distribution of employment not changed during the 1990s but population distributions had undergone their actual change during the decade.

TABLE 6-3. Contribution of Residential and Job Movement to Changing Spatial Mismatch between Blacks and Hispanics and Employment, Metropolitan Areas, 1990–2000

Percent

	Blacks		Hispanics
Index	*Total employment*	*Retail employment*	*Retail employment*
Actual 1990 mismatch index	56.5	58.7	45.5
Job movement: hypothetical index assuming no residential movement[a]	60.4	60.3	45.1
Residential movement: hypothetical index assuming no job movement[b]	52.4	53.7	44.1
Actual 2000 mismatch index	53.3	54.9	43.0

Source: Authors' calculations using data from 1990 and 2000 censuses; 1992 Economic Census; and 1994/1999 ZIP Code Business Patterns.
a. The average values of the indexes presented here are weighted by 1990 metro area population figures.
b. The average values of the indexes presented here are weighted by 2000 metro area population figures.

Our analysis indicates that the residential movement of blacks within metropolitan areas drove declines in the spatial mismatch between blacks and jobs in the 1990s. In fact, we find that in the absence of this movement, changes in the geography of employment opportunities would have aggravated the spatial imbalance between blacks and jobs.

Focusing first on the hypothetical indexes that assume movement of jobs but not blacks, we note that they are higher than the actual mismatch indexes for 2000 (table 6-3). This indicates that had the black population remained in place and had jobs been redistributed as they were during the 1990s, the spatial mismatch index for blacks and total employment would have risen by approximately 4 percentage points. On the other hand, had jobs remained in place and black residences changed as they did over the decade, our second hypothetical index indicates that the spatial mismatch index for total employment would have dropped by approximately 4 percentage points—more than the actual decline. As it turned out, the residential mobility of black households in the 1990s was the more dominant trend, and the overall index declined by a little over 3 percentage points (as shown here and in figure 6-2).

The results for Hispanics were slightly different. The hypothetical retail employment index that assumes mobility of jobs but not people is only slightly lower than the actual average in 2000. The more significant contribution to the reduced mismatch between Hispanics and retail jobs appears to have resulted from the residential mobility of the population. Together, these trends effected a 2.5 percentage point drop in the index over the 1990s.

To summarize, our calculations indicate that nearly all of the reduction in the average geographic imbalance between where blacks live and where jobs are located was driven by within-metropolitan-area improvement in these imbalances during the 1990s (rather than black migration between metropolitan areas). The same is true for the improvement in the imbalance between retail jobs and Hispanics. Behind these within-area improvements, we find that changes in the spatial location of employment opportunities during the decade actually contributed to the further isolation of blacks from jobs. However, the residential movement of blacks within areas was sufficient to both undo the negative affect of job decentralization and create a net reduction in mismatch between blacks and jobs.

CONCLUSION

The patterns observed in the 1990 and 2000 decennial censuses are clear. Black households in both years are consistently the most physically isolated from employment opportunities, followed by Hispanic, Asian, and white households. Although the 1990s did see a reduction in the separation between blacks and jobs, those improvements were modest, and large racial differences in physical access to jobs remained at the close of the century. Moreover, employment growth in central cities over the decade did little to alter this imbalance. In fact, as in past decades, the geography of employment growth in U.S. metropolitan areas was such that, in the absence of black residential mobility, the physical isolation of black households from jobs would have increased.

One encouraging finding from our analysis is that the residential location decisions of black households appear to be determined in part by the geographical distribution in employment opportunities. In fact, all of the improvements in the spatial imbalance between blacks and jobs that we observed can be attributed to black residential mobility. To what extent black residential mobility over the decade was actually driven by black citizens' desire to move closer to employment opportunities or other factors remains an open question.

At the same time, our cautious optimism is tempered by the fact that the socioeconomic distribution of this African American residential mobility was not examined. If residential mobility was concentrated among middle- and upper-income African Americans, the black poor, who arguably are most affected by mismatch conditions, are likely to remain in older, urban, and increasingly jobless neighborhoods. Moreover, the high levels of mismatch for African Americans and the modesty of the improvements in mismatch conditions that we observed indicate that spatial mismatch is a deep structural pattern in U.S. urban areas that survived a period characterized by the strongest economic conditions in decades. Hence, although the news from Census 2000 invites cautious optimism, the problem of geographic access to employment opportunities for minorities has certainly not been solved.

To be sure, policies aimed at fostering residential mobility among blacks are not the only tools that can be used to mitigate the negative consequences of spatial mismatch on African American employment prospects. The far reaches of a metropolitan area can also be made accessible by transportation policies that either improve public transit or that encourage car ownership among black households. Our recent work, for example, shows that blacks who own cars have employment rates that are no lower than whites that own cars, whereas among those without cars, the racial difference in employment rates is substantial.[22] In addition, research suggests that extending public transportation into job-rich suburban corridors can enhance employment opportunities for inner-city minority populations.[23] These findings suggest that much can be accomplished through effective transportation policy.

Alternatively, the mismatch conditions experienced by blacks could be mitigated by effective inner-city development policies. But the results shown here indicate that even in the best of economic circumstances, development was not sufficient to undo the spatial disadvantage of blacks. Our results strongly suggest that promoting black residential mobility seems an effective and efficient policy approach for improving black people's access to jobs. In addition, encouraging the residential mobility of black households may also generate benefits that exceed those that come from greater access to employment opportunities. For example, efforts to mitigate differences in housing quality, school quality, and other local amenities and to foster greater interracial contact may also argue for a residential mobility strategy.

The evidence presented here confirms that despite modest progress in the 1990s, in 2000 America's black and other minority citizens continued to live in places that were physically separated from metropolitan jobs. Whatever the approach, alleviating this stubborn geographic barrier to their well-being merits a serious policy response.

TECHNICAL APPENDIX

To calculate the jobs-people dissimilarity index described in the main text, one needs data on population and job totals for sub-geographic units of the metropolitan area. In this study, we use data measured at the ZIP code level.

22. Raphael and Stoll (2001).
23. Holzer, Quigley, and Raphael (2002).

Dissimilarity Index and Data Sources Used

The actual equation for the dissimilarity index is straightforward. Define *Black$_i$* as the black population residing in ZIP code *i* (where *i* = (1, . . . , n) and indexes the ZIP codes in a given metropolitan area); *Employment$_i$* as the number of jobs in ZIP code *i; Black* as the total black population in the metropolitan area; and *Employment* as the total number of jobs in the metropolitan area. The dissimilarity score between blacks and jobs is given by

(1)
$$D = \frac{1}{2} \sum_i \left| \frac{Black_i}{Black} - \frac{Employment_i}{Employment} \right|.$$

As written, the dissimilarity index ranges between 0 (perfect balance) and 1 (perfect imbalance). We multiply this figure by 100. This permits us to interpret the index values as the percentage of either of the populations that would have to move to yield perfect balance.

We use total population data tabulated at the ZIP code level from the 1990 and 2000 U.S. Census of Population and Housing. The 1990 population data are drawn from the 1990 Summary Tape File 3B; the 2000 population data come from the 2000 Summary Tape File 1. We calculate jobs-people mismatch indexes for four population groups: whites, blacks, Asians, and Hispanics. Because the 2000 census permitted respondents to describe themselves by more than one racial category, a brief discussion of how we defined racial groups in the 2000 census is necessary.

For the year 2000, we experimented with three different sets of criteria for defining race. First, we restricted the population counts to those who chose only a single racial descriptor. Second, we defined racial categories in the most inclusive manner possible, counting all respondents who self-identify as white in the white totals, all respondents who self-identify as black in the black totals, and so on. Finally, we used a hierarchical set of definitions to tabulate populations, defining black as all those who self-identify as black, Asians as all those who self-identify as Asian excluding those who also self-identify as black, and whites as all those who self-identify as white excluding those who also self-identify as either black or Asian. The first set of criteria is the most restrictive, dropping all multi-racial respondents. The second set of criteria is most inclusive and involves double counting multi-racial respondents across categories. The final set of criteria is intended to capture phenotypic differences from the perspective of how others are likely to define the respondent. Because information on whether the respondent is Hispanic was collected in a similar manner in both years, we did not experiment with alternative measures for this group in 2000. All those who self-identify as Hispanic are included in the Hispanic total.

For whites and Asians, the 2000 mismatch index values using the three alternative racial definitions are nearly identical. For blacks, the 2000 index values using the more inclusive definition of black are slightly smaller than the average value using the restrictive single-race-only definition. This pattern indicates that multi-racial blacks live in closer proximity to jobs than blacks that self-identify as being black only. Because one of our critical findings is that the geographic mismatch between blacks and jobs improved during the 1990s, we have chosen to employ the more restrictive definition of race. Hence, we present conservative estimates of these improvements.

Despite this choice, the difference between the 2000 estimates of the black/jobs mismatch using the restrictive and inclusive definitions of black is small, with the dissimilarity scores using the inclusive definition of black roughly 0.6 percentage points lower (for an index ranging from 0 to 100) on average than the comparable index using the more restrictive definition. This difference is also small relative to the black-white differences observed in these indexes (on the order of 20 percentage points) and relative to average improvements in these indexes for blacks observed during the 1990s (on the order of 3 to 4 percentage points). Hence choosing the more conservative definition does not qualitatively alter our conclusions. The alternative calculations using the more inclusive definitions of race are available upon request.

We use employment data from several sources. To measure retail employment, we use ZIP code level data from the 1992 Economic Census and the 1999 ZIP code Business Patterns files. One problem is that although the 1992 Economic Census provides data on total retail employment in each ZIP code in the country, the 1999 ZIP code Business Patterns file provides data on the number of retail establishments by establishment size categories only (in other words, the number of establishments with one to four employees, five to nine employees, ten to nineteen employees, twenty to forty-nine employees, fifty to ninety-nine employees, 100 to 249 employees, 250 to 499 employees, 500 to 999 employees, and 1,000 or more employees). To overcome this discrepancy, we converted the establishment data to total employment counts. To do this, we multiplied the number of establishments in each category by the average of the two endpoints defining the category. For example, for establishments with one to four employees, we multiplied the number of establishments by 2.5 to estimate the number of jobs at firms in this size category. For firms with at least 1,000 employees, we multiplied the number of establishments by 3,000.

The sum of these figures across categories provides an estimate of the number of retail jobs in each ZIP code. To check whether this imputation is reasonable, we imputed retail employment for 1994 using the earliest year of the ZIP code Business Patterns data and compared these imputations to data from the economic census for 1992. The correlation between these two ZIP code level measures of retail employment is 0.97. In addition, we compared the distribution of total retail employment across size categories for 1999 for the nation implied by our 1999 imputation to comparable figures published by the Bureau of Labor Statistics for 2002. Again, our imputations and the published figures are qualitatively similar. The 1999 employed data are matched to the 2000 population data, whereas the 1992 employment data are matched to the 1990 population data.

For total employment, the ZIP code Business Patterns files provide an actual enumeration of the number of jobs located in each ZIP code in the country. Hence, to measure total employment, we used these series from the 1999 and 1994 ZIP code Business Patterns files. Unfortunately, 1994 is the earliest year of the ZIP code Business Pattern data files, and data on total employment by ZIP code is not provided in the 1992 Economic Census. Hence, we were forced to use the 1994 total employment data for the 1990 jobs/total employment mismatch indexes.

For the total employment/population mismatch indexes, we matched the 1999 employment data to the 2000 population data and the 1994 employment data to the 1990 population data. In the main text, we refer to the mismatch indexes by the year from which the population data are drawn and by whether the employment data used are total employment or retail employment.

Spatial Mismatch Decompositions

We decomposed the average change in the mismatch indexes into components attributable to within-metropolitan-area improvements and between-metropolitan-area migration in the following manner: define w_i^{90} as the proportion of the 1990 black population residing in metropolitan area i; w_i^{2000} as the proportion of the 2000 black populations residing in metropolitan area i; I_i^{1990} as the jobs/blacks dissimilarity index value for metropolitan area i in 1990; and I_i^{2000} as the jobs/blacks dissimilarity index value for metropolitan area i in 2000. The weighted averages of the indexes for 1990 and 2000 are given by

$$(2) \qquad \mu_{1990} = \sum_i w_i^{1990} I_i^{1990}, \mu_{2000} = \sum_i w_i^{2000} I_i^{2000},$$

respectively. The change in the average value over the decade is given by the equation

(3) $$Change = \sum_i \left(w_i^{2000} I_i^{2000} - w_i^{1990} I_i^{1990} \right).$$

To decompose the change into the components discussed above, one needs to add and subtract the term $w_i^{2000} I_i^{1990}$ within the parentheses of the change equation. Factoring this equation yields the decomposition of the change:

(4) $$Change = \sum_i \left[w_i^{2000} \left(I_i^{2000} - I_i^{1990} \right) + I_i^{1990} \left(w_i^{2000} - w_i^{1990} \right) \right].$$

The first term in this equation gives the weighted average of the change in the indexes using the 2000 population distribution as a weighting variable. This term gives the portion of the change driven by within-metropolitan-area changes in the index values. The second term provides an estimate of the effect of the change in the weights (in other words, the distribution of blacks across metropolitan areas) on the overall average index using the 1990 index values to calculate the contribution. This second term is the component of the change that is attributable to inter–metropolitan area migration of blacks.

An alternative decomposition would add and subtract $w_i^{1990} I_i^{2000}$ to and from our original expression for the change in the index value. After factoring, this would yield the decomposition

(5) $$Change = \sum_i \left[w_i^{1990} \left(I_i^{2000} - I_i^{1990} \right) + I_i^{2000} \left(w_i^{2000} - w_i^{1990} \right) \right],$$

where again, the first term is the component driven by within-area improvements in the index and the second term is the component driven by between-area migration. These two decompositions may differ slightly depending on the average changes in the index values and the distribution of the changes in weights. To account for these differences, our decomposition in figure 6-5 is based on the average of these two equations (as is the convention). Specifically, our estimate of the within-area improvement component was calculated by computing both decompositions—given by equations (4) and (5)—and taking the average of the first terms from the two equations. Our estimate of the between-area contribution to the improvement was calculated by taking the average of the second terms from the two equations. Because both decompositions yield similar results, our conclusions are not sensitive to the averaging or the choice of decomposition.

TABLE 6A-1. Spatial Mismatch between Hispanics and Asians and Total and Retail Employment in the Twenty Metropolitan Areas with the Largest Black Populations, 1990–2000

Percent

	Total employment				Retail employment			
	Hispanics		Asians		Hispanics		Asians	
Metro area	2000	Change 1990–2000	2000	Change 1990–2000	2000	Change 1990–2000	2000	Change 1990–2000
Atlanta	38.1	3.4	38.8	−0.9	38.3	5.8	36.2	−3.0
Baltimore	33.4	−2.0	38.8	2.2	30.8	−1.8	34.3	1.8
Charlotte	34.8	−4.8	38.8	−10.8	30.4	−5.2	35.6	−10.0
Chicago	57.3	−2.9	45.7	−0.5	57.4	−3.6	43.3	−2.5
Cleveland	53.6	−1.1	29.8	−3.8	57.9	0.0	31.5	−1.9
Dallas	43.2	−1.1	44.8	3.1	42.4	0.2	45.9	3.6
Detroit	50.3	3.0	41.2	2.4	48.6	5.0	43.2	4.8
Ft. Lauderdale	37.4	6.2	40.9	4.9	33.1	2.1	33.3	−0.6
Houston	43.3	0.3	52.2	−0.8	42.7	0.2	47.8	−1.6
Los Angeles–Long Beach	50.3	2.7	48.4	1.6	47.7	−1.2	42.1	−0.2
Memphis	35.9	−6.4	38.5	−4.5	28.9	−11.3	38.4	2.6
Miami	40.3	0.6	43.1	−3.0	33.3	−2.8	37.0	−1.3
New Orleans	38.9	−0.4	49.0	−3.2	34.5	−2.3	44.8	−8.2
New York	58.6	−2.3	57.4	0.8	56.1	−3.7	50.4	1.9
Newark, NJ	52.7	−4.4	34.4	0.5	53.5	−6.2	35.4	0.0
Norfolk	36.5	−4.9	43.5	−2.9	37.9	0.4	44.7	2.0
Oakland	46.8	3.4	43.8	0.2	41.6	4.3	37.3	−0.5
Philadelphia	57.0	−2.5	38.9	−1.2	57.1	−3.9	37.5	−2.6
St. Louis	36.4	−0.1	37.4	2.3	32.9	−1.6	37.9	1.9
Washington, DC	51.8	5.4	42.8	−2.2	46.3	2.0	41.4	0.5

Source: Authors' calculations using data from 1990 and 2000 censuses; 1992 Economic Census; and 1994/1999 ZIP Code Business Patterns.

REFERENCES

Economic Report of the President. 2001. Washington: Government Printing Office.

Frey, William H. 2001. "Melting Pot Suburbs: A Census 2000 Study of Suburban Diversity." Brookings.

Glaeser, Edward L., and Jacob L. Vigdor. 2003. "Racial Segregation in the 2000 Census: Promising News." In *Redefining Urban and Suburban America: Evidence from Census 2000,* vol. 1, edited by Bruce Katz and Robert E. Lang. Brookings.

Holzer, Harry J., Keith R. Ihlanfeldt, and David L. Sjoquist. 1994. "Work, Search, and Travel among White and Black Youth." *Journal of Urban Economics* 35: 320–45.

Holzer, Harry J., John M. Quigley, and Steven Raphael. 2002. "Public Transit and the Spatial Distribution of Minority Employment: Evidence from a Natural Experiment." Working Paper W01–002. Institute of Business and Economic Research, University of California–Berkeley.

Ihlanfeldt, Keith R., and David L. Sjoquist. 1998. "The Spatial Mismatch Hypothesis: A Review of Recent Studies and Their Implications for Welfare Reform." *Housing Policy Debate* 9 (4): 842–92.

Logan, John. 2003. "Ethnic Diversity Grows, Neighborhood Integration Lags Behind." In *Redefining Urban and Suburban America: Evidence from Census 2000,* vol. 1, edited by Bruce Katz and Robert E. Lang. Brookings.

Porter, Michael E. 1995. "The Competitive Advantage of the Inner City." *Harvard Business Review* (May-June): 55–71.

Pugh, Margaret. 1998. "Barriers to Work: The Spatial Divide between Jobs and Welfare Recipients in Metropolitan Areas." Brookings.

Raphael, Steven. 1998. "The Spatial Mismatch Hypothesis of Black Youth Joblessness: Evidence from the San Francisco Bay Area." *Journal of Urban Economics* 43 (1): 79–111.

Raphael, Steven, and Michael A. Stoll. 2001. "Can Boosting Minority Car Ownership Rates Narrow Inter-Racial Employment Gaps?" *Brookings-Wharton Papers on Urban Affairs* 2: 99–137.

Stoll, Michael A. 1999. "Spatial Job Search, Spatial Mismatch, and the Employment and Wages of Racial and Ethnic Groups in Los Angeles." *Journal of Urban Economics* 46: 129–55.

Vigdor, Jacob L. 2002. "Does Gentrification Harm the Poor?" *Brookings-Wharton Papers on Urban Affairs* 3: 133–82.

U.S. Census Bureau. 2002. "Housing Vacancies and Homeownership: Annual Statistics 2001." Washington: U.S. Department of Commerce.

U.S. Department of Housing and Urban Development. 2000. *The State of the Cities 2000.* Washington.

7

Pulling Apart: Economic Segregation in Suburbs and Central Cities in Major Metropolitan Areas, 1980–2000

TODD SWANSTROM, PETER DREIER, COLLEEN CASEY, AND ROBERT FLACK

This chapter provides a Census 2000 examination of municipal economic segregation. Though not studied nearly as much as racial segregation, economic segregation—the degree to which different economic classes live spatially apart from one another—has become an important focus of research in the past twenty years.

Ever since the publication of William Julius Wilson's *The Truly Disadvantaged* (1987), researchers have examined the degree to which poor people have become concentrated in high-poverty neighborhoods—in other words, segregated from the rest of society. For the period 1970–1990, researchers found significant increases in concentrated poverty. Research based on 2000 data however, found encouraging news, including what one researcher called a "dramatic decline" during the 1990s in the number of people living in areas of concentrated poverty.[1]

Concentrated poverty is an important topic to study because poor people living in areas where most of their neighbors are also poor enjoy a lower quality of life than poor people who live in mixed-income neighborhoods. Research has linked living in high-poverty areas (independent of individual characteristics) to such negative outcomes as dropping out of school early,

The authors thank Laura Harris of the Urban Institute and John Logan of Brown University for valuable advice in the early stages of our research; the GIS lab of Saint Louis University and Gary Higgs for equipment and guidance; and Alan Lamberg and Sara Whittington Maevers for help with data analysis and graphics.

1. Jargowsky (2005).

teenage pregnancy, out-of-wedlock births, unemployment, and crime victimization. Areas of concentrated poverty often lack job opportunities, health care services, good shopping, decent schools, and adequate municipal services. Concentrations of poverty violate the fundamental American value of equal opportunity.[2]

Just as many poor people live "worlds apart" from the rest of society, many affluent people do as well. Concentrated wealth is the flip side of concentrated poverty. When affluent households segregate themselves in exclusive suburban enclaves, they sever the social relations that provide low- and moderate-income communities with job networks, role models, and political clout. The damaging effects of the "secession of the successful," as Robert Reich called it, are more pronounced when they move not just into separate neighborhoods, but also into separate municipalities and school districts, siphoning off fiscal and political resources.[3]

Most researchers studying economic segregation have focused on neighborhoods, typically defined as census tracts.[4] In contrast, our research focuses on municipalities. We look at how people with different incomes are sorted among political jurisdictions—central cities and their suburbs. When most poor people lived in central cities, it made more sense to study neighborhoods, most of which were contained within one political jurisdiction. By 2002, however, there were almost as many poor people living in suburbs (13.3 million) as in central cities (13.8 million).[5] Poor families living in suburbs encounter a political environment different from that in central cities—one often divided into hundreds of separate municipalities and school districts. In addition to the neighborhood effects of concentrated poverty, the sorting of economic classes into suburban municipalities and school districts affects access to affordable, high-quality public services, especially schools.

Research on economic segregation must take into account broader economic trends as well. We expect the level of spatial economic segregation to reflect the overall level of inequality in society. At the same time, we know that spatial segregation is also affected by many other factors, including local zoning codes and racial discrimination in housing markets.[6]

---

2. For a synthesis of the literature on the effects of concentrated poverty, see Dreier, Mollenkopf, and Swanstrom (2005).

3. Reich (1992).

4. Massey and Fischer (2003).

5. Proctor and Dalaker (2003). In 2000 the poverty rate in central cities was still more than twice that of suburbs. Berube and Frey (2005).

6. For a recent synthesis of the literature on the causes of economic and racial segregation, see Cashin (2004).

During the period of this study, 1980–2000, economic inequality worsened in the United States. Between 1979 and 2000 the share of income held by the bottom 20 percent of families fell from 5.4 to 4.3 percent, whereas the share of family income held by the top 5 percent of families increased from 15.3 to 21.1 percent.[7]

Thus, although the nation prospered from 1980 to 2000, this prosperity was not shared equally. A disproportionate share of the nation's economic growth benefited those in the top income brackets. National statistics like these give us a good idea of trends in economic inequality, but they do not reflect the degree of inequality across the specific communities in which people live. These local contexts exert significant impacts on the quality of peoples' lives. Economic segregation, especially among local jurisdictions in the same metropolitan area, exacerbates economic inequality.

This chapter analyzes trends in economic segregation among municipalities in fifty major metropolitan areas. We attempt to answer the question: Have the incomes of people living in different municipalities converged, or are the rich and poor increasingly living in different jurisdictions? We begin by examining the economic differences between central cities and their suburbs and then examine economic segregation among suburbs. Our research confirms that economic segregation among municipalities has risen, but that trends varied significantly across time and in different regions of the country.

METHODOLOGY

Economic segregation can be studied in a number of different ways. The most common method examines the spatial distribution of the poor as defined by the federal government. The federal poverty standard, however, has a number of flaws that limit its usefulness.

One problem is that over time the federal standard has tended to undercount the number of families unable to purchase the basic necessities of life.[8] From the viewpoint of our study, a more serious problem is that the federal poverty line ignores differences in the cost of living across metropolitan areas. A report by the National Research Council showed that by using the

---

7. Mishel, Bernstein, and Boushey (2003).

8. The federal poverty standard was originally calculated in the 1960s by measuring how much it cost to purchase a minimally acceptable diet and then multiplying that figure by three (based on evidence at the time that the typical family spent about one-third of its income on food). Since then the poverty standard has been adjusted for inflation using the consumer price index. In 2000, the poverty threshold for a family of three was $13,738. Now that the typical U.S. family spends less than one-seventh of its income on food, the federal poverty standard is anachronistic. U.S. Census Bureau (2002).

same poverty measure for every region in the country, the federal standard pulls poverty out of its regional context.[9] A family of three has a more difficult time making ends meet on a poverty-level income ($14,680 in 2003) in New York City than, for example, in Birmingham, Alabama, or Indianapolis.[10] In a wealthy region, affluent households bid up the cost of living, especially for housing, making it more difficult for the poor to make ends meet.[11]

By using an absolute standard, the federal poverty line also does not capture the spatial and economic gap between rich and poor within a metropolitan area. Poor places may lose middle-class residents, jobs, and investment not just because of the "push" of social and economic deterioration but also because of the "pull" of privileged places in the region. David Rusk postulated that if the per capita income of a central city falls below 70 percent of that of its suburbs, it has reached a "point of no return" and is "no longer a place to invest or create jobs."[12] Although the 70 percent figure is somewhat arbitrary, there is little doubt that if a place falls far enough behind, people and businesses will hesitate to move or invest there, accelerating its decline.

For all these reasons, we employ relative definitions of poverty and affluence, comparing suburbs to each other and to central cities. We use sample ("long form") data from the 1980, 1990, and 2000 censuses, focusing primarily on per capita income. Per capita income is a first approximation of the tax base of a municipality—the capacity to raise revenues needed to provide services. Research shows that having large numbers of low-income people, and thus low per capita income, puts significant spending pressures on local governments.[13]

To assess the gap between central cities and suburbs we computed the ratio of the central city's per capita income to the per capita income of the remainder of the metropolitan area (the suburbs). To measure inequality among suburbs, we compute the number of poor and affluent suburbs. We

9. Citro and Michael (1995).

10. In the New York metropolitan areas in 2003, the typical rent for a two-bedroom apartment was $1,073, while the typical two-bedroom rent in Birmingham and Indianapolis was under $600.

11. Baker (2002) found that between 1995 and 2002 both rents and home purchase prices increased considerably faster than the rate of inflation, with the latter rising nearly 30 percent faster than inflation. In its various *Out of Reach* reports going back to 1989, the National Low Income Housing Coalition has shown that the hourly wage a worker must earn to afford a fair market rent (FMR) apartment has increased steadily. FMR is set by the federal government, and "affordability" is defined according to the generally accepted standard that no household should pay more than 30 percent of its income for housing costs. By 2003 the national hourly wage needed to afford a two-bedroom apartment was $15.21, up from $11.08 in 1999. National Low Income Housing Coalition (2003).

12. Rusk (1993).

13. Ladd and Yinger (1989); Pack (1998).

defined *poor* suburbs as those in which per capita incomes fall below 75 percent of the regional per capita income and *affluent* suburbs as those in which per capita incomes exceed 125 percent of the regional figure. *Middle-income* suburbs include those with per capita incomes between these extremes. Our goal was to evaluate the resources available to a municipality as well as how that municipality compares to surrounding jurisdictions. We were interested not only in the number of places that are poor, middle-income, and affluent but also in the number of people living in these different kinds of places.

We also examined the gap between the lowest-income and highest-income suburbs by computing the ratio between the suburb at the 95th percentile in per capita income (95 percent of all suburbs having lower per capita income) and the suburb at the 5th percentile (near the bottom). This ratio gives a good idea of the spread, or inequality, of incomes among suburbs. A ratio of 5.0 means that the suburb at the 95th percentile has a per capita income five times as large as the suburb at the 5th percentile.

GEOGRAPHIC DEFINITIONS

Our sample draws from the fifty largest metropolitan areas in the country. For Census 2000, the Office of Management and Budget (OMB) and the Census Bureau defined several different types of metropolitan areas. Metropolitan statistical areas (MSAs) are stand-alone metropolitan areas. Because in many parts of the nation metropolitan areas are large or have sprawled out to meet each other, primary metropolitan statistical areas (PMSAs) are parts of larger areas called consolidated metropolitan statistical areas (CMSAs). A good example is the New York-Northern New Jersey-Long Island, NY-NJ-CT-PA CMSA, which stretches from southern Connecticut to central New Jersey.[14]

In choosing our sample of metropolitan areas, we began with the fifty largest CMSAs and MSAs according to Census 2000. CMSAs are so large, however, that they do not represent unified housing and labor markets. So within each CMSA, we examined the largest PMSA. For example, we examined the Dallas, TX PMSA, which had a 2000 population of 3.5 million people—considerably smaller than the Dallas-Fort Worth, TX CMSA, which had a population of 5.2 million.[15]

The unit of analysis in our study is the metropolitan area, not the municipality. Rather than follow a cohort of municipalities over time, we measured the degree of economic segregation within metropolitan areas. For

14. We use metropolitan areas as they were defined by OMB in 1999 (for Census 2000).

15. We chose to study the largest PMSA within each CMSA partly because this gave us broader geographical diversity (rather than studying the largest PMSAs wherever they were located).

this reason, we allowed our metropolitan areas to expand geographically over time as OMB added counties from one census to the next to reflect metropolitan population and economic growth.[16]

In 2000 our fifty metropolitan areas had a total population of over 113 million, representing 40.3 percent of the U.S. population. For the most part, however, our analysis includes only the population in what the Census Bureau designates as "places." In 2000, for example, there were 4,871 total "places" in the fifty metropolitan areas that we studied, with a total population of 95 million; 16.1 percent of the population of these metropolitan areas lived outside municipalities and "census-designated places" (CDPs—see below) in 2000. For our analysis, central cities are defined as the largest cities in their respective metropolitan areas. In 2000, these cities had a combined population of nearly 39 million.

Our sample of places includes areas that are not incorporated as municipalities. Census-designated places are unincorporated communities that are similar to municipalities (and may become municipalities in the future) but do not have a general-purpose local government. CDPs represented 21.2 percent of all our places in 1980, 23.0 percent in 1990, and 26.3 percent in 2000.[17] Presumably, residents of poor CDPs do not face the same fiscal stress and accompanying public service issues that residents of poor municipalities face, because local services are not funded from the tax base of the CDP alone; for example, many unincorporated areas receive services from county governments.[18] But residents of poor CDPs may be subject to the same social and economic problems, such as high crime and low levels of private investment, as residents of poor municipalities.

16. The criterion for adding an outlying county is that it "must have a specified level of commuting to the central counties and also must meet certain standards regarding metropolitan character, such as population density, urban population, and population growth" (U.S. Census Bureau 2001). Note also that the analysis treats some PMSAs and MSAs differently. When OMB introduced the CMSA concept in the 1980s, it resulted in some metropolitan areas actually *shrinking* in size, even though they were still growing in population. For example, the Chicago metropolitan area changed from a six-county standard metropolitan statistical area (SMSA—a now-defunct concept) in 1980, to a three-county PMSA in 1990, to a nine-county PMSA in 2000. For the eight PMSAs in 2000 that were actually smaller than their corresponding SMSAs in 1980, we employ constant 2000 boundaries. The remaining ten PMSAs "grew" in the same way as the MSAs over time.

17. For more information about CDPs see the Census Bureau's web page on the Participant Statistical Areas Program, available at www.census.gov/geo/www/psapage.html. Adding together those living in CDPs and those living outside all "places," as defined by the census, it is clear that the percentage of the population living in unincorporated parts of metropolitan areas rose significantly between 1980 and 2000.

18. We say "presumably" because little research has been done on the cost and quality of local services in the unincorporated parts of metropolitan areas, which represent a growing percentage of the population.

FINDINGS

Our research reveals that overall, the 1990s saw less growth in economic segregation than the 1980s. However, inequality among suburbs increased in
the 1990s, as the proportion of population living in middle-income suburbs
continued to decline.

The Income Gap between Cities and Suburbs Stabilized in the 1990s

A study of eighty-five large metropolitan areas found that in 1960 the per
capita income of central cities, on average, was actually slightly higher than
the per capita income of their suburbs. In 1980, however, the per capita
income of central cities had fallen to 89 percent of suburban per capita
income, and the downward trend continued in the 1980s.[19] The 2000 census
data provide an opportunity to see if this trend persisted during the 1990s.

In our sample of fifty metropolitan areas, the per capita income of central cities relative to that of their suburbs fell from 86.3 percent in 1980 to
85.4 percent in 1990. In the 1990s, however, the downward trend abated and
this figure remained stable at 85.5 percent by 2000.

In this respect, the 1990s were better for cities than the 1980s. In the
1980s, all three of the cities that were below Rusk's "point of no return"
(having only 70 percent of their suburbs' per capita income) at the beginning of the decade fell further behind. In the 1990s, by contrast, four of the
ten cities that were below the 70 percent standard at the beginning of the
decade actually improved their standing by 2000 (Chicago, Cleveland, Detroit,
and Miami).[20]

Overall, the good news is that twenty-two of the fifty central cities improved
their income relative to that of their suburbs in the 1990s (compared to sixteen of fifty in the 1980s). In 2000, nine central cities had higher per capita
incomes than their suburbs (see table 7A-1 in appendix). In this group, the
best-off cities were Charlotte and Seattle, which had per capita incomes
25 percent and 22 percent higher, respectively, than their suburbs. Every
central city that had a higher per capita income than its suburbs lay in a
rapidly growing metropolitan area in the South or the West. Many of them

---

19. Ledebur and Barnes (1992).

20. The six cities that did not improve their standing relative to that of their suburbs were
Buffalo, Hartford, Milwaukee, New York, Philadelphia, and St. Louis. Our results mirror what
Rusk found in the third edition of his book, updated with 2000 census data, where he amends
his rule to read "the point of (almost) no return." In the 1990s, Rusk reports, eleven of twenty-
four cities that were below the 70 percent standard at the beginning of the decade improved
relative to their region. Rusk (2003).

fit Rusk's definition of "elastic cities," which expand their boundaries as their metropolitan area grows, annexing growing suburban areas.[21]

Despite this improvement, the ratio of city to suburban income actually fell in twenty-eight of the fifty metropolitan areas during the 1990s. This was a better performance than in the 1980s, when thirty-four cities fell further behind their suburbs, but it is hardly evidence of a dramatic "comeback."[22] In 2000, nine cities had per capita incomes lower than 70 percent of the per capita income of their suburbs, and one—Hartford—fell below 50 percent. All of these cities are located in the Northeast or Midwest.

Thus the national trend masks the fact that the gap between central cities and suburbs varies significantly by region. As figure 7-1 shows, city/suburban income gaps in the Northeast and Midwest are wide and still growing, whereas smaller gaps in the South and West are narrowing. The city/suburban gap is widest in the Northeast, and it continued to widen in the 1990s. In the Midwest, on the other hand, the gap increased only slightly over the decade. The South and the West started with smaller income gaps between their central cities and suburbs, and cities in these regions experienced increased incomes relative to those of their suburbs in the 1990s.

Of course, per capita income measures cannot capture the significant spatial inequalities that exist within cities. In most central cities, older neighborhoods near downtowns are still losing population.[23] Although the number of neighborhoods with extreme levels of poverty shrank in most cities over the decade, most inner-city neighborhoods still have poverty rates far exceeding those found in their suburbs.[24] Increases in cities' relative incomes could in part reflect a shift of poverty to the suburbs, not an improvement in the standing of lower-income city residents. If the poor end up in poor suburbs that lack good schools and job opportunities, they may be no better off than before.

An increase in a city's per capita income relative to that of its suburbs does not necessarily indicate that *absolute* conditions have improved. Per capita income gaps could narrow in the context of declining conditions metro-wide. One study finds that the most distressed cities in 1980 were actually worse off twenty years later.[25]

Finally, in some cities gentrification may play a role in relative income improvements. Although most cities have not witnessed large increases in

21. Rusk (1993).
22. For discussion of the "comeback cities" thesis, see Grogan and Proscio (2000).
23. Berube and Forman (2003).
24. Jargowsky (2005).
25. Furdell, Wolman, and Hill (2005).

FIGURE 7-1. Central City per Capita Income as a Percentage of Suburban per Capita Income, by Region, Fifty Metropolitan Areas, 1980–2000

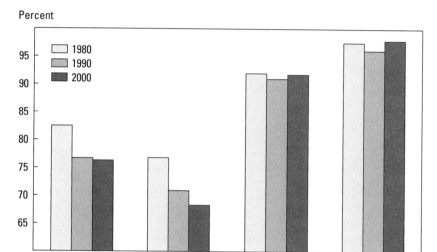

Source: Authors' calculations using 1980, 1990, and 2000 census data.

the number of affluent households, the 1990s saw a resurgence of gentrification in cities such as San Francisco, Seattle, and Boston, where soaring housing prices squeezed low-income families out of downtown neighborhoods, in some cases to less expensive suburbs or substandard accommodations.[26]

Suburban Inequality Increased in the 1980s but Declined Slightly in the 1990s

Defining a poor suburb as any suburb with per capita income lower than 75 percent of that of its metropolitan area, we find that the number of poor suburbs in the fifty metropolitan areas increased dramatically in the 1980s (from 607 to 1,099) and continued to increase in the 1990s, reaching a total of 1,189 by 2000. Of course, as metropolitan areas grow, the number of suburbs grows as well. As a proportion of all suburbs, therefore, poor suburbs

26. Wyly and Hammel (1999). For evidence that rents and homeownership costs went up much faster than inflation from the mid-1990s on, see Joint Center for Housing Studies (2004) and Baker (2002). For specific evidence on affordability problems and displacement in Boston and San Francisco, see Carey Goldberg, "Massachusetts City Plans to Destroy Public Housing," *New York Times*, April 2, 2001, p. A11; and Matt Richtel, "Bay Area Real Estate Prices Too Hot for Some to Touch," *New York Times*, May 29, 2002, p. C1.

increased significantly in the 1980s (from 16.2 to 26.0 percent), but then fell slightly in the 1990s to 24.7 percent (figure 7-2).

As the number of poor suburbs grew in the 1980s and 1990s, an increasing share of the metropolitan population lived in these places.[27] Figure 7-3 shows that in the 1980s the number of people (poor and nonpoor) living in poor U.S. suburbs more than doubled, from 3.5 million to 8.7 million, and the proportion of suburbanites living in poor suburbs soared from 8.4 percent to 17.4 percent. During the 1990s, the number of people living in poor suburbs rose by about 1.5 million (to 10.2 million), and their proportion of the metropolitan population grew modestly to 18.1 percent. Obviously, not all people living in poor suburbs are themselves poor, but they are likely to experience greater disadvantage by living in municipalities with low per capita incomes, fiscal stress, and the various economic and social problems that may result.

David Rusk's "point of no return" hypothesis argued that when a city's per capita income falls below 70 percent of that in its suburbs, it reaches a "point of no return" at which it tends to be shunned by investors and middle-class residents.[28] Our analysis suggests that poor suburbs did not experience this type of cycle of decline. Per capita income in suburbs considered poor in 1980 (those with per capita income below 75 percent of the income in their metropolitan area) grew at about the same rate between 1980 and 2000 as per capita income in their metropolitan area.[29]

The trend in affluent suburbs mirrored that for poor suburbs. The number of affluent suburbs (those with per capita income exceeding 125 percent of that in their metropolitan area) in our fifty metropolitan areas increased continuously throughout our time period (figure 7-4). In the 1980s affluent

27. When calculating percentages of suburban residents, we used the suburban population that lives in "places" as defined by the census. We excluded the suburban population living outside municipalities and census-designated places.

28. Rusk (1993) presents no arguments as to why he used a 70 percent cutoff rather than some other number. We chose to use cut-off points of 75 percent and 125 percent because they provided a slightly better sample of poor and affluent places in all metropolitan areas.

29. This result excludes one outlier: in the Raleigh, North Carolina, area, one suburb (Holly Springs) rated poor in 1980 enjoyed per capita income growth that was 215 percent greater than that of its region. The nationwide average, however, masks the fact that in some parts of the country, poor suburbs performed significantly worse than their metropolitan areas, falling further behind the rest of the region. In eleven metropolitan areas, the growth in per capita income of poor suburbs in 1980 was less than 90 percent of the growth in their metropolitan area, with seven growing at less than 80 percent of the metropolitan area rate—leaving them considerably poorer by comparison. In several cases—such as the San Francisco, Charlotte, and San Antonio areas—these regions experienced booming high-tech economies in the 1990s. Thus one downside of this rapid economic growth could be that poorer parts of the region are left further behind.

FIGURE 7-2. Number and Proportion of Suburbs That Were Poor, Fifty Metropolitan Areas, 1980–2000

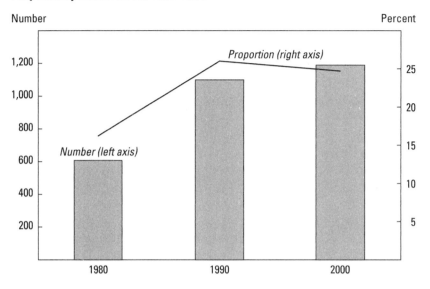

Source: Authors' calculations using 1980, 1990, and 2000 census data.

FIGURE 7-3. Number and Proportion of Suburban Residents in Poor Suburbs, Fifty Metropolitan Areas, 1980–2000

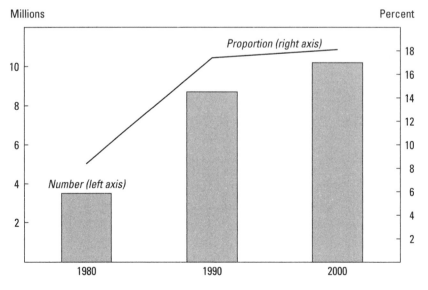

Source: Authors' calculations using 1980, 1990, and 2000 census data.

FIGURE 7-4. Number and Proportion of Suburbs That Were Affluent, Fifty Metropolitan Areas, 1980–2000

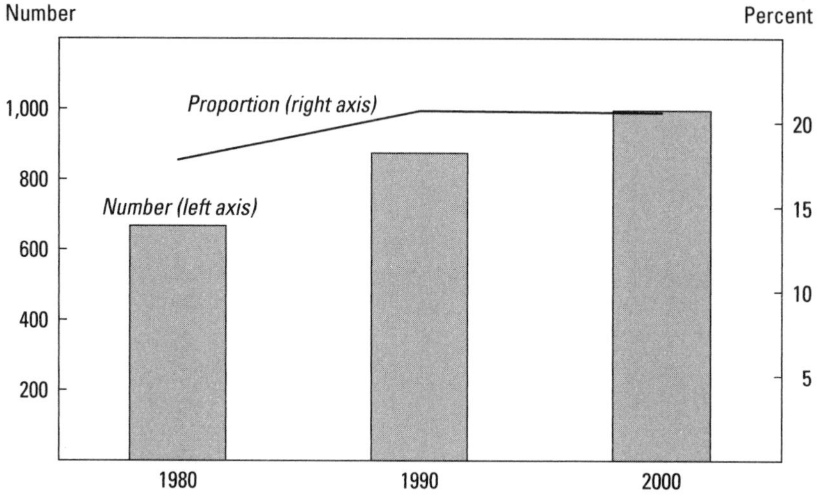

Number   Percent

Source: Authors' calculations using 1980, 1990, and 2000 census data.

suburbs as a proportion of all suburbs increased from 17.8 to 20.7 percent and remained at that level during the 1990s. Note that overall we identified somewhat fewer affluent suburbs in 2000 (995) than poor suburbs (1,189).

However, a somewhat larger share of metropolitan residents live in affluent suburbs than in poor suburbs, and the trend continues upward. Residents of affluent suburbs increased steadily in number, from 7.0 million in 1980 to 9.6 million in 1990, finally reaching 11.9 million in 2000 (figure 7-5). This translated into a consistent rise in the proportion of metropolitan residents living in these suburbs, from 16.7 percent in 1980 to 21.1 percent in 2000. Again, not all the people living in affluent suburbs are themselves affluent, but the quality of their lives is enhanced by living in municipalities with high per capita income, fiscal health, and higher-performing schools. It seems that higher-income individuals and families may increasingly be relocating to suburban jurisdictions where conditions are different from those in poor suburbs.

By definition, the growth of poor and affluent suburbs accompanied a decline in the number of middle-income suburbs. In 1980, 74.9 percent of suburban residents lived in middle-income suburbs; by 1990, it had declined to 63.4 percent; and the proportion further fell to 60.8 percent in 2000 (figure 7-6). The number of people living in middle-income suburbs increased

FIGURE 7-5. **Number and Proportion of Suburban Residents in Affluent Suburbs, Fifty Metropolitan Areas, 1980–2000**

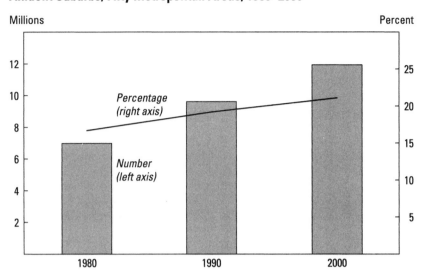

Source: Authors' calculations using 1980, 1990, and 2000 census data.

from 31.2 million in 1980 to 31.8 million in 1990, to 34.3 million in 2000, but their share of the overall suburban population declined due to faster growth occurring in both poor and affluent suburbs.

Gaps between Rich and Poor Suburbs Have Widened

Not only are an increasing number of suburbs inhabiting the extremes of the per capita income distribution, but the extremes themselves also have grown further apart. To measure the gap between poor and affluent suburbs, we computed the ratio of the per capita income of the suburb in the 95th percentile (95 percent of suburbs scoring lower) to the per capita income of the suburb near the bottom at the 5th percentile.

As noted earlier, the suburbs rated poor in 1990 enjoyed income growth roughly equal to that for their metropolitan area during the 1990s. This suggests that the widening gap between the top and the bottom owes not to the poorest suburbs falling further down the income scale but to wealthy suburbs pulling farther away from the others. This is consistent with national analyses finding that the wealthy benefited disproportionately from the economic prosperity of the 1980s and 1990s.

The economic polarization of suburbs varies significantly across the country, with the 95th/5th ratio in 2000 varying from a high of 9.92 in the

FIGURE 7-6. Proportion of Suburban Residents Living in Middle-Income, and Affluent Suburbs, Fifty Metropolitan Areas, 1980, 1990, 2000

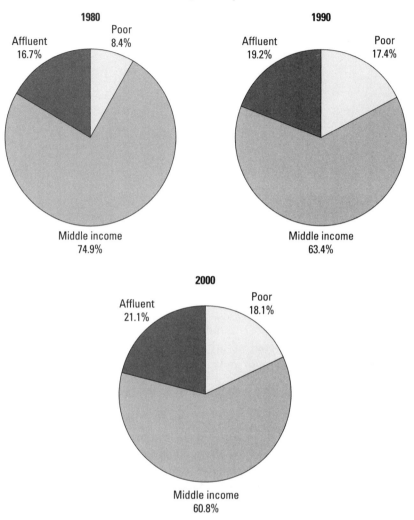

Source: Authors' calculations using 1980, 1990, and 2000 census data.

West Palm Beach-Boca Raton, FL MSA to a low of 1.44 in the Norfolk, VA MSA (see table 7A-2 in the appendix).

Many of the metropolitan areas that have low levels of suburban inequality surround older cities in the Northeast, such as Buffalo, Hartford, and Providence. Conversely, most regions with the widest gaps between rich and poor suburbs are booming areas in the Sun Belt, such as Phoenix, Los Angeles, Miami, and Houston. As further evidence of this, on average, only 13 percent of suburbs in Northeastern metropolitan areas are classified as poor, whereas 29 percent of Southern suburbs are.[30] Notably, though, many of the poor suburban places in the South and West are CDPs, which may not face the same fiscal disadvantages as poor incorporated municipalities in the Northeast and Midwest.

The most fragmented metropolitan areas, those with more municipalities relative to population, tend to be in the Northeast and the Midwest, where the gap between central city and suburban incomes is greatest.[31] The fact that most low-income families are confined to central cities may explain the relatively low degree of suburban inequality in these metropolitan areas.

In less fragmented metropolitan areas in the West and the South, by contrast, lower-income people are not as confined to central cities and live in the suburbs at higher rates. For example, the San Diego and Los Angeles metropolitan areas have central cities that are among the best off relative to their suburbs, but they also exhibit some of the highest levels of suburban inequality. Some of these suburbs never employed the sort of restrictive racial covenants once commonplace in older metropolitan areas of the Northeast and Midwest that long kept minorities confined to central cities. Moreover, in many Sun Belt metropolitan areas, new immigrants are moving directly to the suburbs.[32] Having suburbs that are more open to low-income families, including immigrants, could potentially benefit these families by expanding their residential options, but it may also create greater suburban inequality. In addition, booming Sun Belt economies may help to generate some wealthy suburbs that leave poor suburbs behind, exacerbating inequalities.

Growing Suburban Inequality Resulted from Transitions in Middle-Income Suburbs

One question raised by this analysis is whether the growth in poor and affluent places represents existing suburbs becoming poorer or more affluent or whether these places were added to metropolitan areas by new incorporations or modifications to metropolitan definitions. As table 7-1 shows, the vast majority of the growth in affluent places represents the shift of previously middle-income places into the affluent category, rather than new incorporations or the addition of new counties and places to metropolitan areas.

---

30. The average was 22 percent for the Midwest and 23 percent for the West. These are unweighted averages for the metropolitan areas in each region.

31. Orfield (2002).

32. Singer (2004).

TABLE 7-1. Sources of Increase in Poor and Affluent Suburbs in the Fifty Largest Metropolitan Areas, 1980s and 1990s

	Poor suburbs		Affluent suburbs	
	1980s	1990s	1980s	1990s
Original metropolitan counties	363	49	167	76
Share of total change (percent)	74	55	81	63
Suburbs in new metro area counties	108	124	9	18
Share of total change (percent)	22	138	4	15
New incorporations and CDPs	21	15	31	27
Share of total change (percent)	4	17	15	22
Total change	492	90	207	121

Source: Authors' calculations using 1980, 1990, and 2000 census data.

The latter two categories represented 19.2 percent of the growth in the 1980s and 37.3 percent of growth in the 1990s (with most of that being new incorporations or the designation of affluent areas as CDPs).

The same pattern prevailed for poor suburbs in the 1980s, when most of the growth in poor places (74 percent) represented the relative income decline of previously middle-income places. The pattern for the growth of poor places in the 1990s was different, however. In the 1990s the growth of poor suburbs occurred entirely in counties added to metropolitan areas ("new metropolitan area counties"); indeed, the number of poor places in existing counties actually declined in the 1990s. At the same time, a small number of suburbs that were poor in 1990 moved out of that category by 2000.

Two conclusions from this analysis stand out. First, the 1990s were kinder to poor suburban places, some of which were able to improve their relative economic standing during that decade. Second, new low-income metropolitan suburbs typically are not located in the inner ring near the central city; more often they are found on the outer edges.

This deeper analysis of how poor and affluent suburbs evolved puts a more optimistic spin on trends in the 1990s, a much more promising decade in terms of suburban inequality trends than the 1980s. If the borders of metropolitan areas had remained fixed, we would have witnessed a decline of approximately 4.5 percent in the number of poor suburban places in the 1990s.[33] On the other hand, the growth in affluent places in both the 1980s

33. Taking into account new incorporations and the creation of CDPs, we estimate that about 49 places that were in our sample in 1990 and that were "poor" in 1990 were not poor in 2000. In other words, about 4.5 percent of poor places became nonpoor in the 1990s. This is only an approximation, however, because we have not counted the number of new incorporations or CDPs in our metropolitan areas that did not expand their boundaries (in a very small number of cases, suburbs actually go out of existence).

and 1990s was not due primarily to adding counties but to existing suburbs moving up into the affluent category.[34] This explains the continued growth of suburban inequality in the 1990s.

Even though the recent growth of poor places owes to expanding metropolitan area boundaries, this remains an important phenomenon. First, because our goal is to measure the degree of inequality among places within metropolitan areas, it is appropriate that the analysis acknowledge the continued evolution of these areas. If metropolitan areas grow and therefore include more poor places, they are by definition characterized by greater levels of economic inequality.

Second, although there are differences between poor towns in predominantly rural areas and poor suburbs in growing metropolitan areas, poor suburbs added to metropolitan areas in the 1990s are not sleepy rural towns. On average they experienced 19 percent population growth in the 1990s.[35] As they are integrated into the metropolitan fabric, their costs of living, especially for housing, will rise. With growing populations, they will face fiscal challenges to build new schools and other needed infrastructure. At the same time, they will face increasingly stiff competition from more prosperous parts of the region for jobs, investment, and middle-class residents.

CONCLUSION

This study of economic inequality in major metropolitan areas confirms that, as with the trend in concentrated poverty, the 1990s were much better for cities and suburbs overall than the 1980s.[36] What's more, after thirty years of relative decline, central cities finally stopped falling further behind their suburbs in per capita income. Indeed, some central cities appear to be making a comeback. The national statistics, however, hide the fact that the gaps between cities and suburbs in the Northeast and Midwest are wide and still growing.

In contrast to neighborhood poverty trends, moreover, we do not find a dramatic decline in economic inequality among places in the 1990s. Following the huge increase in inequality among suburban places in the 1980s, the 1990s brought little improvement and in some ways—notably the growth of population in affluent places—continued the trends of the 1980s. Although the

---

34. The data also show that affluent places are more likely than poor places to incorporate or to be designated by the Census Bureau as CDPs. It is not surprising that affluent places often incorporate to protect their advantaged position, whereas poor places rarely do.

35. Suburban population in existing metropolitan counties grew at an average rate of 26.0 percent in the 1990s.

36. Jargowsky (2005); Kingsley and Pettit (2003).

prosperous 1990s benefited many poor places, including many central cities, suburban inequality persisted. In the Northeast and Midwest suburban inequality is lower, but the gap between the central cities and the suburbs is larger. On the other hand, the West and the South have greater suburban inequality, but the gap between the suburbs and the central cities is smaller. It appears that in these regions, immigrants and the poor have greater access to the suburbs, though they may often be confined to lower-income suburbs.

Suburban inequalities vary across time as well as space. Although a rising tide does not necessarily lift all boats, it certainly helps to keep many afloat. The year 2000 represented one of the most prosperous in U.S. history, with one of the lowest unemployment rates (4.0 percent) in a generation. A number of scholars have noted that the decline in concentrated poverty at the neighborhood level must be attributed in large part to a prosperous economy and tight regional job markets that pulled up distressed areas.[37] When the economy falters, however, as it always does at some point in the business cycle, the trends could revert to the 1980s pattern of rapidly rising inequality among places. The 2000–02 recession, the increase in the nation's poverty rate, and the weak recovery since then suggests that we might now be closer to the 1980s pattern than the 1990s pattern. Indeed, poverty rates in both cities and suburbs increased steadily from 2000 to 2003.

The stubborn persistence of inequality among suburbs, even in the booming 1990s, suggests that municipal boundaries act as powerful mechanisms for sorting economic classes across space. Spatial inequalities can set in motion a snowball effect that harms regional competitiveness by fueling the abandonment of older parts of regions, accelerating sprawl and its many costs, and making it more difficult for regions to form the broad coalitions necessary to address these problems.

Rising economic segregation among suburbs has broad policy implications. If suburban sorting were based on free choice in housing markets, there would be little cause for concern. No one wants to tell people where they can live. But there is a great deal of evidence to suggest that suburban governments are already doing this (or at least restricting the choices of the poor).[38] Suburbs use "snob zoning" to exclude poor households by zoning out apartments and requiring minimum-lot sizes for single-family homes. Suburban governments can exclude in other ways, such as by refusing to sign cooperation agreements with the local housing authority or by excluding local public transit.

---

37. William Julius Wilson, "There Goes the Neighborhood," *New York Times,* June 16, 2003, A19.

38. Pendall (2000); Powell (2000).

Suburban exclusion also inhibits labor mobility and economic productivity by physically separating low-income households from areas of job growth in the region. A large body of evidence points to the existence of a geographical mismatch between lower-skill jobs and affordable housing in many metropolitan areas.[39]

Another public policy issue raised by economic segregation in suburbs is unequal access to public goods. In 2000, local governments, including schools systems, spent $996 billion on local public goods and services.[40] The cost and quality of local public goods depend primarily on where one lives. Racial segregation of schools has increased in many areas not because schools discriminate against minorities, but because segregated living patterns sort races into different school districts. Similarly, lower-income households have inferior access to public goods not so much because they are discriminated against by their governments, but because they are stuck in jurisdictions with fewer taxable resources and greater spending demands.

In the end, the problems normally associated with declining central cities are increasingly moving to the suburbs.[41] This chapter shows that middle-class suburbs are being squeezed by the growth in affluent and poor suburbs, and the gap between these suburbs is wider than ever. Of course, central cities still have a disproportionate share of the poor. But they also have valuable assets, including central business districts, tourist destinations, and urban amenities such as parks, sports stadiums, museums, and universities. The sheer size of central cities and their highly visible mayors guarantee them some degree of attention in the policy process.[42]

Poor suburbs arguably have it worse. They usually lack the valued amenities, political visibility, and professional staff of central cities. They also often lack public policies attuned to their special needs.[43] Rather than pitting poor cities against poor suburbs in a zero-sum game, federal and state governments should be poised to offer assistance to fiscally strapped municipalities wherever they exist.

39. Of six literature reviews on spatial mismatch, three find substantial support for the hypothesis, two find moderate support, and one finds the evidence too mixed to reach a conclusion. Ellen and Turner (2003).
40. U.S. Census Bureau (2002).
41. Puentes and Orfield (2002).
42. As the proportion of the population living in central cities has declined, however, their political clout in Washington, D.C., and in state capitals has also declined, along with urban revitalization and anti-poverty programs. Wolman and others (2004).
43. Puentes and Orfield (2002).

T A B L E   7 A - 1 .   Central City/Suburban Per Capita Income Gap in Fifty Metropolitan Areas, 1980, 1990, 2000[a]

Metro area	2000 Index	2000 Rank	1990 Index	1990 Rank	1980 Index	1980 Rank
Hartford	49.2	1	53.7	3	60.6	1
Detroit	54.6	2	53.6	2	66.9	3
Milwaukee	58.3	3	62.9	4	76.9	11
Cleveland	59.9	4	53.5	1	63.1	2
Philadelphia	61.2	5	65.8	5	73.7	7
New York	65.2	6	67.6	8	72.5	5
Rochester	67.4	7	71.1	11	78.5	12
St. Louis	67.9	8	68.7	9	72.7	6
Buffalo	68.6	9	68.9	10	78.7	13
Providence	70.0	10	74.8	12	87.4	24
Chicago	73.1	11	67.4	7	71.2	4
Memphis	75.4	12	77.9	16	98.0	40
Boston	76.7	13	77.7	15	76.4	10
Miami	79.0	14	67.3	6	74.5	8
Louisville	79.3	15	80.0	18	83.2	16
West Palm Beach	79.3	16	77.4	14	79.3	14
Sacramento	80.2	17	87.0	26	92.9	31
Columbus, OH	81.1	18	83.9	22	83.2	17
Grand Rapids	81.7	19	79.2	17	86.2	21
Jacksonville	82.6	20	89.5	30	88.4	27
San Antonio	82.7	21	75.7	13	75.4	9
Richmond	83.0	22	85.2	23	86.3	22
Norfolk	83.3	23	83.6	21	87.7	25
Cincinnati	83.5	24	81.5	19	89.0	28
Minneapolis	84.8	25	86.2	24	90.4	30
Phoenix	85.0	26	89.6	31	95.6	35
Kansas City	85.8	27	88.7	28	87.8	26
Dallas	87.2	28	98.5	41	102.3	45
New Orleans	87.5	29	90.3	33	85.9	19
Indianapolis	87.7	30	91.6	35	94.6	34
Pittsburgh	88.4	31	87.5	27	86.7	23
Denver	89.4	32	92.1	37	94.5	33
San Francisco	90.1	33	82.1	20	83.3	18
Houston	91.8	34	89.9	32	96.1	37
Nashville	93.5	35	108.9	47	101.4	43
Washington, DC	93.7	36	86.4	25	86.1	20
Portland	96.0	37	94.5	38	95.9	36
Austin	97.0	38	96.2	39	97.7	38
Oklahoma City	97.4	39	103.7	45	107.8	46
Los Angeles	99.9	40	100.4	42	102.1	44
Orlando	99.9	41	92.0	36	93.8	32
Tampa	100.9	42	91.3	34	89.4	29
Raleigh	102.2	43	106.4	46	109.2	48
Atlanta	103.3	44	89.1	29	80.4	15
San Diego	105.4	45	102.0	43	101.3	42
Salt Lake City	105.7	46	114.5	49	110.7	49
Las Vegas	105.9	47	96.3	40	97.7	39
Greensboro	109.2	48	109.2	48	108.8	47
Seattle	121.8	49	102.9	44	99.7	41
Charlotte	124.8	50	124.6	50	115.0	50

Source: Authors' calculations using 1980, 1990, and 2000 census data.

a. Index is central city per capita income divided by suburban per capita income for metropolitan area noted. Metropolitan area names are abbreviated.

T A B L E   7 A - 2 .   Per Capita Income Ratio of 95th/5th Percentile Suburbs in Fifty Metropolitan Areas, 2000

Rank	Metro area	Index
1	West Palm Beach–Boca Raton, FL MSA	9.9
2	Phoenix-Mesa, AZ MSA	6.7
3	Los Angeles–Long Beach, CA PMSA	6.3
4	Miami, FL PMSA	6.0
5	Houston, TX PMSA	4.9
6	San Francisco, CA PMSA	4.7
7	Cleveland-Lorain-Elyria, OH PMSA	4.5
8	Denver, CO PMSA	4.5
9	New York, NY PMSA	4.4
10	San Diego, CA MSA	4.4
11	San Antonio, TX MSA	4.1
12	Austin, TX MSA	4.1
13	Tampa–St. Petersburg–Clearwater, FL MSA	4.0
14	St. Louis, MO-IL MSA	3.8
15	Chicago, IL PMSA	3.8
16	Detroit, MI PMSA	3.8
17	Indianapolis, IN MSA	3.8
18	Nashville, TN MSA	3.7
19	Orlando, FL MSA	3.6
20	Las Vegas, NV-AZ MSA	3.6
21	Washington, DC-MD-VA-WV PMSA	3.6
22	Memphis, TN-AR-MS MSA	3.5
23	Dallas, TX PMSA	3.5
24	Louisville, KY-IN MSA	3.4
25	Atlanta, GA MSA	3.3
26	Kansas City, MO-KS MSA	3.2
27	Minneapolis–St. Paul, MN-WI MSA	3.0
28	Columbus, OH MSA	2.9
29	Pittsburgh, PA MSA	2.9
30	Seattle-Bellevue-Everett, WA PMSA	2.9
31	Oklahoma City, OK MSA	2.9
32	Cincinnati, OH-KY-IN PMSA	2.9
33	Sacramento, CA PMSA	2.8
34	Jacksonville, FL MSA	2.8
35	Philadelphia, PA-NJ PMSA	2.7
36	Charlotte-Gastonia–Rock Hill, NC-SC MSA	2.7
37	Richmond, VA MSA	2.7
38	Salt Lake City–Ogden, UT MSA	2.6
39	Milwaukee-Waukesha, WI PMSA	2.6
40	New Orleans, LA MSA	2.5
41	Boston, MA-NH PMSA	2.5
42	Portland-Vancouver, OR-WA PMSA	2.4
43	Grand Rapids, MI	2.4
44	Raleigh-Durham–Chapel Hill, NC MSA	2.3
45	Providence–Fall River–Warwick, RI-MA MSA	2.3
46	Greensboro–Winston-Salem–High Point, NC MSA	2.1
47	Hartford, CT MSA	2.0
48	Rochester, NY MSA	1.9
49	Buffalo–Niagara Falls, NY MSA	1.8
50	Norfolk–Virginia Beach–Newport News, VA-NC MSA	1.4

Source: Authors' calculations using 1980, 1990, and 2000 census data.

REFERENCES

Baker, Dean. 2002. "The Run Up in Home Prices: Is It Real or Is It Another Bubble?" Washington: Center for Economic and Policy Research.

Berube, Alan, and Benjamin Forman. 2003. "Patchwork Cities: Patterns of Urban Population Growth in the 1990s." In *Redefining Urban & Suburban America: Evidence from Census 2000*, vol. 1, edited by Bruce Katz and Robert E. Lang. Brookings.

Berube, Alan, and William H. Frey. 2005. "A Decade of Mixed Blessings: Urban and Suburban Poverty in Census 2000." In *Redefining Urban and Suburban America: Evidence from Census 2000*, vol. 2, edited by Alan Berube, Bruce Katz, and Robert E. Lang. Brookings.

Cashin, Sheryll. 2004. *The Failures of Integration: How Race and Class Are Undermining the American Dream*. New York: Public Affairs.

Citro, Constance F., and Robert T. Michael, eds. 1995. *Measuring Poverty: A New Approach*. Washington: National Academy Press.

Dreier, Peter, John Mollenkopf, and Todd Swanstrom. 2005. *Place Matters: Metropolitics for the Twenty-first Century*, rev. ed. University Press of Kansas.

Ellen, Ingrid Gould, and Margery Austin Turner. 2003. "Do Neighborhoods Matter and Why?" In *Choosing a Better Life: Evaluating the Moving to Opportunity Social Experiment*, edited by John Goering and Judith D. Feins. Washington: Urban Institute Press.

Furdell, Kimberly, Harold Wolman, and Edward W. Hill. 2005. "Did Central Cities Come Back? Which Ones, How Far, and Why?" *Journal of Urban Affairs* 27 (3): 283–305.

Grogan, Paul, and Tony Proscio. 2000. *Comeback Cities*. Boulder, Colo.: Westview Press.

Jargowsky, Paul. 2005. "Stunning Progress, Hidden Problems: The Dramatic Decline of Concentrated Poverty in the 1990s." In *Redefining Urban and Suburban America: Evidence from Census 2000*, vol. 2, edited by Alan Berube, Bruce Katz, and Robert E. Lang. Brookings.

Joint Center for Housing Studies. 2004. *The State of the Nation's Housing 2004*. Harvard University.

Kingsley, G. Thomas, and Kathryn L. S. Pettit. 2003. "Concentrated Poverty: A Change in Course." Washington: Urban Institute.

Ladd, Helen F., and John Yinger. 1989. *America's Ailing Cities: Fiscal Health and the Design of Urban Policy*. Johns Hopkins University Press.

Ledebur, Larry C., and William R. Barnes. 1992. "City Distress, Metropolitan Disparities, and Metropolitan Growth." Washington: National League of Cities.

Massey, Douglas S., and Mary J. Fischer. 2003. "The Geography of Inequality in the United States, 1950–2000." In *Brookings-Wharton Papers on Urban Affairs 2003*, edited by William G. Gale and Janet Rothenberg Pack. Brookings.

Mishel, Lawrence, Jared Bernstein, and Heather Boushey. 2003. *The State of Working America 2002/2003*. Cornell University Press.

National Low Income Housing Coalition. 2003. *Out of Reach: America's Housing Wage Climbs*. Washington.

Orfield, Myron. 2002. *American Metropolitics*. Brookings.

Pack, Janet Rothenberg. 1998. "Poverty and Urban Public Expenditures." *Urban Studies* 35 (11): 1995–2019.

Pendall, Rolf. 2000. "Local Land Use Regulation and the Chain of Exclusion." *Journal of the American Planning Association* 66 (2): 125–42.

Powell, John. 2000. "Addressing Regional Dilemmas for Minority Communities." In *Reflections on Regionalism,* edited by Bruce Katz. Brookings.

Proctor, Bernadette D., and Joseph Dalaker. 2003. *Poverty in the United States: 2002.* Washington: U.S. Census Bureau.

Puentes, Robert, and Myron Orfield. 2002. "Valuing America's First Suburbs: A Policy Agenda for Older Suburbs in the Midwest." Brookings.

Reich, Robert B. 1992. *The Work of Nations.* New York: Random House.

Rusk, David. 1993. *Cities without Suburbs.* Johns Hopkins University Press.

———. 2003. *Cities without Suburbs: A Census 2000 Update.* Baltimore: Woodrow Wilson Center Press.

Singer, Audrey. 2004. "The Rise of New Immigrant Gateways." In *Redefining Urban and Suburban America: Evidence from Census 2000,* vol. 2, edited by Alan Berube, Bruce Katz, and Robert E. Lang. Brookings.

U.S. Census Bureau. 2001. *Census 2000 Summary File 1 Technical Documentation.*

———. 2002. *Statistical Abstract of the United States 2002.*

Wolman, Hal, and others. 2004. "The Calculus of Coalitions: Cities and States and the Metropolitan Agenda." Brookings.

Wyly, Elvin K., and Daniel J. Hammel. 1999. "Islands of Decay in Seas of Renewal: Housing Policy and the Resurgence of Gentrification." *Housing Policy Debate* 10 (4): 711–71.

8

Vacating the City: An Analysis of New Home Construction and Household Growth

THOMAS BIER AND CHARLIE POST

The 1990s were an unusual decade in the recent history of U.S. cities. As the country experienced the greatest economic expansion in its history, a number of major central cities, particularly in the Midwest and Northeast, had their smallest population loss since the 1960s. A few, including Chicago and Minneapolis, actually gained residents.[1] The price of housing on the East and West coasts skyrocketed, whereas in the Midwest it elevated moderately. And concentrated urban poverty lessened in many big cities but grew in suburbs.[2]

The high price of housing on the coasts, population growth in the large metropolitan areas of the South, Southwest, and West, and the issue of "affordability" for low- and moderate-income households across the country fueled the view that housing production was insufficient and that the shortfall was contributing to rising prices and a limited choice of housing.

Indeed, underlying all of the housing-related changes and issues of the 1990s were the factors of supply and demand. The nation grew by 13.5 million households, whereas 13.2 million building permits were filled. Nationally, housing supply was just about in balance with population growth. But substantial variation existed across the country. Although people flocked to Phoenix and the housing industry there boomed, few went to Syracuse and

The authors thank Winifred Weizer and Rick Seifritz, our graduate assistants, who were invaluable aides during the course of this project, and, at the Brookings Institution, Amy Liu, Kurt Sommer, Mark Muro, and particularly Rob Puentes, for their suggestions and guidance.

1. Katz and Lang (2003).
2. Jargowsky (2005).

the builders there felt it. The question of how well supply and demand are balanced can be answered only at the local level.

Our analysis is based on the proposition that the relationship between housing construction and household growth is a fundamental and potent factor in the dynamics of urban change. Cities whose metropolitan areas consistently produce more housing than growth (and some do) face continuing, inescapable population loss and real estate abandonment. Cities whose areas consistently produce less housing than growth face a "tight" housing market and escalating prices. Sound policy will recognize the difference.

This chapter examines the extent to which new housing construction kept pace with household growth in seventy-four large metropolitan areas between 1980 and 2000 (with particular focus on the 1990s). The chapter assesses the impact of supply and demand on these areas and considers consequent policy issues.

BACKGROUND

Housing analysts have studied the relationship between new housing and growth for some time, particularly in the years immediately following World War II.[3] The housing boom that followed the war, the initial development of suburbs, the concern over slums, and the spread of urban deterioration prompted efforts to research and illuminate the dynamics of housing markets and neighborhood change.

The basic model emerging from that work holds that in a typical metropolitan area, the amount of new housing built in a year exceeds the increase in the number of households living in the area. This results in a housing surplus, with most new housing located at the outer edges of the metropolitan area. The purchase (or rental) of new construction by people moving up the property ladder enables households with lower income to move in their wake—which in turn enables others to move, and so on down the income ladder. After all moves have occurred, and because the number of new units exceeds household growth for the entire area, some housing is left vacant. The surplus is evident at the bottom of the market where the least preferred places are abandoned—most likely in old central city neighborhoods. In the process, some existing housing "filters down" in value relative to most other properties, the likely end point of which is eventual abandonment. This model of metropolitan housing dynamics is most evident in Midwestern and Northeastern metropolitan areas.[4]

3. See, for example, Ratcliff (1949); Lowry (1960); and Grigsby (1963).
4. For examples of recent movement patterns, see Bier (2001).

The driving force in the process emanates from the surplus; without it, many moves would not occur and "new" housing opportunities for lower-income households would not open up. As one analyst puts it, "one of our main purposes in studying the dynamics of the housing market is to see to what extent and by what means the market might be manipulated to produce a surplus of homes."[5] This was the explicit policy mechanism born in the Great Depression for improving conditions for the low-income residents of cities: enable them to move from bad to better housing in the private market, which required people with higher incomes to move before them, led by buyers and renters of new construction.

The resulting surplus and depreciation were considered beneficial. The worst housing was being eliminated and society was better off. The remaining challenge was "residential renewal" of fully depreciated and abandoned locations. It was assumed that renewal, in combination with a continuous surplus, would eradicate slums and breathe new life into cities. But renewal did not happen at a scale consistent with the extent of decline and abandonment.

The constant movement of population through an ever-expanding metropolitan supply of housing creates continuous erosion. However, for some cities in recent years immigration has provided a degree of salvation. Chicago, for example, gained 207,792 Hispanic residents in the 1990s, whereas the city's overall population grew by 112,290.[6] Immigrants thus occupied housing that otherwise would have been empty. If Buffalo or Detroit had had the same rate of immigration as Chicago in the 1990s, they too might have had population growth. The effect of housing "oversupply" is starkly evident in many Midwest cities because of the lack of immigrants moving in to occupy housing being vacated by out-movers. The domino-like process of decline has progressed to where it now affects older suburbs in the Midwest and Northeast that have low-value housing stock.

METHODOLOGY

As defined here, the measure of surplus (or shortage) is the difference between change in the number of households living in an area and change in the size of the area's housing stock. This chapter uses U.S. Census Bureau data on building permits (Current Construction Reports Series C-40) as the measure of change in stock. For several reasons, those data provide an approximation of stock change rather than the true change. Change in an area's housing supply is the net result of the number of new units constructed, the number demolished, and the number converted in use to or from housing.

5. Grigsby (1963).
6. Berube (2003).

This chapter does not take into account demolitions, conversions, or units lost to aging, which in some places can be significant over the course of a decade.[7] Manufactured housing is not included in the analysis. Further, not all building permits necessarily result in newly constructed housing units, although the vast majority do, and the number of permits may not have been accurately reported. On the "demand" side, the decennial census is known to undercount population in major cities.[8] These various factors together produce an unknown amount of distortion in the analysis.

A further assumption in the analysis may introduce additional error. For each metropolitan area, it was assumed that the entire supply of suburban housing was occupied (except for normal vacancy) and that all surpluses (if any) would be located in the central city. In other words, the "worst" housing and least desirable locations in the area were assumed to exist only in the central city and not in suburbs. That assumption probably holds true for all practical purposes in most areas—where it does not, some additional error results. For example, a Cleveland suburb, East Cleveland, has approximately 3,500 abandoned units, 13 percent of Cleveland's 27,000.[9] East St. Louis, Illinois, has 4,000 abandoned units, 9 percent of St. Louis's 42,500.

The analysis also can be distorted by having two or more major or comparable cities in the same metropolitan area. If there is a surplus, where is it located? For each metropolitan area this analysis considered all "central cities" as defined by the U.S. Census Bureau. We retained the central city with the largest number of households in 2000, plus any other central city having at least half as many households as the largest city. In eleven cases, cities were in effect combined to function as the "central city" (for example, Tampa-St. Petersburg, Florida, and Raleigh-Durham, North Carolina); in others, one city was designated as the "central city" because of the likelihood it would contain the bulk of surplus housing (for example, Norfolk rather than Virginia Beach, Virginia).

Further distortion can result from the close proximity of two metropolitan areas. For this reason, the analysis employs primary metropolitan statistical areas (PMSAs) rather than consolidated metropolitan statistical areas (CMSAs). For example, Cleveland and Akron are just forty miles apart, in the same metropolitan housing market, the Cleveland-Akron-Lorain, OH CMSA. This analysis treats them as two separate PMSAs: the Akron and the Cleveland-

7. One important reason these are excluded is because data on units removed from the housing stock are generally not reliable. As the National Association of Home Builders points out, "a direct source of data for removals is not available." Mitchum (2003).

8. Edmonston (1999).

9. Units abandoned during the decade were estimated to equal the change in the number of units between 1990 and 2000 plus the number vacant in 2000 that exceeded an assumed normal vacancy rate of 3 percent.

Lorain-Elyria PMSA. For metropolitan areas not part of CMSAs, the analysis uses metropolitan statistical area (MSA) data.

Although the initial intent of this study was to analyze the 100 largest metropolitan areas, for various reasons, twenty-six metropolitan areas were eliminated. All single-county metropolitan areas were excluded, because some, such as Los Angeles County and Miami-Dade County, were embedded in larger metropolitan areas.[10] They (and New York) were dropped because of their complexity (one could not reasonably assume where household loss, if any, would be located). Areas without a major city were excluded (for example, Nassau-Suffolk, New York, and Bergen-Passaic, NJ), as were some that had missing data. The final sample of seventy-four metropolitan areas (MSAs and PMSAs) ranged in size from two to eighteen counties.

Some counties were dropped from the analysis because of obviously incomplete numbers of building permits, but the rest of their metropolitan areas were retained. Although those areas consequently do not correspond to the Office of Management and Budget (OMB) official metropolitan definitions, the excluded counties were small and had little effect on the analysis.[11] Mobile, Alabama, had missing data for the 1980s and was excluded from analysis of that decade but was included in analysis of the 1990s.

The first step in the analysis was to compute for each metropolitan area the ratio of the total number of building permits (units) recorded in a decade to the total number of new households living in the area and to compute the percentage difference between permits and household change. A ratio greater than 1.0 indicated a housing surplus—the number of units built exceeded household growth. The higher the ratio, the greater the surplus.

If the assumption that the central city would be the location of most of the surplus was accurate, then cities within metropolitan areas with ratios greater than 1.0 should have lost households and had an increase in housing vacancies. A ratio less than 1.0 indicated a tight housing market in which more households than new units were added to the area. In such a situation, the city vacancy rate was assumed to have declined and the number of households to have increased.

10. Metropolitan areas omitted from the analysis include Albuquerque, New Mexico; Bakersfield, California; Bergen-Passaic, New Jersey; Birmingham, Alabama; Colorado Springs, Colorado; El Paso, Texas; Fort Lauderdale, Florida; Fort Worth-Arlington, Texas; Honolulu, Hawaii; Jersey City, New Jersey; Los Angeles-Long Beach, California; McAllen-Edinburg-Mission, Texas; Miami, Florida; Nassau-Suffolk, New York; New Haven-Meriden, Connecticut; New York, New York; Orange County, California; San Diego, California; San José, California; Stockton-Lodi, California; Tacoma, Washington; Tucson, Arizona; Ventura, California; and West Palm Beach-Boca Raton, Florida.

11. One or more counties were dropped from the analysis of seven metropolitan areas: Atlanta, Cincinnati, Dallas, Houston, Kansas City (Missouri), St. Louis, and Washington, D.C.

FINDINGS

In comparing housing construction to household growth, this analysis reveals that the fate of cities relates very closely to these supply and demand dynamics. In particular, a surplus of units in a number of older metropolitan areas fueled central city abandonment, while households have grown in cities situated in metropolitan areas without such dramatic imbalances.

Building Permits Exceeded New Households from 1980 to 2000

In the seventy-four metropolitan areas analyzed, the total number of building permits issued outpaced the number of new households by more than 2 million, or 19 percent. The cumulative ratio of permits to household change in all metropolitan areas surveyed was 1.2. However, there were wide variations between the two decades. During the 1980s, building permit issuance outpaced household growth by 29 percent. During the 1990s, the difference was just 9 percent. Clearly, the pace of housing construction is not always geared to the magnitude of household change (table 8-1).

The dramatic difference between the 1980s and the 1990s probably resulted from the Tax Reform Act of 1986, which reduced financial incentives for investing in multi-family housing. Prior to the act, investments in multi-family real estate could be sheltered from income tax. Indeed, multi-family permits in the metropolitan areas in this study declined from 42 percent of all permits in the 1980s to 24 percent in the 1990s, suggesting that the pre-1986 tax code may have stimulated the issuance of more multi-family permits than the market truly demanded.

Assuming that that was the case, this chapter focuses primarily on the 1990s, when the difference between households and permits, although still striking, was not as severe. During the 1990s, the increase in building permits outpaced the increase in households by just over half a million.

In addition to the variation between decades, there were major differences in the ratio of building permits to household growth from region to region. From 1980 to 2000, the highest ratios existed in the Midwestern metropolitan areas, which showed a 35 percent difference between permits and household growth. During the 1980s, the Midwestern disparity peaked at almost 50 percent. Although that figure declined by about half in the 1990s, Midwestern and Northeastern rates continued to far outpace the national average. By contrast, although building permits exceeded household growth in the West by 16 percent during the 1980s, the situation was actually reversed in the next decade. During the 1990s, household growth

T A B L E   8 - 1 .   Building Permits and Household Change, by Region, Seventy-Four Metropolitan Areas

Period and region	Metro areas	Building permits	Household change	Ratio	Difference, permits minus households (percent)
1980s					
Midwest	19	1,384,214	928,041	1.49	49.2
Northeast	15	989,195	722,891	1.37	36.8
South	28	3,304,612	2,584,399	1.28	27.9
West	12	1,745,069	1,500,953	1.16	16.3
United States	74	7,423,090	5,736,284	1.29	29.4
1990s					
Midwest	19	1,659,743	1,335,038	1.24	24.3
Northeast	15	721,253	596,890	1.21	20.8
South	28	2,840,301	2,685,984	1.06	5.8
West	12	1,589,173	1,624,712	0.98	−2.2
United States	74	6,810,470	6,242,624	1.09	9.1
Total					
Midwest	19	3,043,957	2,263,079	1.35	34.5
Northeast	15	1,710,448	1,319,781	1.30	29.6
South	28	6,144,913	5,270,383	1.17	16.6
West	12	3,334,242	3,125,665	1.07	6.7
United States	74	14,233,560	11,978,908	1.19	18.8

Source: Authors' analysis of data from decennial censuses and Census Bureau Current Construction Reports.

in Western metropolitan areas actually surpassed the number of permits by 2 percent.[12]

Of course, these federally defined regions are quite large, and there are stark differences between metropolitan areas in the same region: Buffalo versus Boston in the Northeast and Baltimore versus San Antonio in the South. But in the aggregate, the regional statistics tell an important story.

Homebuilders construct what they think they can sell; they do not consult demographers and then align their production volume with projected household growth. They build even when household growth is nearly zero (which was the case, for example, in the Youngstown, Ohio, metropolitan area in the 1980s). The Buffalo metropolitan area presents a clear example of the effect of new construction exceeding household growth by a wide margin. In the 1990s, housing construction in the Buffalo metropolitan area exceeded household growth by nearly 4 to 1, leading inevitably to a housing surplus. Somewhere in the Buffalo area, housing that was occupied in 1990 became vacant by 2000. During that period, not surprisingly, the city of Buffalo's vacancy rate increased 5.5 percentage points to 15.7 percent, and

12. Myers and Park (2002).

the city lost 10 percent of its households. At the same time, the number of households living in the suburbs grew by 6.3 percent.

At the other end of the spectrum, construction and growth in the Denver metropolitan area during the 1990s were out of balance, with *less* new housing than household growth. In that "shortage" situation, the city of Denver's vacancy rate declined by 7.1 percentage points, whereas its households grew by 13.4 percent (figure 8-1).

Two factors may explain most of the variation in the disparity between building permits and household growth among areas: land costs and strength of the local economy. Housing surpluses occurred where the local economy was weak and land costs low (Buffalo in the 1990s represented this extreme), whereas shortages occurred where the economy was strong and land prices high (for example, San Francisco). Because of the "roughness" of the data used in this analysis, the extremes may be more discernable than those places where supply and demand were fairly close to being in balance.

Building Permit Surpluses Contributed to Increased Central City Abandonment

Table 8-2 demonstrates one important effect of new housing exceeding household growth. Although the number of households in Southern and Western central cities grew and vacancy rates dropped, cities in the Midwest and Northeast either lost households or gained only slightly, and vacancy rates generally stalled.

Of course, all metropolitan areas throughout the country must accommodate some degree of new housing (there must be some replacement of fully depreciated structures). Areas with little or no household growth still have substantial movement and demand for new housing. How much new housing can be located in a central city? If a city, such as Phoenix, has large amounts of undeveloped land, much can be built. But if all a city's land has been developed (in other words, the city is built out, with no remaining virgin land) then it must reuse sites, making development more difficult.

With more new housing than growth, abandonment is unavoidable—and the more that construction exceeds growth, the greater the abandonment. In most cases, particularly in the Northeast and Midwest, the central city bears the brunt of abandonment, although suburbs are generally fully occupied through movement up.

Table 8A-1 (in the appendix) displays the seventy-four metropolitan areas ranked on their 1990s ratio of building permits to household growth. Again, Midwestern and Northeastern metropolitan areas such as Buffalo and Pittsburgh are at the top of the list. In Pittsburgh, almost three units of

FIGURE 8-1. Household Change and Housing Unit Permits, Selected Metropolitan Areas, 1990–2000[a]

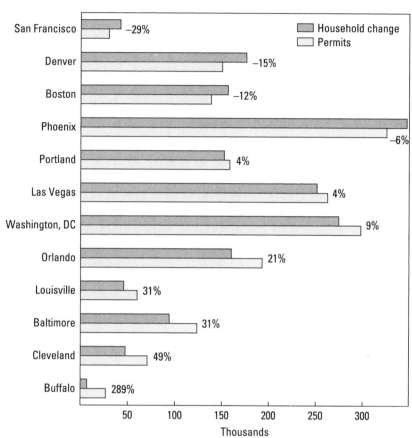

Source: Authors' analysis using data from decennial censuses and Census Bureau Current Construction Reports.

a. Percentages indicate difference between permits and household change.

TABLE 8-2. Central City Household and Vacancy Rate Change, by Region, Seventy-Four Metropolitan Areas, 1990–2000

Region	Number of metro areas	Ratio of permits to household change	Central city household change (percent)	Change in vacancy rate (percentage points)
Midwest	19	1.24	1.8	−0.2
Northeast	15	1.21	−2.3	0.6
South	28	1.06	12.2	−3.4
West	12	0.98	16.3	−2.5
United States	74	1.09	7.6	−1.8

Source: Authors' analysis of data from decennial censuses and Census Bureau Current Construction Reports.

new housing were built for each net addition to the area's households: 55,936 housing permits were recorded, although the area grew by only 19,252 households. Partly as a consequence, the city of Pittsburgh lost 6.3 percent of its households, and its vacancy rate increased 2.2 percentage points.

This trend of central city abandonment follows a common theme. All but two of the cities (Akron, Ohio, and Kansas City, Missouri) in metropolitan areas where permits exceeded household growth by the highest percentages (above 25 percent) lost households, whereas most cities in areas below that threshold gained households or lost slightly. With the minor exception of Newark, New Jersey, all cities in metropolitan areas where household growth outnumbered permits gained households. Changes in city vacancy rates between 1990 and 2000 followed a similar pattern.

If a metropolitan area grows in households over the course of a decade, and if *all* of the area's new housing is located in the central city, then those additional households would presumably have to live in the city. As the city's share of new construction decreases, the city's potential household gain diminishes (assuming all suburban housing is occupied). If a city's share is large enough, it can reduce or even eliminate the negative effect of a high ratio of permits-to-household growth. All but one of the twenty-seven cities that lost households in the 1990s (Toledo, Ohio, being the exception) had a small share (less than 10 percent) of their area's building permits, and twenty cities had less than 5 percent. Kansas City, Missouri, had a high ratio but gained households (4 percent), in part because the city captured 15 percent of its area's building permits in the 1990s.

Most cities, however, probably cannot escape the second negative effect of a high permit-to-household-change ratio: abandonment. A high ratio means that housing must become vacant somewhere in the area. This analysis assumes that the central city contains the housing that is at the bottom of the market throughout the area, and surplus housing resulting from new construction exceeding household growth leads to vacancies and abandonment in that segment of the market—irrespective of the city's share of the area's new housing.

The negative effects of "oversupply" in a metropolitan area can also involve suburbs—particularly older, inner-ring suburbs. A recent study of suburban population change in the thirty-five largest metropolitan areas between 1990 and 2000 found that although 63 percent of all suburbs grew, 37 percent actually lost population or stayed the same.[13] The areas with the

13. Lucy and Phillips (2003).

largest percentage of suburbs that declined were Buffalo, Philadelphia, Pittsburgh, Cincinnati, Cleveland, Detroit, and St. Louis. Six of those areas had permit-to-household-change ratios of 1.46 or higher.[14]

In addition to having homes that may not meet contemporary tastes and standards, older or "first" suburbs are also hurt by consumers' desire to buy "up and out." For instance, from 1997 to 1998, about 86 percent of the homeowners who moved in the Cleveland, Columbus, and Cincinnati metropolitan areas bought homes that were 57 to 69 percent more expensive than the homes that they had left. In all three of these regions, most higher-priced homes were lo'cated "farther out."[15] Homes in the first suburbs tend to be occupied by lower-income households, negatively affecting the local tax base.[16] This phenomenon can be exacerbated by a large and continuous metropolitan "oversupply," leading to an excess of housing stock in first suburbs that eventually is abandoned.[17]

Although cities in metropolitan areas with high ratios confront household loss and increasing vacancy overall, growth can occur at the sub-city level. Among twenty-four major cities, six experienced downtown population growth in the 1990s even though the city as a whole lost population.[18] All six of these cities—Baltimore, Cleveland, Detroit, Milwaukee, Norfolk, and Philadelphia—had high permit-to-household-change ratios in the 1990s. Similarly, seventeen of the twenty largest cities experiencing overall population declines during the decade experienced population increases in their central business districts.[19]

Central Cities Gained Households in Metropolitan Areas Where Demand Exceeded Supply

Several hypotheses were tested to explore the relationship between household change, the location of new housing (city or suburbs), and permit-to-household-change ratio:

—Hypothesis 1: *The central city will not lose households if the area ratio is less than 1.0.* For the 1980s, there were no cases in which both the ratio was

---

14. For a detailed discussion of these places, see Puentes and Orfield (2002).

15. Bier (2001).

16. Bier and Howe (1998).

17. This is a particular problem for slow-growing metropolitan areas such as Philadelphia, St. Louis, Detroit, Milwaukee, and Pittsburgh, where population either grew very slowly or not at all in the 1990s, but land continued to be developed on the fringe (Fulton and others 2001).

18. Sohmer and Lang (2003).

19. Berube and Forman (2003).

less than 1.0 and the central city lost households. For the 1990s, there was one case, Newark, New Jersey, which had a ratio of 0.99 and central city household decline of 170—a marginal exception.

—Hypothesis 2: *The higher the ratio, the more likely the central city will lose households, and, conversely, the lower the ratio, the more likely the city will gain households.* A simple correlation test between ratio and percent household change for the 1980s resulted in a very weak correlation (−0.15); the test for the 1990s resulted in a moderately strong correlation (−0.46).

Table 8A-1 (in the appendix) shows the seventy-four metropolitan areas and their central cities ranked by ratio and grouped by household loss quartile. If hypothesis 2 holds, the percentage of cities within each quartile that lost households should decrease from the top of the table (highest ratios) to the bottom (lowest ratios). The top quartile ranges from Buffalo (ratio 3.89) to Louisville (1.31). All but two of the seventeen cities lost households. The second quartile ranges from Rochester (1.30) to Raleigh-Durham (1.08). Seven of these cities, or a little over one-third, lost households. In the third ratio quartile, about one in six cities lost households, and in the bottom quartile, no cities did. In general, then, hypothesis 2 holds: the higher the ratio, the more likely the central city will lose households.

—Hypothesis 3: *The larger a city's share of metropolitan building permits, the lower the city's household loss (if the metropolitan ratio is above 1.0) or the more households it will gain (if the ratio is below 1.0).* Where new housing is located in a metropolitan area affects city household change. Theoretically, if all new housing was suburban and the area ratio was above 1.0, the central city would be unable to gain households (assuming no abnormal surplus existed in the suburbs). At the other extreme, if all new housing was located in the city (and the suburban supply remained fixed), the city would receive all of the area's household growth—but still bear the brunt of the consequent abandonment. Thus, we hypothesize that higher city shares of metropolitan permits will be associated with lower city household loss (where the ratio is above 1.0).

A statistical test provides support for this hypothesis. Fifty-four metropolitan areas had a ratio above or equal to 1.0 for the 1990s, and in this group the correlation between city share of metropolitan permits and city household loss is 0.61. Twenty areas had a ratio less than 1.0 for the 1990s, and for this group the correlation was 0.49. The average city that lost households in the 1990s needed to capture 17 percent of its metropolitan area's permits but received only 4 percent (table 8-3). Cities with higher-than-average

TABLE 8-3. Cities That Lost Households in the 1990s and New Housing Needed to Eliminate the Loss

Metro area	Region	Metro area ratio of permits to household change	Central city permits as percentage of metro area permits		Central city household change (percent)
			Needed to break even	Actual	
Buffalo, NY	NE	3.89	59	8	−10
Youngstown-Warren, OH	MW	2.35	41	3	−10
Syracuse, NY	NE	1.69	38	4	−8
Scranton–Wilkes-Barre, PA	NE	2.53	25	5	−5
Detroit, MI	MW	1.48	24	2	−10
Toledo, OH	MW	1.48	22	12	−5
Pittsburgh, PA	NE	2.91	21	3	−6
St. Louis, MO	MW	1.70	18	2	−11
Dayton, OH	MW	2.21	18	2	−7
Milwaukee, WI	MW	1.39	18	5	−4
Rochester, NY	NE	1.30	18	3	−5
Cleveland, OH	MW	1.49	18	5	−5
Baltimore, MD	S	1.31	17	2	−7
Albany-Schenectady, NY	NE	1.35	16	5	−4
Philadelphia, PA	NE	1.22	13	3	−2
Hartford, CT	NE	1.79	11	1	−13
Cincinnati, OH	MW	1.46	11	4	−4
Springfield, MA	NE	1.26	11	7	−1
Gary, IN	MW	1.49	9	0	−7
Louisville, KY	S	1.31	9	7	−2
Norfolk, VA	S	1.30	7	3	−4
Harrisburg, PA	NE	1.18	5	1	−5
Richmond, VA	S	1.15	5	3	−1
Greenville-Spartanburg, SC	S	1.05	5	4	−1
Allentown, PA	NE	1.06	2	2	−2
Washington, DC	S	1.09	1	1	−1
Average		1.63	17	4	−5

Source: Authors' analysis of data from decennial censuses and Census Bureau Current Construction Reports.

ratios (above 1.63) generally needed a larger share than that, and cities with lower ratios generally needed a smaller share.[20]

DISCUSSION

A recent article asked whether there is an undersupply of housing in the United States. The author noted that for several reasons (mainly the Tax

20. The method for determining the city's share of new housing that would have been needed in the 1990s to produce zero household loss is as follows: the number of households actually lost by the city in the 1990s was added to the number of city building permits; the resultant number, divided by the total area permits (times 100), gives the city's "needed" share. This method assumes the total metropolitan permits to be constant (in other words, the city's increase in permits results in an equal decrease in the suburban portion of the area).

Reform Act of 1986) housing production in the 1990s decreased from that in the 1980s and that "another decade of undersupplied housing could make already unaffordable markets even less accessible." The article focused on major coastal cities such as San Francisco and Boston.[21] But in the 1980s, when production volumes were indeed larger than in the 1990s, sixty-four of the seventy-four cities in this study (87 percent) had increases in vacancy. Analytically speaking, the last thing that Northeastern and Midwestern cities such as Buffalo, St. Louis, Detroit, and Pittsburgh needed was more housing in their suburbs.

The results of this study confirm that housing is undersupplied in some areas, oversupplied in others, and appropriately supplied in still others. Whether housing is undersupplied is too broad a question. A more pertinent question might be "What is the right amount of new housing for a particular metropolitan area?" But is an answer other than "What the market will absorb" feasible? Should homebuilding in the Buffalo area during the 1990s have been 75 percent less than it was in order to have matched the area's household growth? Only *extreme* governmental control—extreme in relation to the nation's practice of free enterprise—could have achieved such a limitation.

At the same time, policies to boost production are taken for granted. The above-cited article reflects that purpose: "Before housing affordability reaches crisis dimensions in many places, it is possible that the market will undergo a major correction. But it is unlikely that market forces alone will solve the undersupply problem. There are, however, several policy initiatives [such as expanding low-income tax credits for multi-family construction] that could immediately facilitate more housing production."[22]

As our research suggests, clearly there is a supply problem in some major markets. However, calls for more production must consider the metropolitan housing market and should be accompanied by attention to the possible negative consequences of increased production. New multi-family housing for low-income households in an area where production exceeds growth will likely result in more abandonment, but that may be judged to be an acceptable consequence, particularly if the construction is located near suburban centers of employment growth.

An issue that has yet to be explicitly addressed in the still-young life of U.S. cities is that of who should be responsible for redevelopment of obsolete, bottom-of-the-market, fully depreciated real estate. Thus far the

---

21. The article points out that housing is not undersupplied "equally throughout the nation. The undersupply problem is most acute along the east and west coasts." Lang (2002).
22. Lang (2002).

answer has been the host jurisdiction—with some assistance from the federal government and possibly some from state government. The total community in which the real estate is located—the metropolitan area—is held harmless (although, as state and federal taxpayers, residents indirectly pay something). Though the primary responsibility lies with the community as a whole—the metropolitan area—it is invariably denied by means of jurisdictional boundaries and perceptions of home rule, which cultivate the attitude that each unit of government is independent and wholly accountable for its condition.

A prominent exception is the Minneapolis-St. Paul metropolitan area, which for more than twenty-five years has practiced tax-base sharing. There, an increment of property tax revenues produced by commercial and industrial development is shared with jurisdictions whose tax revenues are relatively weak, reducing fiscal disparities.[23] The policy represents one of the most direct and responsible ways for a metropolitan area to address problems created by obsolete and seriously depreciated real estate. However, tax sharing is contentious; communities that give up revenues do not necessarily like it. As some of them eventually age to the point where they possess troubled real estate and deteriorated infrastructure, resistance to such policies could fade.

Other less contentious actions can serve the objective of increasing urban redevelopment. The state of Maryland's "smart growth" program has become a featured example due to its emphasis on using state resources and policies to strengthen older communities and reduce urban sprawl. A growing number of states are following suit. In a sense, they all are grappling with how to influence or control private investment in real estate as suburban sprawl, urban decline, and traffic congestion have intensified. These initiatives are emerging within the context of a national attitude that holds that government has no business interfering with the free market and the rights of property owners. But the negative consequences of ever-outward suburban development—and, in many places, inner abandonment—are forcing attitude change. Like tax-base sharing, as the benefits of new ways of influencing the location of investment in real estate become apparent, attitudes will change.

The state that has gone the furthest with comprehensive efforts to manage growth is Oregon, where "growth boundaries" around metropolitan areas are required.[24] Coupled with policies that strongly support urban

---

23. Orfield (1997).

24. Oregon Department of Land Conservation and Development, "Oregon's Statewide Planning Goals and Guidelines. Goal 14: Urbanization," OAR 660–015–0000(14) (2000).

redevelopment and maintenance, a growth boundary generates forces that stimulate urban core investment—which is exactly what a city in an area with a consistently high ratio needs. "Inward forces" (as opposed to outward forces associated with unbridled suburban development) draw to the urban core private investment that otherwise would not exist or be considered. Public funds to address unusual costs associated with redevelopment may still be required, but the amount required would be less than without containment. Containment of outer development may raise the cost of housing and real estate in general, but the alternative can be a steady stream of abandonment that is not matched by redevelopment.[25] Containment costs nothing—it is just policy—but it is as politically challenging as tax-base sharing, if not more so.

The figures reported in this study for the Portland, Oregon, area, with its growth boundary, are striking: the ratio of housing construction to household growth in the 1990s was 1.04; the city's share of building permits in the area was 11.9 percent, its households grew by 19.5 percent, and its vacancy rate hardly changed. Those figures suggest that Portland and its area in the 1990s were in optimal development balance.

As long as Detroit, Philadelphia, St. Louis, Baltimore, Rochester, Cleveland, Pittsburgh, Buffalo, Cincinnati, Milwaukee, Syracuse, and others are faced with consistently large disparities throughout the area between new housing and growth, initiatives to strengthen those cities need to be as potent as the destructive power of the disparity. An Oregon-style approach coupled with tax-base sharing would likely be effective. That solution probably is a remote possibility at best. However, a feasible and significant step in that policy direction would be a smart growth program such as Maryland's. Time will tell if Maryland's program is potent enough to lower the permits-to-growth ratio in the Baltimore area and/or increase substantially the city's share of new housing. If it is, then other states will have evidence to act accordingly.

As discussed, abandonment is an inescapable consequence of new housing exceeding growth, but to the extent that a city can increase its share of the area's new housing, it can reduce its household loss.[26] That can be a sizable challenge if the city is "old" and built-out. Extensive redevelopment usually

---

25. Critics of Oregon's urban growth boundary claim it has caused home prices to be higher than they otherwise would be. If that has been the result, the increase, relative to that in other cities, has not been large enough to confirm that position. Downs, Nelson, and Fischel (2002).

26. Household loss is not necessarily a serious negative effect for cities with high population densities. However, cities typically lose their higher-income residents and do not experience sufficient redevelopment to compensate for the loss.

is the only option, although some existing structures can be upgraded or converted to residential use, substituting for new construction.

Redevelopment, however, typically costs more than "greenfield" suburban development because of expenses associated with creating "new"
construction sites (for example, demolition, site assembly, brownfield
cleanup).[27] Cities with the greatest needs usually lack the resources required
to redevelop at a scale sufficient to offset abandonment and household loss.
St. Louis (ratio of 1.70) had 20,000 units abandoned in the 1990s and lost
18,000 households. Philadelphia (ratio of 1.22) is spending $160 million to
demolish 10,000 structures; Detroit (1.48) has targeted 12,000 structures at
a cost of $120 million.[28] However, although redevelopment may be expen-
sive, what is becoming increasingly clear in these places is that the cost of
doing nothing is even greater.

Cities in areas with a ratio slightly higher than 1.0 probably would be
best served by no change. The ideal ratio might be around 1.05, which
would create some brake on prices and would allow for abandonment of
some of the worst housing. A small amount of annual abandonment and
household loss (depending on the city's share of new supply) should be
manageable.

By contrast, metropolitan areas with a ratio under 1.0 undoubtedly need
more housing (Boston in the 1990s was 0.88). In their cities, little if any
housing is being abandoned and nonresidential buildings may be converted to residential use. Increasing the ratio to 1.0 or slightly more than
1.0 would result in no negative consequences (assuming the city's share of
production is sufficient to prevent household loss). Pressure on housing
costs would be reduced.

CONCLUSION

Low household growth in a metropolitan area does not necessarily result in
correspondingly low housing construction, as recent experience in numerous Midwestern and Northeastern areas makes clear. Although the Buffalo
area had household growth of only 1.5 percent for the entire decade of the
1990s, almost four units of housing were built for each additional household. Builders may give some attention to growth figures, but they do not
equate them and production volume. Again, builders produce what they can
sell—irrespective of actual or projected growth.

27. Koebel (1996); Suchman (1997).
28. Jodi Wilgoren, "Detroit Urban Renewal without the Renewal," *New York Times*,
July 7, 2002, p. A9.

The variation in ratios among areas stems from variation in economic conditions. Economic growth attracts households, and where growth is strong (as it was in the West and South during the 1990s), expansion of the housing supply is more likely to keep pace with growth (accompanied by upward pressure on housing prices). Where economic growth is not strong, neither is household growth, but demand for new housing still exists.

This chapter also points out that imbalance between an area's household growth and expansion of the supply of housing through construction can exert negative effects on the central city. The more that new housing exceeds growth, the greater the impact in terms of household loss and abandonment (and depreciated real estate).

The only recourse available to a city in an area with a high ratio of housing construction to household growth is to increase the size of its share of the area's new housing (which can include upgrading or converting existing stock such that it substitutes, in effect, for new construction). Of course, housing production is not an automatic solution. People who could otherwise live in a suburb have to want the product in the central city, including the specific location and associated local conditions—safety, availability and quality of services, and schools typically influence move decisions. The relationship between housing construction and household growth may seem like an arcane academic consideration, but it is a fundamental and potent factor in the dynamics of urban change.

T A B L E 8 A - 1 . Metropolitan Area and Central City Building Permits, Household Change, and Vacancy Change, Seventy-Four Metropolitan Areas, 1990–2000

		Metropolitan area				Central city					
Rank	Name	Region	Permits	Household change	Ratio	Name	Household change	Percentage change in households	Change in vacancy rate (percentage points)	Permits	Central city permits as a percentage of metro area permits
First quartile											
1	Buffalo–Niagara Falls, NY MSA	NE	26,881	6,916	3.89	Buffalo, NY	–13,716	–10.1	5.5	2,109	7.8
2	Pittsburgh, PA MSA	NE	55,936	19,252	2.91	Pittsburgh, PA	–9,744	–6.3	2.2	1,781	3.2
3	Scranton–Wilkes-Barre Hazleton, PA MSA	NE	13,462	5,331	2.53	Scranton, PA; Wilkes-Barre, PA	–2,808	–5.4	4.3	610	4.5
4	Youngstown-Warren, OH MSA	MW	15,505	6,613	2.34	Youngstown, OH; Warren, OH	–5,886	–10.3	3.6	393	2.5
5	Dayton-Springfield, OH MSA	MW	33,888	15,326	2.21	Dayton, OH	–5,261	–7.2	3.2	716	2.1
6	Hartford, CT MSA	NE	67,227	37,660	1.79	Hartford, CT	–6,478	–12.6	2.9	767	1.1
7	St. Louis, MO-IL MSA	MW	109,944	64,650	1.70	St. Louis, MO	–17,855	–10.8	1.2	1,869	1.7
8	Syracuse, NY MSA	NE	16,222	9,627	1.69	Syracuse, NY	–5,463	–8.4	3.6	627	3.9
9	Cleveland-Lorain-Elyria, OH PMSA	MW	70,718	47,376	1.49	Cleveland, OH	–9,149	–4.6	0.7	3,173	4.5
10	Gary, IN PMSA	MW	30,304	20,375	1.49	Gary, IN	–2,724	–6.6	–0.6	57	0.2
11	Detroit, MI PMSA	MW	170,516	115,268	1.48	Detroit, MI	–37,629	–10.1	1.5	3,490	2.0
12	Toledo, OH MSA	MW	18,914	12,818	1.48	Toledo, OH	–1,958	–1.5	–0.1	2,257	11.9
13	Cincinnati, OH-KY-IN PMSA	MW	91,999	62,881	1.46	Cincinnati, OH	–6,247	–4.0	2.1	3,686	4.0
14	Kansas City, MO-KS MSA	MW	108,751	78,036	1.39	Kansas City, MO	6,374	3.6	–2.9	16,413	15.1
15	Milwaukee-Waukesha, WI PMSA	MW	69,184	49,935	1.39	Milwaukee, WI	–8,352	–3.5	1.5	3,730	5.4
16	Akron, OH PMSA	MW	34,650	25,010	1.39	Akron, OH	193	0.2	0.7	3,855	11.1
17	Albany-Schenectady-Troy, NY MSA	NE	25,704	19,066	1.35	Albany, NY; Schenectady, NY	–2,895	–4.1	2.8	1,315	5.1
18	Baltimore, MD PMSA	S	123,254	93,926	1.31	Baltimore, MD	–18,488	–6.7	5.2	1,997	1.6
19	Louisville, KY-IN PMSA	S	59,805	45,686	1.31	Louisville, KY	–1,651	–1.5	–0.7	3,880	6.5

(continued)

185

TABLE 8A-1. Metropolitan Area and Central City Building Permits, Household Change, and Vacancy Change, Seventy-Four Metropolitan Areas, 1990–2000 (continued)

		Metropolitan area				Central city					
Rank	Name	Region	Permits	Household change	Ratio	Name	Household change	Percentage change in households	Change in vacancy rate (percentage points)	Permits	Central city permits as a percentage of metro area permits
Second quartile											
20	Rochester, NY MSA	NE	31,215	23,984	1.30	Rochester, NY	-4,608	-4.9	3.4	861	2.8
21	Norfolk–Virginia Beach–Newport News, VA-NC MSA	S	86,192	66,523	1.30	Norfolk, VA	-3,268	-3.7	-0.7	2,714	3.1
22	Springfield, MA MSA	NE	16,622	13,147	1.26	Springfield, MA	-639	-1.1	0.8	1,151	6.9
23	Wichita, KS MSA	MW	29,854	23,912	1.25	Wichita, KS	15,838	12.9	-0.2	16,064	53.8
24	Mobile, AL MSA	S	39,409	31,572	1.25	Mobile, AL	3,038	4.0	0.0	5,235	13.3
25	Philadelphia, PA-NJ PMSA	NE	138,274	113,087	1.22	Philadelphia, PA	-13,004	-2.2	0.2	4,585	3.3
26	Omaha, NE-IA MSA	MW	43,199	35,416	1.22	Omaha, NE	22,896	17.1	-1.4	24,782	57.4
27	Indianapolis, IN MSA	MW	121,655	99,841	1.22	Indianapolis, IN	28,161	9.6	1.6	41,209	33.9
28	Sarasota-Bradenton, FL MSA	S	55,433	45,844	1.21	Sarasota, FL; Bradenton, FL	3,113	7.5	-1.6	4,792	8.6
29	Fresno, CA MSA	W	48,063	39,792	1.21	Fresno, CA	18,272	15.0	0.1	21,749	45.3
30	Orlando, FL MSA	S	192,813	159,973	1.21	Orlando, FL	15,180	23.1	-1.9	18,267	9.5
31	Knoxville, TN MSA	S	35,824	30,418	1.18	Knoxville, TN	6,677	9.5	1.3	8,410	23.5
32	Harrisburg-Lebanon-Carlisle, PA MSA	NE	26,518	22,578	1.17	Harrisburg, PA	-959	-4.5	3.0	318	1.2
33	Charleston-North Charleston, SC MSA	S	34,917	30,289	1.15	Charleston, SC; North Charleston, SC	16,322	30.1	-1.2	9,150	26.2
34	Richmond-Petersburg, VA MSA	S	65,094	56,828	1.15	Richmond, VA	-788	-0.9	-1.0	2,173	3.3
35	Columbus, OH MSA	MW	109,618	97,259	1.13	Columbus, OH	44,538	17.3	0.3	44,472	40.6
36	New Orleans, LA MSA	S	36,242	32,815	1.10	New Orleans, LA	16	0.0	-4.1	4,108	11.3

#	Metropolitan area	Region									
37	Washington, DC-MD-VA-WV PMSA	S	297,915	274,435	1.09	Washington, DC	−1,296	−0.5	−0.7	2,510	0.8
38	Raleigh-Durham-Chapel Hill, NC MSA	S	132,315	122,251	1.08	Raleigh-Durham, NC	45,766	32.3	−0.6	48,664	36.8

Third quartile

#	Metropolitan area	Region									
39	Jacksonville, FL MSA	S	88,356	82,058	1.08	Jacksonville, FL	43,115	17.9	−1.8	50,482	57.1
40	Seattle-Bellevue-Everett, WA PMSA	W	165,970	154,260	1.08	Seattle, WA	21,797	9.2	−0.5	24,893	15.0
41	Tampa-St. Petersburg-Clearwater, FL MSA	S	149,584	139,835	1.07	Tampa, FL; St. Petersburg, FL	13,918	6.3	−3.6	20,396	13.6
42	Wilmington-Newark, DE-MD PMSA	S	33,187	31,272	1.06	Wilmington, DE	61	0.2	2.4	853	2.6
43	Allentown-Bethlehem-Easton, PA MSA	NE	22,483	21,317	1.05	Allentown, PA	−743	−1.7	2.3	498	2.2
44	Atlanta, GA MSA	S	410,774	389,530	1.05	Atlanta, GA	12,395	8.0	−4.7	18,398	4.5
45	Greenville-Spartanburg-Anderson, SC MSA	S	60,592	57,962	1.05	Greenville, SC; Spartanburg, SC	−442	−1.1	2.2	2,600	4.3
46	Las Vegas, NV-AZ MSA	W	262,412	251,236	1.04	Las Vegas, NV	77,015	77.2	−1.7	83,427	31.8
47	Chicago, IL PMSA	MW	313,245	300,150	1.04	Chicago, IL	36,754	3.6	−1.6	29,859	9.5
48	Grand Rapids-Muskegon-Holland, MI MSA	MW	64,582	62,136	1.04	Grand Rapids, MI	4,188	6.1	−0.3	4,057	6.3
49	Portland-Vancouver, OR-WA PMSA	W	158,144	152,335	1.04	Portland, OR	36,469	19.5	0.1	18,895	11.9
50	Vallejo-Fairfield-Napa, CA PMSA	W	21,818	21,064	1.04	Vallejo, CA; Fairfield, CA; Napa, CA	10,727	12.4	−1.6	9,541	43.7
51	Minneapolis-St. Paul, MN-WI MSA	MW	181,936	176,445	1.03	Minneapolis, MN	1,670	1.0	−3.2	3,769	2.1
52	Salt Lake City-Ogden, UT MSA	W	86,692	84,509	1.03	Salt Lake City, UT	4,804	7.2	−2.4	3,942	4.5
53	Tulsa, OK MSA	S	30,736	30,213	1.02	Tulsa, OK	10,296	6.6	−4.2	11,980	39.0
54	Greensboro-Winston-Salem-High Point, NC MSA	S	81,742	80,502	1.02	Greensboro, NC; Winston-Salem, NC	33,817	25.1	−0.4	20,533	25.1
55	Nashville, TN MSA	S	100,012	100,284	1.00	Nashville-Davidson, TN	28,818	14.5	−3.3	28,272	28.3
56	Newark, NJ PMSA	NE	42,812	43,030	0.99	Newark, NJ	−170	−0.2	−1.9	3,981	9.3

(continued)

TABLE 8A-1. Metropolitan Area and Central City Building Permits, Household Change, and Vacancy Change, Seventy-Four Metropolitan Areas, 1990–2000 (continued)

		Metropolitan area				Central city					
Rank	Name	Region	Permits	Household change	Ratio	Name	Household change	Percentage change in households	Change in vacancy rate (percentage points)	Permits	Central city permits as a percentage of metro area permits
Fourth quartile											
57	Ann Arbor, MI PMSA	MW	41,281	41,591	0.99	Ann Arbor, MI	4,036	9.7	–2.1	3,323	8.0
58	Sacramento, CA PMSA	W	99,150	100,447	0.99	Sacramento, CA	10,137	7.0	–0.1	8,103	8.2
59	Monmouth–Ocean, NJ PMSA	NE	58,099	58,921	0.99	Dover Township, NJ	6,153	22.5	–4.8	5,131	8.8
60	Dallas, TX PMSA	S	250,028	254,711	0.98	Dallas, TX	49,773	12.4	–7.0	46,622	18.6
61	Houston, TX PMSA	S	179,825	183,772	0.98	Houston, TX	101,068	16.4	–6.9	65,079	36.2
62	Baton Rouge, LA MSA	S	18,361	18,802	0.98	Baton Rouge, LA	5,633	6.8	–5.5	3,435	18.7
63	Riverside–San Bernardino, CA PMSA	W	163,881	168,008	0.98	Riverside, CA; San Bernardino, CA	8,390	6.5	0.9	10,850	6.6
64	Columbia, SC MSA	S	37,670	40,118	0.94	Columbia, SC	8,326	24.5	0.3	4,467	11.9
65	Phoenix–Mesa, AZ MSA	W	325,990	347,536	0.94	Phoenix, AZ	95,913	25.9	–6.3	80,577	24.7
66	Oklahoma City, OK MSA	S	40,605	44,150	0.92	Oklahoma City, OK	25,772	14.4	–5.5	21,979	54.1
67	Little Rock–North Little Rock, AR MSA	S	23,956	26,686	0.90	Little Rock, AR	4,779	6.6	–1.6	8,314	34.7
68	Providence–Fall River–Warwick, RI-MA MSA	NE	41,559	46,716	0.89	Providence, RI	3,484	5.9	–3.7	911	2.2
69	Boston, MA-NH PMSA	NE	138,245	156,258	0.88	Boston, MA	11,064	4.8	–4.0	3,848	2.8
70	Oakland, CA PMSA	W	77,057	87,689	0.88	Oakland, CA	6,269	4.3	–2.3	4,383	5.7
71	Denver, CO PMSA	W	150,117	175,887	0.85	Denver, CO	28,283	13.4	–7.1	16,505	11.0
72	Austin–San Marcos, TX MSA	S	106,422	125,879	0.85	Austin, TX	73,501	38.3	–7.4	51,231	48.1
73	San Antonio, TX MSA	S	69,238	89,650	0.77	San Antonio, TX	78,713	24.1	–4.2	52,199	75.4
74	San Francisco, CA PMSA	W	29,879	41,949	0.71	San Francisco, CA	24,116	7.9	–2.1	13,280	44.4

Source: Authors' analysis of data from decennial censuses and Census Bureau Current Construction Reports.

REFERENCES

Berube, Alan. 2003. "Racial Change in the Nation's Largest Cities." In *Redefining Urban and Suburban America: Evidence from Census 2000,* vol. 1, edited by Bruce Katz and Robert E. Lang. Brookings.

Berube, Alan, and Benjamin Forman. 2003. "Patchwork Cities: Patterns of Urban Population Growth in the 1990s." In *Redefining Urban and Suburban America: Evidence from Census 2000,* vol. 1, edited by Bruce Katz and Robert E. Lang. Brookings.

Bier, Thomas. 2001. "Moving Up, Filtering Down: Metropolitan Housing Dynamics and Public Policy." Brookings.

Bier, Thomas, and Steven R. Howe. 1998. "Dynamics of Suburbanization in Ohio Metropolitan Areas." *Urban Geography* 19 (8): 695–713.

Downs, Anthony, Arthur C. Nelson, and William A. Fischel. 2002. "Have Housing Prices Risen Faster in Portland Than Elsewhere?" *Housing Policy Debate* 13 (1): 7–50.

Edmonston, Barry. 1999. "The 2000 Census Challenge." *Population Reference Bureau Reports on America* (February): 1–18.

Fulton, William, and others. 2001. "Who Sprawls the Most? How Growth Patterns Differ Across the U.S." Brookings.

Grigsby, William. 1963. *Housing Markets and Public Policy.* University of Pennsylvania Press.

Jargowsky, Paul. 2005. "Stunning Progress, Hidden Problems: The Dramatic Decline of Concentrated Poverty in the 1990s." In *Redefining Urban and Suburban America: Evidence from Census 2000,* vol. 2, edited by Alan Berube, Bruce Katz, and Robert E. Lang. Brookings.

Katz, Bruce, and Robert E. Lang, eds. 2003. *Redefining Urban and Suburban America: Evidence from Census 2000,* vol. 1. Brookings.

Koebel, C. Theodore. 1996. "Urban Redevelopment, Displacement, and the Future of the American City." Richmond, Va.: Federal Reserve Bank of Richmond.

Lang, Robert E. 2002. "Is the United States Undersupplying Housing?" *Housing Facts and Findings* 4 (2). Washington: Fannie Mae Foundation.

Lowry, Ira. 1960. "Filtering and Housing Standards: A Conceptual Analysis." *Land Economics* 36 (4): 362–70.

Lucy, William H., and David L. Phillips. 2003. "Suburbs and the Census: Patterns of Growth and Decline." In *Redefining Urban and Suburban America: Evidence from Census 2000,* vol. 1, edited by Bruce Katz and Robert E. Lang. Brookings.

Mitchum, Drew A. 2003. "Housing Removal Rates." *Housing Economics* (February): 13.

Myers, Dowell, and Julie Park. 2002. "The Great Housing Collapse in California." Washington: Fannie Mae Foundation.

Orfield, Myron. 1997. *Metropolitics: A Regional Agenda for Community and Stability.* Brookings.

Puentes, Robert, and Myron Orfield. 2002. "Valuing America's First Suburbs: A Policy Agenda for Older Suburbs in the Midwest." Brookings.

Ratcliff, Richard. 1949. *Urban Land Economics.* London: McGraw-Hill.

Sohmer, Rebecca, and Robert E. Lang. 2003. "Downtown Rebound." In *Redefining Urban and Suburban America: Evidence from Census 2000,* vol. 1, edited by Bruce Katz and Robert E. Lang. Brookings.

Suchman, Diane R. 1997. *Developing Infill Housing in Inner-City Neighborhoods.* Washington: Urban Land Institute.

9

Tracking American Trends into the Twenty-First Century: A Field Guide to the New Metropolitan and Micropolitan Definitions

WILLIAM H. FREY, JILL H. WILSON,
ALAN BERUBE, AND AUDREY SINGER

The term "metropolitan area" is one of the few statistical terms that show up in common conversation. A metropolitan area is not a political jurisdiction with a mayor or police department, but an economically and socially linked collection of large and small communities. Residing in a metropolitan area provides identification with an understood broader community, often eliciting civic pride promoted by local chambers of commerce and economic development commissions. Regional newspapers, sports teams, and cultural institutions all serve to reaffirm the existence of the metropolitan area. Moreover, the metropolitan designation of an area confers on it something of an urbane or cosmopolitan status, placing it in a league with other recognized economic regions.

Such commonly held perceptions of metropolitan areas are reflected in rigorous statistical definitions of the metropolitan concept developed by the U.S. Office of Management and Budget (OMB). Other federal agencies, such as the U.S. Census Bureau, use these standards to collect and disseminate area-based statistics in publications such as the *United States Statistical Abstract*. They are incorporated into federal and state policies to allocate public resources to local areas. They are also used widely in the private sector and the research community to identify consumer, labor, and housing markets. And OMB-defined metropolitan areas are often ranked in the popular press and publications such as *Places Rated Almanac*.

The authors are grateful to Michael Ratcliffe, Elizabeth Grieco, and Amy Liu for their comments on earlier drafts of the chapter and to Cathy Sun for her technical assistance.

The federal government defined metropolitan statistical areas as early as the late 1940s,[1] and it has updated them several times, primarily to take into account shifts in demographic trends and modest changes in nomenclature.[2] However, in the early 1990s the OMB initiated a decade-long effort to reassess the metropolitan classification system, in light of the many changes in U.S. settlement patterns that had taken place over the previous fifty years.[3]

The original metropolitan statistical area concept was predicated on the model of a large central city of over 50,000 residents that served as a hub of social and economic activity for surrounding counties. Together, the city and counties formed a stand-alone metropolitan area. Since 1950, however, the decentralization of both employment and population in many urban areas has served to disperse the "core" well beyond the largest city into smaller clusters of previously "suburban" communities. As metropolitan populations expanded, it became evident that hierarchies were forming within metropolitan areas. Large metropolitan areas developed somewhat self-contained sub-areas (for example, Newark and Long Island within the greater New York region), and existing neighboring metropolitan areas became, for some purposes, part of a larger super-region (for example, Washington, D.C., and Baltimore). It also became apparent that many communities, considered too small to be part of a metropolitan area, should nonetheless be recognized as part of the settlement system rather than omitted completely.

After a series of commissioned studies, meetings with user communities, and interagency meetings, the OMB's wide-ranging effort in the 1990s resulted in the adoption of new standards for metropolitan and micropolitan areas. The OMB has urged all federal agencies that collect and publish data for these areas to use the most recent definitions.

1. In 1947, the Bureau of the Budget (predecessor of the current Office of Management and Budget), in coordination with the Census Bureau, the Bureau of Labor Statistics, and other agencies, coordinated efforts to define the initial standard metropolitan areas (SMAs). They were formed on the basis of a large population nucleus together with adjacent components (counties, or in New England, towns). Prior to that time, metropolitan-like entities were defined variously by different agencies with names such as "metropolitan districts," "industrial areas," "labor market areas," and "metropolitan counties." Fitzsimmons and Ratcliffe (2004).

2. Subsequent to the identification of standard metropolitan areas (SMAs) in 1949, different terms and slight changes in definitions were incorporated to establish the basic areas as standard metropolitan statistical areas (SMSAs) in 1958, and metropolitan statistical areas (MSAs) in 1983. Concepts associated with larger metropolitan regions (groupings of metropolitan areas) identified for use in previous censuses included the standard consolidated area, used in the 1960 Census; the standard consolidated statistical area (SCSA), identified in 1975 for use in the 1980 census; and the consolidated metropolitan statistical area (CMSA) in 1983. Frey and Speare (1995).

3. Fitzsimmons and Ratcliffe (2004).

FIGURE 9-1. Old versus New Terminology

OLD
Consolidated metropolitan statistical area (CMSA)
Primary metropolitan statistical area (PMSA)
Metropolitan statistical area (MSA)
New England county metropolitan area (NECMA)
Central city

NEW
Metropolitan statistical area (MetroSA)
Micropolitan statistical area (MicroSA)
New England city and town area (NECTA)
Combined statistical area (CSA)
Metropolitan division
Principal city

Source: Office of Management and Budget.

The changes are significant, not only in terminology (see figure 9-1) but also in the geographic sweep of classified areas. Figure 9-2 displays the metropolitan or nonmetropolitan status of U.S. counties according to the old and new standards. Under the old system, only 20 percent of the country's territory was defined. The new standards double the coverage, classifying 46 percent of U.S. land area. "Micropolitan areas"—a new classification—account for most of the increased coverage and fill in a noticeable portion of the "empty" space across the country.

Given these significant changes, many researchers and policymakers will have to alter the way they think about and use metropolitan area data. This chapter provides a "field guide" to help the average consumer of these statistics understand how the new metropolitan and micropolitan areas differ from those used previously and what they imply for planning, research, and policy.[4] First, we compare the classification of metropolitan statistical areas under the old and new standards, describing the terminology, criteria, and options for defining a metropolitan area. Second, we introduce the OMB's new concept— the micropolitan statistical area—and describe its geographic and demographic scope. Third, we discuss how the transition in standards changes the composition of metropolitan areas, illustrating four main types of change.

4. This survey does not attempt to review all of the substantive and technical decisions made during this extensive effort. See Office of Management and Budget (2000); Fitzimmons and Ratcliffe (2004); and U.S. General Accounting Office (2004).

FIGURE 9-2. County Classifications, Old and New Standards

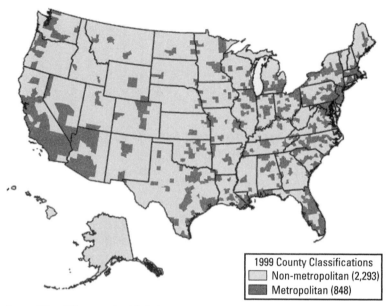

1999 County Classifications
Non-metropolitan (2,293)
Metropolitan (848)

Source: Office of Management and Budget.

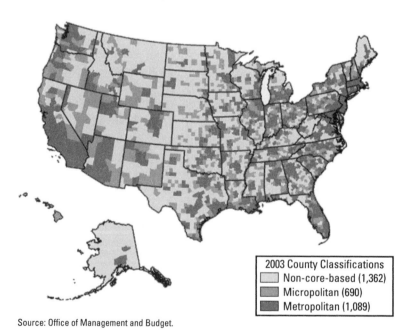

2003 County Classifications
Non-core-based (1,362)
Micropolitan (690)
Metropolitan (1,089)

Source: Office of Management and Budget.

Fourth, we discuss the new principal cities and how these affect metropolitan area titles. Fifth, we analyze how the change in standards alters the socio-economic attributes and rankings of metropolitan areas. Finally, we discuss the implications of the new system for research and policy.

METHODOLOGY

To elucidate important features of the new metropolitan and micropolitan areas, much of this chapter contrasts the areas defined according to the "new standards" (released in June 2003, with updates in December 2003) with comparable areas defined under the previous standards, published in 1999 ("old standards" in this chapter).[5] We draw comparative statistics from decennial U.S. censuses for areas located in the 50 states.[6] Practically all Census 2000 publications and data products to date utilized the old standards for metropolitan areas as we employ them here. This also holds for metropolitan statistics distributed by most other federal agencies during this period.

The reader should note that metropolitan areas, under both old and new standards, are not, strictly speaking, urban areas; similarly, the metropolitan/nonmetropolitan dichotomy is not the same as the urban/rural dichotomy. The OMB defines the metropolitan areas used by all federal agencies to represent functional areas. They are composed of large statistically linked sub-areas (counties) that form socially and economically integrated regions. The OMB determines the composition of metropolitan areas by analyzing commuting patterns within a given region, along with population and employment levels. In contrast, the Census Bureau defines urban areas, which reflect a physical (rather than functional) distinction, mostly on a smaller scale; urban or urbanized areas are required to pass population size and density thresholds.[7] Thus most metropolitan areas contain both urban and rural territory, as do most parts of the country that are located outside of metropolitan areas. In 2000, approximately 12 percent of the nation's metropolitan population was rural and approximately 41 percent of its nonmetropolitan population was urban.

5. Note that we are comparing metropolitan areas—where old metropolitan standards were used to define areas with pre-2000 population and commuting data—to the new standards that were used to define areas with 2000 census commuting data and 2000 census and 2002 population estimate data. Thus some changes to metropolitan areas result solely from changes to OMB's classification system, whereas others reflect population and economic dynamics taking place over the course of the 1990s.

6. Metropolitan areas have also been defined for the territory of Puerto Rico, but those have been omitted from our comparisons.

7. The U.S. Census Bureau defines as urban any densely settled area that has a population of at least 2,500. All territory not included in an urbanized area of 50,000 or more people or an urban cluster of 2,500 to 49,999 people (the two types of urban areas) is considered rural.

Nonetheless, practitioners and even federal agencies have commonly applied the term "urban" to metropolitan areas and "rural" to all non-metropolitan territory.[8] It is likely that this practice will continue under the new standards, although the new micropolitan areas (designated here as "MicroSAs") may blur the line between urban and rural. In like manner the term "suburban" is often applied to portions of metropolitan areas that lie outside of major cities despite the fact that neither the old nor new OMB standards make reference to the terms "suburban" or "suburb."[9] Researchers are also likely to use the new standards—with new "principal cities" defining major cities—to distinguish suburban populations.

FINDINGS

Comparing the new metropolitan classification system to the old one highlights several ways in which researchers' use of metropolitan geographies is likely to change. Furthermore, detailed analysis of individual metropolitan areas indicates that while many retained their basic form, others have changed so substantially that their relative ranking on demographic indicators has changed as well.

Metropolitan Statistical Areas Are the Standard Tool for Analyzing Metropolitan Geographies

This section discusses how the new standards and the old standards for metropolitan areas, the basic components of the OMB's classification system, differ; the next section describes the new micropolitan areas. A comparison of the old and new settlement area concepts is diagrammed in figure 9-3, and the terminology is defined in the appendix.

Metropolitan Area Choices under the Old Standards

In the old system, metropolitan America consisted of individual metropolitan statistical areas (MSAs) and another set of areas that could be defined either as consolidated metropolitan statistical areas (CMSAs) or their component parts, primary metropolitan statistical areas (PMSAs). CMSAs could be defined only for large metropolitan areas with more than 1 million people and where additional criteria allowed for subdivision of those areas into component PMSAs. For example, the Washington-Baltimore, DC-MD-VA-WV CMSA was subdivided into the Washington, DC-MD-VA-WV PMSA; the Baltimore, MD PMSA; and the Hagerstown, MD PMSA.

8. See, for example, Brown and Swanson (2004).
9. See, for example, Frey and Berube (2002).

FIGURE 9-3. Metro Area Choices under Old and New Standards

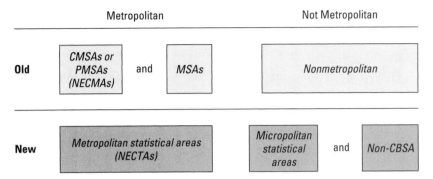

Source: Office of Management and Budget.

Nationally, the combined population of all CMSAs equaled the combined population of all PMSAs, and when either was added to the combined MSA population, the result equaled the total U.S. metropolitan population.

Consumers of these statistics who wished to compare metropolitan areas on some measure had a choice between analyzing all MSAs and CMSAs or all MSAs and PMSAs. In other words, PMSAs and CMSAs could not be used together in the same analysis. However, consumers of statistics for a local CMSA region could choose which level—CMSA or PMSA—best represented their "metropolitan area" (for example, Washington, D.C., analysts could decide between using the Washington-Baltimore CMSA or the Washington PMSA, depending on their purposes).

National rankings of metropolitan areas could legitimately employ either the MSA/CMSA combined list (276 areas, including 258 MSAs and eighteen CMSAs), which was favored by the OMB and the Census Bureau, or the MSA/PMSA combined list (331 areas, including 258 MSAs and 73 PMSAs), which common practice tended to favor. Statistical rankings including metropolitan growth rates, crime statistics, employment patterns, and quality of life indicators found in publications such as *Places Rated Almanac* used the MSA/PMSA system, as have most publications in Brookings's Living Cities Census Series. For the remainder of this chapter, we also use MSAs and PMSAs as benchmarks for comparison with the new system.

An additional choice faced analysts of metropolitan areas in the six New England states. The OMB defined MSAs, PMSAs, and CMSAs for these states, as well as an alternative set of areas known as *New England county metropolitan areas* (NECMAs). New England MSAs, CMSAs, and PMSAs were based on city and town components rather than counties, but many analysts were unable to obtain relevant information at the town level. Hence, NECMAs were developed as county-based counterparts to New England's conventional metropolitan areas. Many national analyses, therefore, used MSAs, CMSAs, and PMSAs, outside of New England, along with NECMAs inside the region.

Finally, the previous standards did not define any settlements outside of the metropolitan areas. All of the residual counties in the United States (or towns in New England) were labeled "nonmetropolitan." Some analysts chose to use individual counties as a means of distinguishing areas within nonmetropolitan territory.[10] Researchers at the U.S. Department of Agriculture created Rural-Urban Continuum Codes (Beale Codes) to distinguish among nonmetropolitan counties based on their urban population and adjacency to metropolitan areas.[11]

Metropolitan Area Choices under the New Standards

For those interested in comparing metropolitan areas across the country, there is now really only one choice: the *metropolitan statistical area* (MetroSA). Although the new system allows for some hierarchical choices for analyses of individual areas (discussed below), intermetropolitan analyses are best conducted using the MetroSA, which now is based exclusively on county-level components in both New England and non–New England states. MetroSAs are defined using somewhat different criteria than those used for the old MSAs, CMSAs, and PMSAs. As a consequence, both the size and number of metropolitan areas have changed.

According to the new standards, metropolitan area central counties are now determined exclusively by their overlap with urban areas—the more restrictive "urbanized areas or cities of 50,000 or more" criterion is no longer part of their definition.[12] The extent of urban areas has also changed, due to population growth and new definitional criteria. Together, these changes have increased the number of central counties, thus enlarging the potential commuting fields of many large metropolitan areas.

At the same time, new commuting criteria for adding outlying counties to a region's central counties are more restrictive than those used previously. Thus, forty-one counties that previously served as outlying counties of

10. Johnson (1999).
11. "Measuring Rurality: Rural-Urban Continuum Codes," USDA Economic Research Service (www.ers.usda.gov/briefing/rurality/RuralUrbCon/ [November 2004]).
12. Although the existence of an urbanized area with a population of over 50,000 is required for each MetroSA, the central counties are defined in terms of urban populations, including both urbanized areas and urban clusters. Central cities are no longer part of the new definitions.

metropolitan areas do not qualify as such under the new rules but have now become part of new micropolitan areas.[13]

One result of the change in criteria for defining metropolitan areas is that the larger MetroSAs are more comparable in size and area to the former CMSAs than to the former PMSAs.[14] As a consequence, users who are accustomed to employing the PMSA/MSA definitions under the old system will find that the number of metropolitan areas with populations exceeding 1 million drops from sixty-one to forty-nine in the new system. At the same time, the number of metropolitan areas with populations below 250,000 rises from 149 to 195. Yet the forty-nine large MetroSAs make up about the same share of the U.S. population—53 percent—as the sixty-one large MSAs/PMSAs (see figure 9-4). At the other end of the spectrum, the 195 small MetroSAs represent only a slightly larger share of U.S. population than the 149 small MSAs/ PMSAs (10 percent versus 8 percent). Altogether, the new standards describe 361 MetroSAs, compared to 331 MSAs/PMSAs under the old system.

As with the previous standards, the OMB defines an alternative set of areas in the six New England states. Unlike under old standards, however, these alternative areas are defined at the city and town level and are called *New England city and town areas* (NECTAs). MetroSAs in New England are made up of counties, making counties the basic "building blocks" of metropolitan areas both inside and outside the New England states.

Finally, the most recognizable change with the new standards is the identification of smaller "metropolitan-like" communities. These new areas, called "micropolitan areas," define meaningful "core-based" areas with cores too small to qualify as MetroSAs. They are discussed below.

The New Hierarchy Options for Local Areas

Although the new standards provide a single unit, the MetroSA, for comparing metropolitan areas across the country, they provide additional choices when the focus turns to local areas (see figure 9-5). *Combined statistical areas* (CSAs) represent two or more adjoining MetroSAs or MicroSAs. They range

13. The previous criteria for adding outlying counties included both density and commuting requirements. The new criteria have dropped the density requirements but made the commuting requirements more stringent. A consequence of the more stringent commuting requirements was the elimination of outlying counties that would have qualified under the old system; however, in some cases new counties with low population densities that now qualify as outlying counties under the new standards would have been omitted under the previous ones.

14. The new system does not define a PMSA counterpart for large areas with populations exceeding one million (as was the case for CMSAs in the old system). However, for 11 MetroSAs, with populations exceeding 2.5 million, the new system creates "metropolitan divisions," which in some cases approximate the former PMSAs. These are discussed later in the text.

FIGURE 9-4. Number of Metropolitan Areas and Share of U.S. Population, by Size of Metropolitan Area Population, 2000

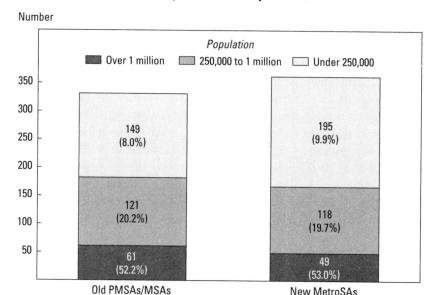

Source: Authors' analysis of Census 2000 data.

in size from the two-county Clovis-Portales, NM CSA (population 63,000), which consists of the Clovis MicroSA and the Portales MicroSA, to the thirty-county New York-Newark-Bridgeport, NY-NJ-CT-PA CSA (population 21.4 million), made up of six MetroSAs and one MicroSA. The OMB designates CSAs where certain cross-area commuting requirements are met and in specified circumstances where local input favors the designation. There are currently 120 CSAs (those associated with the greater Atlanta area, the Dallas-Fort Worth area, and the New York area are illustrated below). Forty-five percent (163) of all MetroSAs are located in a CSA.

These areas are useful primarily for local analyses, as they give users a more expansive way to define their particular region. CSAs are ill-suited for cross-metropolitan analyses, because CSAs and MetroSAs are different analytic units.

The other innovation in the new standards that may assist local area analyses is the *metropolitan division*. The OMB designated metropolitan divisions within each of eleven MetroSAs with populations of over 2.5 million, and they reflect single- or multi-county areas with close commuting ties. Examples include the Washington-Arlington-Alexandria, DC-VA-MD-WV

FIGURE 9-5. New Hierarchy Options for Local Areas[a]

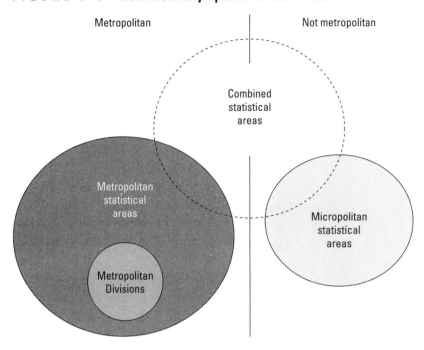

Source: Office of Management and Budget.

a. These options are not available for all 361 metropolitan areas and 573 micropolitan areas. There are 120 combined statistical areas, which encompass 163 metropolitan and 153 micropolitan areas. Twenty-nine metropolitan divisions exist within 11 metropolitan areas.

metropolitan division and the Bethesda-Frederick-Gaithersburg, MD metropolitan division within the Washington-Arlington-Alexandria, DC-VA-MD-WV MetroSA; and the Dallas-Plano-Irving, TX metropolitan division and Fort Worth-Arlington, TX metropolitan division within the Dallas-Fort Worth-Arlington, TX MetroSA.

These metropolitan divisions, as components of MetroSAs, somewhat resemble PMSAs under the old system. However, PMSAs were much more common; because only a few very large MetroSAs contain metropolitan divisions, metropolitan divisions are less practical geographic units for nationwide analyses. The higher population threshold for establishing metropolitan divisions (at least 2.5 million)—opposed to the threshold of at least 1 million to establish PMSAs—means that the new system contains twenty-nine metropolitan divisions within eleven MetroSAs, compared to seventy-three PMSAs within eighteen CMSAs under the old system. Nevertheless, metropolitan divisions provide increased flexibility for local analyses. Thus, in some metropolitan areas users are able to choose among a metropolitan hierarchy that includes CSAs, MetroSAs, and metropolitan divisions.

Micropolitan and Metropolitan Areas Represent 93 Percent of the U.S. Population and 46 Percent of U.S. Land Area

The *micropolitan statistical area* (MicroSA) is perhaps the most innovative concept created under the new standards. The OMB developed MicroSAs in response to arguments that smaller communities located outside of metropolitan areas deserved recognition as self-contained settlements. They and MetroSAs are defined in a parallel manner in that they are core-based, meaning that they consist of one or more counties centered on a contiguous urban area. MicroSAs and MetroSAs differ primarily in the population of their core areas: between 10,000 and 50,000 for MicroSAs, and at least 50,000 for MetroSAs. Some MicroSAs have larger populations than the smallest MetroSAs, but they are classified as the former because their core urban areas have fewer than 50,000 people. MicroSAs range in size from about 13,000 (Andrews, TX) to over 180,000 (Torrington, CT); MetroSAs range in size from just over 50,000 (Carson City, NV) to 18.3 million (New York-Northern New Jersey-Long Island, NY-NJ-PA).

The new standards define 573 MicroSAs in addition to the 361 MetroSAs. The 573 MicroSAs incorporate 690 counties, indicating that the majority of these areas include just one county. Because of the way they were defined, the OMB refers to both types of areas as *core-based statistical areas* (CBSAs). Together, these core-based areas cover a much larger share of the nation's population and land mass than metropolitan areas alone under the old standards. The combined MetroSAs and MicroSAs now represent 93 percent of the U.S. population and 46 percent of the land area. In comparison, the old metropolitan areas constituted 80 percent of the nation's population and just 20 percent of its land area (table 9-1).

For analysts accustomed to distinguishing between metropolitan and nonmetropolitan populations, MicroSAs belong to the latter category. However, they represent only part of the nation's nonmetropolitan territory. The remaining portion of nonmetropolitan land is defined by the somewhat cumbersome term "non-core-based areas." Because MicroSAs constitute 60 percent of the total nonmetropolitan population, it is now less appropriate to think of the nonmetropolian population as wholly "rural."

Researchers from the Census Bureau and other federal agencies will incorporate the new micropolitan area concept into a range of national statistics, opening up a new field of study for demographers, planners, and policy-

T A B L E   9 - 1 .   Geographic and Demographic Coverage, Old and New Standards

Standard	Number of counties	Share of national land area (percent)	Population, 2000	Share of national population
Old				
Metropolitan	848	20	226,207,070	80.4
Nonmetropolitan	2,293	80	55,214,836	19.6
New				
Metropolitan	1,089	25.3	232,579,940	82.6
Micropolitan	690	20.3	29,412,298	10.5
Non-core-based	1,362	54.4	19,429,668	6.9

Source: Authors' analysis of Census 2000 data.

makers. The locations and profiles of MicroSAs are quite varied. Table 9-2 shows that states containing the largest number of MicroSAs are not the nation's largest states, but they are heavily concentrated in the Midwest and South and constitute a larger share of overall population there. Texas, Ohio, North Carolina, Indiana, and Georgia lead all other states in micropolitan areas, whereas the highly urbanized states of Massachusetts, Rhode Island, and New Jersey do not have any. Small states with numerous counties, such as Iowa, Nebraska, and South Dakota, each have more MicroSAs than California.

Recent analyses—one by Lang and Dhavale and one by Frey—highlight the variations in micropolitan area demographic profiles. They find that the fastest-growing MicroSAs are located near large growing MetroSAs, whereas the more remote MicroSAs are generally smaller and slow-growing. Overall, MicroSA populations tend to be older, poorer, more conservative, less educated, and less racially diverse than their metropolitan counterparts.[15]

Most of the Largest Metropolitan Areas Underwent Changes in Territory and Population

Analysts (and even casual observers) first encountering the new metropolitan areas will likely ask how different the new standards are from the old ones. The simple answer is "Quite a bit." The changes are especially pronounced in the nation's larger metropolitan areas, which form the focus of many Brookings Metropolitan Policy Program analyses. This section first describes the changes from the old to new systems viewed from the county level, then explores how those county transitions reshaped the nation's largest metropolitan areas.

15. Lang and Dhavale, chapter 10 of this volume; Frey (2004a).

T A B L E 9 - 2 . Number of Micropolitan Statistical Areas, by State[a]

Rank	State	Micro areas
1	Texas	41
2	Ohio	29
3	North Carolina	26
4	Indiana	25
5	Georgia	24
6	Illinois	23
7	Pennsylvania	21
8	Missouri	20
9	Mississippi	20
10	Tennessee	20
11	Michigan	18
12	Minnesota	18
13	Kentucky	17
14	Louisiana	17
15	Oklahoma	17
16	Kansas	15
17	New York	15
18	Iowa	15
19	Arkansas	14
20	New Mexico	14
21	Oregon	13
22	South Carolina	13
23	Wisconsin	13
24	Alabama	13
25	Florida	11
26	Nebraska	10
27	South Dakota	9
28	Washington	9
29	California	9
30	Idaho	8
31	Colorado	7
32	Wyoming	7
33	West Virginia	6
34	New Hampshire	6
35	Arizona	5
36	Montana	5
37	North Dakota	5
38	Vermont	5
39	Utah	5
40	Maryland	4
41	Nevada	4
42	Alaska	3
43	Hawaii	3
44	Virginia	3
45	Connecticut	2
46	Maine	2
47	Delaware	1
48	District of Columbia	0
49	Massachusetts	0
50	New Jersey	0
51	Rhode Island	0

Source: Office of Management and Budget.
a. Micropolitan areas that cross state boundaries are counted once in each state.

County Shifts

Because both the old and new systems are county-based, it is possible to view the extent of change between the two systems from the county level. Counties could make six possible transitions between the systems, shown in table 9-3. Of the 3,141 counties that make up the United States, a plurality (43 percent) remained "undefined"—that is, they were nonmetropolitan under the old system and they are non-core-based under the new system. They include the vast number of small, rural counties found mostly in the interior states. The next largest proportion of counties (26 percent) remained metropolitan under the new system, and of these the vast majority (92 percent) remained within the same metropolitan area. Thus roughly 70 percent of counties retained a comparable position in the transition to the new standards.

Other counties changed classification due to the introduction of the micropolitan concept, new rules for defining metropolitan areas, changes in commuting patterns, or simple population growth and decentralization. Counties that changed from nonmetropolitan to micropolitan were fairly common, accounting for 21 percent of all counties and nearly 10 percent of U.S. population. Nine percent of U.S. counties jumped from nonmetropolitan to metropolitan status. Far smaller proportions moved down the hierarchy from metropolitan to micropolitan (1 percent) and from metropolitan to non-core-based status (just five counties).

As a result of these transitions, a greater share of the nation's population is now considered metropolitan (83 percent, up from 80 percent). On net, 242 counties moved from nonmetropolitan to metropolitan standing (46 from metropolitan to nonmetropolitan and 288 from nonmetropolitan to metropolitan). Some became part of the forty-five new metropolitan areas announced under the new system, whereas others were added to the fringes of existing metropolitan areas. Of the forty-six counties that changed status from metropolitan to nonmetropolitan, only five did not become part of a MicroSA. The forty-one previously metropolitan counties that became micropolitan did not necessarily shrink in size but generally failed to meet the new, more stringent commuting threshold for inclusion in metropolitan areas.

Metropolitan Shifts

Despite the fact that a majority of the nation's counties have effectively the same designations under the new system, the county composition of most of the nation's largest metropolitan areas changed in some way. In fact, eighty-one of the 102 metropolitan areas with populations of at least 500,000 under the old system (in 2000) are defined somewhat differently under the new system. As a result, two-thirds (fifty-six) of the eighty-one metropolitan

TABLE 9-3. County Transitions

Old classification	New classification	Number	Percent of counties	Population, 2000	Percent of population
Metropolitan	Metropolitan	801	25.5	223,113,722	79.3
Metropolitan	Micropolitan	41	1.3	2,856,237	1.0
Metropolitan	Non-core-based	5	0.2	105,216	0.0
Nonmetropolitan	Metropolitan	288	9.2	9,466,218	3.4
Nonmetropolitan	Micropolitan	649	20.7	26,556,061	9.4
Nonmetropolitan	Non-core-based	1357	43.2	19,324,452	6.9

Source: Authors' calculations of Census 2000 data.

areas gained population, whereas the rest (twenty-five) lost population. We provide examples of the several different ways in which metropolitan areas have been redefined by the new standards. Table 9-4 shows the extent of each of these types of changes among the 102 metropolitan areas when the old MSAs/PMSAs are compared to the new MetroSAs.

Adding Counties to Metropolitan Areas: Atlanta

Twenty-nine of the 102 largest metropolitan areas experienced a net addition of counties in the transition to the new system. Most of these metropolitan areas are located in the middle and southern regions of the country, where population is growing and spreading out quickly.[16]

Atlanta offers the most dramatic example of a metropolitan area with additional counties in its definition. Metropolitan Atlanta is undergoing rapid population growth, mostly in its suburbs, which grew by 44 percent in the 1990s. The new definition of metropolitan Atlanta reflects this sprawling suburban pattern and offers more than one choice for delineating the area. Under the old standards, Atlanta was a single MSA made up of twenty counties. The new system creates the twenty-eight-county Atlanta-Sandy Springs-Marietta, GA MetroSA (the original twenty counties plus eight more). It also gives the option of using the thirty-three-county Atlanta-Sandy Springs-Gainesville, GA-AL combined statistical area (CSA), which includes the Gainesville MetroSA (one county) and four MicroSAs (one county each) (see figure 9-6).

Removing Counties from Metropolitan Areas: Knoxville, Las Vegas, and Washington, D.C.

Most of the thirteen metropolitan areas that experienced a net loss of counties are located in the eastern half of the United States. In the West, only Las

16. Springfield, Massachusetts, and Providence, Rhode Island, were the only New England metropolitan areas to experience a net addition of counties.

T A B L E   9 - 4 .   Metropolitan Transitions, Areas with Populations of 500,000 or Greater, 2000

Transition Type	Number of metro areas	Percent of top 102
Geographical changes		
Added counties (net)	29	28.4
Removed counties (net)	13	12.7
Split into two or more metros	9	8.8
Combined into one metro	23	22.5
Changed in more than one way	7	6.9
Stayed the same	21	20.6
Total	102	100.0
Population changes[a]		
Gained population	56	54.9
Lost population	25	24.5
Same population	21	20.6
Total	102	100.0

Source: Authors' analysis of Office of Management and Budget and Census 2000 data.
a. Comparing total metro area population in 2000 according to old and new definitions.

Vegas lost counties from its metropolitan definition. As noted earlier, the vast majority of counties removed from metropolitan areas became part of micropolitan areas, so they do not necessarily represent areas that are losing population. In almost all cases in which micropolitan areas were created on the outskirts of metropolitan areas, CSAs also were defined, often matching the former metropolitan definition.

Knoxville, Tennessee, is a typical example. Under the old system, the Knoxville, TN MSA consisted of six counties. Under the new standards, the OMB removed outlying Sevier County from the metropolitan area and named it the Sevierville, TN MicroSA. Together, the metropolitan area and micropolitan area form the newly defined Knoxville-Sevierville-La Follette, TN CSA (see figure 9-7).

Not all counties that made the transition from metropolitan to micro-politan status became part of a CSA. For example, the Las Vegas, NV-AZ MSA consisted of three counties under the old standards (Mohave County in Arizona and Clark and Nye counties in Nevada). Under the new standards, only Clark County remains in the Las Vegas-Paradise, NV MetroSA. Nye County becomes the Pahrump, NV MicroSA, which, together with the Las Vegas metropolitan area, makes up the Las Vegas-Paradise-Pahrump, NV CSA. Mohave County, Arizona, is now the Lake Havasu City-Kingman MicroSA, outside of any CSA.

The Washington, D.C., metropolitan area provides a unique example in that two of its counties changed from metropolitan to non-core-based. The Washington, DC-MD-VA-WV PMSA saw three counties removed in the

FIGURE 9-6. Atlanta-Sandy Springs-Gainesville, GA-AL Combined Statistical Area

transition: two in Virginia and one in West Virginia. Although Berkeley County, West Virginia, became part of a separate metropolitan area (Hagerstown-Martinsburg, MD-WV MSA), Culpeper and King George counties in Virginia became non-core-based areas. These examples demonstrate the greater simplicity of the new classification system, which eliminated from some MetroSAs far-flung counties with little economic relationship to the core.[17]

17. For example, the county seat of fully rural King George County, Virginia, is a full seventy miles from the District of Columbia. In 2000, only 3 percent of the county's workers commuted to the district.

FIGURE 9-7. Knoxville-Sevierville-La Follette, TN Combined Statistical Area

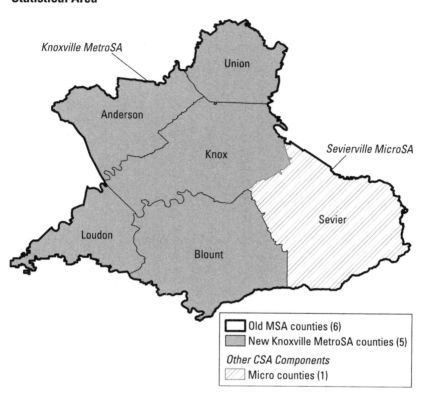

Knoxville MetroSA

Union

Anderson

Knox

Sevierville MicroSA

Sevier

Loudon

Blount

Old MSA counties (6)
New Knoxville MetroSA counties (5)
Other CSA Components
Micro counties (1)

Separating a Metropolitan Area into New Areas: Raleigh-Durham

Of the 102 largest MSAs/PMSAs, nine split into two or more metropolitan areas under the new system. These metropolitan areas are scattered around the country. Similar to those metropolitan areas that lost counties, the cleaving of these metropolitan areas reflects the stricter commuting thresholds under the new system and perhaps an emerging economic independence separating formerly close-knit neighbors.

Under the old standards, the area of North Carolina known as the Research Triangle—the Raleigh-Durham-Chapel Hill, NC MSA—consisted of six counties. The new standards split the triangle into two metropolitan areas: the Durham, NC MetroSA and the Raleigh-Cary, NC MetroSA. Together, the two metropolitan areas consist of the same six counties plus one additional county in the Durham metropolitan area. The Raleigh-Durham-Cary, NC CSA combines these two MetroSAs with the new one-county Dunn, NC MicroSA (see figure 9-8). As with Raleigh-Durham, the new standards split the former

FIGURE 9-8. Raleigh-Durham-Cary, NC Combined Statistical Area

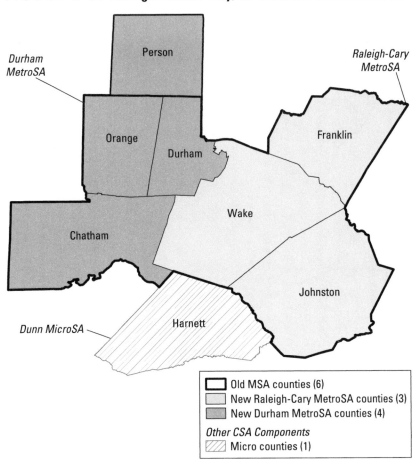

Vallejo-Fairfield-Napa, CA PMSA into two MetroSAs, and the Grand Rapids-Muskegon-Holland, MI MSA into three MetroSAs and one MicroSA.

Combining Two or More Metropolitan Areas into One Area: Dallas-Fort Worth and New York

Twenty-three MSAs and PMSAs under the old system combined with neighboring areas to form new, larger MetroSAs. In Dallas-Fort Worth, the combination produced a region with several different layers. Under the old standards, Dallas-Fort Worth was a twelve-county CMSA divided into two PMSAs: Dallas (with eight counties) and Fort Worth-Arlington (with four counties) (figure 9-9). The new standards created the unified Dallas-Fort Worth-Arlington, TX MetroSA, made up of twelve counties (two of which are

FIGURE 9-9. Dallas-Forth Worth, TX Combined Statistical Area

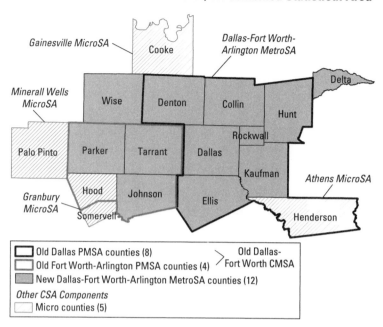

different from the originals). And because the metropolitan area contains over 5 million people, the OMB further delineated two metropolitan divisions within the region: Dallas-Plano-Irving and Fort Worth-Arlington. These divisions resemble the old PMSAs and recognize that each of the areas retains some individual economic character. In addition, the new Dallas-Fort Worth, TX CSA includes the MetroSA and four surrounding micropolitan areas.

If the Dallas-Forth Worth changes are complex, the changes to the New York metropolitan area might rank as mind-boggling. Yet the new metropolitan geography that results is arguably more satisfying than the old one.[18] The old New York PMSA consisted of eight counties—the five New York City boroughs and three New York State counties north of the city. Suburbs just across the Hudson River in New Jersey and those just a county or two away on Long Island occupied different PMSAs altogether. In cross-metropolitan analyses, the New York metropolitan area (PMSA) often seemed an outlier because the city so dominated the area's demographic and economic characteristics.

With the release of the new standards, several former PMSAs in the New York CMSA combined to form the New York-Northern New Jersey-Long Island, NY-NJ-PA MetroSA, consisting of twenty-three counties in three

18. Of the twenty-two metropolitan areas under the old system that have combined in the new system, seven are located in the New York region.

FIGURE 9-10. New York-Newark-Bridgeport, NY-NJ-CT-PA Combined Statistical Area

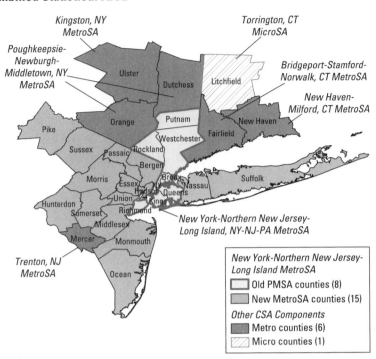

states. This expansive new MetroSA incorporates four metropolitan divisions. Even the division that includes New York City (the New York-Wayne-White Plains, NY-NJ metropolitan division) contains eleven counties in two states, and it is larger than the old PMSA. At the "macro" level, the New York-Newark-Bridgeport, NY-NJ-CT-PA CSA contains thirty counties in four states (figure 9-10). As in Dallas-Fort Worth, the New York region can now be viewed at three hierarchical levels of geography (figure 9-11). Instead of one CMSA made up of fifteen PMSAs, the new CSA includes six MetroSAs, further subdivided into four metropolitan divisions, and one MicroSA.

National metropolitan analyses are likely to adopt the New York MetroSA, and some demographic consequences of that transition are explored below. At the same time, researchers focusing specifically on the New York region now benefit from a wider variety of options codified in the OMB's metropolitan definitions.

Multiple Changes

The new metropolitan standards changed some metropolitan areas in more than one way. Detroit provides the most complicated example: The old

FIGURE 9-11. New York's Components, Old and New Definitions

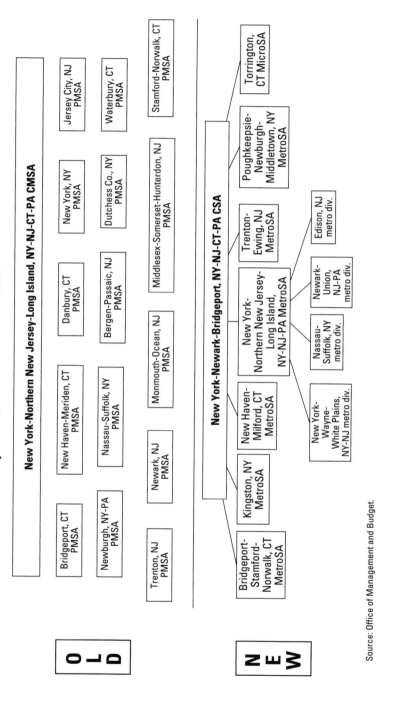

Source: Office of Management and Budget.

Detroit PMSA gained a county, lost a county, and split into two separate MetroSAs in the new system. The Detroit, MI PMSA consisted of six counties: Lapeer, Macomb, Monroe, Oakland, St. Clair, and Wayne. The new Detroit-Warren-Livonia, MI MetroSA still consists of six counties, but one changed. Livingston County, formerly in the Ann Arbor, MI PMSA, moved into the Detroit metropolitan area. Meanwhile, Monroe County became its own metropolitan area. Besides Detroit, six other MSAs/PMSAs have a new composition through a mix of county additions and subtractions or metropolitan splits and combinations.

These examples show that the transition to a new classification system reshuffled many pieces of the metropolitan puzzle. Yet the basic contours of most metropolitan areas remain largely intact. The streamlined rules for defining metropolitan areas have resulted in some sensible changes (a slightly smaller Washington metropolitan area, a larger New York metropolitan area, and a combined Dallas-Forth Worth metropolis), and they offer researchers a richer variety of options for analyzing some of the nation's largest regions. In a later section, we explore how the new metropolitan areas rank on basic demographic attributes compared to their previous counterparts.

Principal Cities Replaced Central Cities in Metropolitan and Micropolitan Areas

Some of the examples above highlight the implications of another significant change between the old and new standards: the identification of new *principal cities* for MetroSAs and MicroSAs. These replace the old system's central cities and designate prominent places within these areas; specifically, the OMB uses principal cities and census-designated places (CDPs) to derive the official names for all MetroSAs and MicroSAs.[19]

Although the concept of principal cities may seem familiar to most analysts, these places differ somewhat from central cities. First, the term "principal" (rather than "central") denotes that these cities are no longer as critical to the identification of metropolitan areas and their commuting fields. The current standards employ urban areas rather than cities or incorporated places as "cores" to define their central and outlying counties. Nonetheless, most urbanized areas contain recognizable cities, which developers of the new standards determined should be identified because their names are well known as important jurisdictions within MetroSAs and MicroSAs.

---

19. This change has brought recognition to large suburban economic centers that have been featured for the first time in the names of metropolitan areas (for example, Paradise, Nevada; Sandy Springs, Georgia; and Towson, Maryland.).

Second, the rules for identifying principal cities are slightly different from those used to identify central cities. The principal city or cities of an area always include the largest incorporated place or census-designated place, as well as additional cities that meet population and employment thresholds.[20] The new standards identify 646 principal cities among the 361 MetroSAs, up from 554 central cities under the old system. The OMB also recognizes 609 principal cities among the 573 MicroSAs.

As noted earlier, some analysts have used central cities to identify suburban populations, by subtracting central city populations from metropolitan area populations and designating the result as "suburban." This fairly crude means of defining the suburbs has figured in several Brookings analyses.[21] Although neither the previous nor the new metropolitan standards confer "suburban" status on this residual territory, it is likely that analysts will continue to employ a similar technique with principal cities to derive their suburbs.[22] The introduction of a new and larger set of cities within metropolitan areas may therefore shrink somewhat the differences between "urban" and "suburban" territories overall.[23]

On this note, figure 9-12 provides a comparison of the share of metropolitan populations residing in central cities and principal cities. Principal cities make up a somewhat larger share of metropolitan population than did central cites (39.8 percent versus 35.5 percent). This is due to the identification of additional principal cities within existing metropolitan areas and to the creation of many smaller metropolitan areas that now have their own principal cities. Figure 9-12 also shows the share of the micropolitan population living in principal cities. Principal cities' smaller share of MicroSA population (33.2 percent) reflects the more dispersed settlements common in these smaller areas.

20. Additional principal cities within a metropolitan area include any with more than 250,000 people or 100,000 workers. Places with more than 50,000 people can also be principal cities if the number of jobs located there meets or exceeds the number of employed residents. Finally, principal cities also include places with more than 10,000 people that are at least one-third the size of the largest place in the metropolitan area and that have at least as many jobs as employed residents.

21. See, for example, Frey (2001); Berube and Frey (2002); Singer (2004).

22. See Frey (2004b) for a critique of employing this practice to designate the suburban population.

23. At the same time, many Brookings analyses have employed a modified set of central cities in the largest metropolitan areas, recognizing only cities that appear within the metropolitan area name—and in some cases, only those that exceed certain population thresholds. See, for example, Frey and Berube (2002) and Suro and Singer (2002). This approach discounted small employment centers in large regions, such as Frederick, Maryland (Washington-Baltimore CMSA), and Port Huron, Michigan (Detroit CMSA); future Brookings analyses may employ a similar approach with principal cities.

FIGURE 9-12. Share of Core-Based Population in Central or Principal Cities, 2000

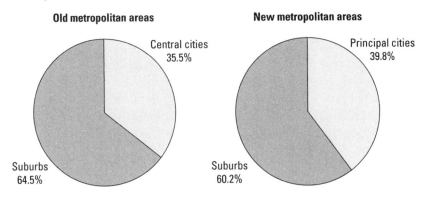

Old metropolitan areas

Central cities
35.5%

Suburbs
64.5%

New metropolitan areas

Principal cities
39.8%

Suburbs
60.2%

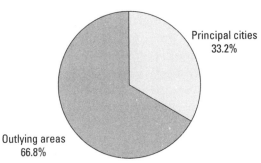

New micropolitan areas

Principal cities
33.2%

Outlying areas
66.8%

Source: Authors' analysis of Census 2000 data.

Although the population or demographic changes caused by the shift to principal cities may intrigue researchers, these new principal cities make even more noticeable changes to the names of MetroSAs. As with central cities, most metropolitan area titles now incorporate the names of the three largest principal cities in descending population size.[24] However, because some new cities are identified in existing areas and some metropolitan areas split or combined with others, title changes are common. Among the 102 largest MSAs and PMSAs, two-thirds (sixty-seven) registered some change in their official names in the transition to

24. There are some exceptions to this rule, where local opinion favored a different name. See the Discussion section.

T A B L E   9 - 5 .   Title Changes of Selected Metropolitan Areas

Former title	New title
Austin-San Marcos, TX MSA	Austin-Round Rock, TX MetroSA
Boulder-Longmont, CO PMSA	Boulder, CO MetroSA
Bryan-College Station, TX MSA	College Station-Bryan, TX MetroSA[a]
Chicago, IL PMSA	Chicago-Naperville-Joliet, IL-IN-WI MetroSA
Fort Myers-Cape Coral, FL MSA	Cape Coral-Fort Myers, FL MetroSA[a]
Houston, TX PMSA	Houston-Baytown-Sugar Land, TX MetroSA
Las Vegas, NV-AZ MSA	Las Vegas-Paradise, NV MetroSA
Los Angeles-Long Beach, CA PMSA	Los Angeles-Long Beach-Santa Ana, CA MetroSA
Minneapolis-St. Paul, MN-WI MSA	Minneapolis-St. Paul-Bloomington, MN-WI MetroSA
New Orleans, LA MSA	New Orleans-Metairie-Kenner, LA MetroSA
New York, NY PMSA	New York-Northern New Jersey-Long Island, NY-NJ-PA MetroSA
Norfolk-Virginia Beach-Newport News, VA-NC MSA	Virginia Beach-Norfolk-Newport News, VA-NC MetroSA[a]
Phoenix-Mesa, AZ MSA	Phoenix-Mesa-Scottsdale, AZ MetroSA
San Diego, CA MSA	San Diego-Carlsbad-San Marcos, CA MetroSA
San Francisco, CA PMSA	San Francisco-Oakland-Fremont, CA MetroSA
San Jose, CA PMSA	San Jose-Sunnyvale-Santa Clara, CA MetroSA
Ventura, CA PMSA	Oxnard-Thousand Oaks-Ventura, CA MetroSA[a]
Washington, DC-MD-VA-WV PMSA	Washington-Arlington-Alexandria, DC-VA-MD-WV MetroSA

Source: OMB

a. Order of place names in the title changed.

MetroSAs. Examples of these changes appear in table 9-5. In most cases, the result is a longer name, sometimes incorporating places not well-known to outsiders. The New Orleans MSA, for example, is now the New Orleans-Metairie-Kenner MetroSA.

A city's inclusion in its metropolitan area's title may promote name recognition and enhance its status. Scottsdale, Arizona, for example, gained prominence by entering the title of the Phoenix-Mesa metropolitan area. Although Scottsdale did not meet the old population threshold, its rank as the third-largest principal city in the Phoenix area thrust it into the new metropolitan title.[25] Places such as Naperville and Joliet, Illinois, in the Chicago metropolitan area, and Carlsbad and San Marcos, California, in the San Diego metropolitan area, realized similar benefits from the change in naming convention.

The order of city names in a metropolitan area title is also significant, because sometimes the first-named city is the only one used to refer to a metropolitan area. In the case of the Norfolk-Virginia Beach-Newport News, VA-NC MSA, the city of Norfolk has been eclipsed by Virginia Beach, switching the order of the two in the new MetroSA title. Without changing

25. According to the old standards, metropolitan area names included the largest central city and each additional city with at least 250,000 persons. Under the new standards, the names of the second- and third-largest principal cities are included in metropolitan area titles.

its geographical components, the Ventura, CA PMSA became the Oxnard-Thousand Oaks-Ventura, CA MetroSA. And in Austin, Texas, Round Rock replaced San Marcos as the second-named city in the metropolitan area title, thanks to the more streamlined rules for defining principal cities (versus central cities).[26]

New Definitions Alter Social and Economic Attributes of Some Metropolitan Areas

The new classification system provides a single choice for analyzing or ranking metropolitan areas across the country, but several ways for local analysts to define their areas. In this section, we first compare the options available for analysis in one large region, New York, and compare the region's attributes under the old and new systems. We then contrast demographic rankings of metropolitan areas using the MetroSA concept to those provided by the old MSAs and PMSAs.

Local Choices and Changes: New York

As was the case under the old standards, how one defines a local area for study can significantly affect the results. For New York, there are now three ways to define the metropolitan area, rather than two. Table 9-6 compares population sizes and socioeconomic attributes for the former New York CMSA and PMSA with the new CSA, MetroSA, and metropolitan division containing New York City. The former CMSA and the current CSA are similar in size, whereas the former PMSA is similar to the current metropolitan division. Interestingly, the current MetroSA, the geography likely to be used most often, has no parallel in the old standards. Whereas the former PMSA constituted only 44 percent of the CMSA's population, the current MetroSA accounts for 86 percent of the CSA. Even the smaller geographical unit, the division, makes up more than half of its CSA's population.

Thus it is not surprising that there are noticeable differences between the profile of the "new" New York (MetroSA) and the "old" New York (PMSA). The MetroSA is wealthier, whiter, more educated, and has a higher percentage of its population in married-couple households. These differences reflect

26. Under the old standards, Austin and San Marcos were the two central cities in the Austin, TX MSA. Round Rock was not a central city because it did not have an employment/residence ratio of at least 0.75 and at least 40 percent of its employed residents working within the city. Under the new standards, Round Rock qualifies as a principal city because its population is over 50,000 and its employment/residence ratio is at least 1.0. Because San Marcos's population is less than 50,000 and it does not have both an employment/residence ratio of at least 1.0 and a population of at least one-third that of Austin's, it did not qualify as a principal city and thus was dropped from the metropolitan area title.

TABLE 9-6. **Comparing "Old" and "New" New York**

Percent, except as indicated

Definition	Population (millions)	Households with annual income Below $25,000	Households with annual income Above $75,000	White	Hispanic	Black	Asian-Pacific Islander	Less than high school	Bachelor's or higher
Old									
CMSA	21.1	25.5	32.4	56.2	18.2	16.1	6.7	20.7	30.5
PMSA	9.3	32.7	25.6	39.6	25.1	22.7	9.0	26.0	29.2
New									
CSA	21.3	25.5	32.3	56.6	18.1	16.0	6.7	20.6	30.4
MetroSA	18.3	26.2	32.0	53.4	19.5	17.0	7.3	21.3	30.3
Division	11.3	31.0	27.0	42.4	25.0	20.3	8.9	25.2	29.4

Source: Authors' analysis of Census 2000 data.

the new area's reach into the far suburbs of northern and central New Jersey, Long Island, and even eastern Pennsylvania. By far the greatest disparity between the two metropolitan area definitions appears in race and ethnicity attributes. The new MetroSA is majority non-Hispanic white (53 percent), whereas the old PMSA was only 40 percent white.

National Changes: Metropolitan Rankings

New York presents one of the more extreme examples of how the new classification system may alter our understanding of who lives in a particular metropolitan area. But significant changes are evident in other parts of the nation, where new metropolitan areas were created, expanded, or combined.

The demographic consequences of the new system are apparent across the nation's largest metropolitan areas, too. Table 9-7 presents rankings of old and new metropolitan areas (MSAs/PMSAs/NECMAs vs. MetroSAs) by population, income, and educational attributes using Census 2000 data. One immediately apparent change is that New York replaces Los Angeles as the most populated metropolitan area in the country, with nearly 6 million more people than its West Coast counterpart. Dallas's rank, meanwhile, jumps from 10 to 5, due to its combination with Fort Worth. Although Detroit's population increases slightly, its rank declines from 6 to 9. Miami makes it into the top ten (from its previous rank of 24), thanks to its new grouping with Fort Lauderdale and West Palm Beach, whereas Atlanta just misses the top ten, falling to 11 in rank.

The new system also significantly alters the list of wealthiest metropolitan areas, as measured by the share of households with annual income above $75,000. Formerly, half of the top twelve metropolitan areas were in the

TABLE 9-7. Rankings of Old and New Metropolitan Areas, 2000

Rank	OLD MSAs/PMSAs	Total population (000)	Rank	NEW MetroSAs	Total population (000)
1	Los Angeles-Long Beach, CA PMSA	9,519	1	New York-Northern New Jersey-Long Island, NY-NJ-PA	18,323
2	New York, NY PMSA	9,314	2	Los Angeles-Long Beach-Santa Ana, CA	12,366
3	Chicago, IL PMSA	8,273	3	Chicago-Naperville-Joliet, IL-IN-WI	9,098
4	Boston, MA-NH NECMA	6,058	4	Philadelphia-Camden-Wilmington, PA-NJ-DE-MD	5,687
5	Philadelphia, PA-NJ PMSA	5,101	5	Dallas-Fort Worth-Arlington, TX	5,162
6	Detroit, MI PMSA	4,442	6	Miami-Fort Lauderdale-Miami Beach, FL	5,008
7	Washington, DC-MD-VA-WV PMSA	4,923	7	Washington-Arlington-Alexandria, DC-VA-MD-WV	4,796
8	Houston, TX PMSA	4,178	8	Houston-Baytown-Sugar Land, TX	4,715
9	Atlanta, GA MSA	4,112	9	Detroit-Warren-Livonia, MI	4,453
10	Dallas, TX PMSA	3,519	10	Boston-Cambridge-Quincy, MA-NH	4,391
11	Nassau-Suffolk, NY PMSA	2,754	11	Atlanta-Sandy Springs-Marietta, GA	4,248
12	Riverside-San Bernardino, CA PMSA	3,255	12	San Francisco-Oakland-Fremont, CA	4,124
13	Minneapolis-St. Paul, MN-WI MSA	2,969	13	Riverside-San Bernardino-Ontario, CA	3,255
14	San Diego, CA MSA	2,814	14	Phoenix-Mesa-Scottsdale, AZ	3,252
15	St. Louis, MO-IL MSA	2,604	15	Seattle-Tacoma-Bellevue, WA	3,044

Rank	Old MSAs/PMSAs	Households with income over $75,000 (percent)	Rank	New MetroSAs	Households with income over $75,000 (percent)
1	San Jose, CA PMSA	49.6	1	San Jose-Sunnyvale-Santa Clara, CA	49.3
2	Nassau-Suffolk, NY PMSA	45.0	2	Bridgeport-Stamford-Norwalk, CT	43.6
3	Middlesex-Somerset-Hunterdon, NJ PMSA	43.6	3	Washington-Arlington-Alexandria, DC-VA-MD-WV	40.7
4	San Francisco, CA PMSA	42.3	4	San Francisco-Oakland-Fremont, CA	39.9
5	Washington, DC-MD-VA-WV PMSA	40.1	5	Oxnard-Thousand Oaks-Ventura, CA	37.8
6	Bergen-Passaic, NJ PMSA	38.9	6	Trenton-Ewing, NJ	36.1
7	Oakland, CA PMSA	38.1	7	Boulder, CO	35.3
8	Ventura, CA PMSA	37.8	8	Santa Cruz-Watsonville, CA	34.6
9	Orange County, CA PMSA	37.4	9	Boston-Cambridge-Quincy, MA-NH	34.3
10	Newark, NJ PMSA	37.0	10	Ann Arbor, MI	32.8
11	Bridgeport, CT NECMA	36.2	11	Anchorage, AK	32.1
12	Trenton, NJ PMSA	36.1	12	New York-Northern New Jersey-Long Island, NY-NJ-PA	32.0
13	Boulder-Longmont, CO PMSA	35.3	13	Vallejo-Fairfield, CA	31.8
14	Santa Cruz-Watsonville, CA PMSA	34.6	14	Napa, CA	31.8
15	Monmouth-Ocean, NJ PMSA	34.4	15	Hartford-West Hartford-East Hartford, CT	31.7

(continued)

T A B L E   9 - 7 .   Rankings of Old and New Metropolitan Areas, 2000 (continued)

Rank	OLD MSAs/PMSAs	Bachelor's degree or higher (percent)	Rank	NEW MetroSAs	Bachelor's degree or higher (percent)
1	Boulder-Longmont, CO PMSA	52.4	1	Boulder, CO	52.4
2	Iowa City, IA MSA	47.6	2	Ann Arbor, MI	48.1
3	Corvallis, OR MSA	47.4	3	Ithaca, NY	47.5
4	San Francisco, CA PMSA	43.6	4	Corvallis, OR	47.4
5	Lawrence, KS MSA	42.7	5	Ames, IA	44.5
6	Washington, DC-MD-VA-WV PMSA	41.8	6	Lawrence, KS	42.7
7	Columbia, MO MSA	41.7	7	Washington-Arlington-Alexandria, DC-VA-MD-WV	42.5
8	Madison, WI MSA	40.6	8	Iowa City, IA	42.0
9	San Jose, CA PMSA	40.5	9	Bridgeport-Stamford-Norwalk, CT	39.9
10	Charlottesville, VA MSA	40.1	10	Columbia, MO	39.9
11	Santa Fe, NM MSA	39.9	11	San Jose-Sunnyvale-Santa Clara, CA	39.8
12	Bloomington, IN MSA	39.6	12	Fort Collins-Loveland, CO	39.5
13	Fort Collins-Loveland, CO MSA	39.5	13	Durham, NC	38.8
14	Raleigh-Durham-Chapel Hill, NC MSA	38.9	14	San Francisco-Oakland-Fremont, CA	38.8
15	Gainesville, FL MSA	38.7	15	Charlottesville, VA	38.3

Source: Authors' analysis of Census 2000 data.

greater New York region, but because four of these are now incorporated into the New York MetroSA, they leave room for other metropolitan areas to move up the list. Hartford and Anchorage, for example, now break into the top fifteen. Simultaneously, the combination of former PMSAs into the New York-Northern New Jersey-Long Island MetroSA moved New York up in the wealth rankings from 51 to 12.

On the share of adults with at least a bachelor's degree, many college towns are among the highest-ranked metropolitan areas under both the old and new systems, but some ordering did change. The Ann Arbor, MI MetroSA retained only the county from its old PMSA that contains the University of Michigan, elevating it from 19 to 2 in the ranking. Iowa City, on the other hand, added another county outside the University of Iowa, dropping it from 2 to 8. Similarly, Bloomington, Indiana, and Madison, Wisconsin, each added two counties to their metropolitan definitions, causing them to fall out of the top fifteen. And Ithaca, New York, one of the forty-nine new metropolitan areas and home to Cornell University, now ranks 3. Perhaps the most notable change in the educational rankings is the drop that San Francisco took from 4 to 14, due to its combination with Oakland.

In summary, these examples demonstrate that the rules governing metropolitan area definitions may greatly influence our understanding of which regions are biggest, richest, or brightest.

DISCUSSION

The real-world implications of the new metropolitan classifications discussed here have yet to be determined, in large part because many individuals and organizations are still relying on the old (and in some cases, even earlier) definitions in research and practice. Brookings's studies using Census 2000 data still employ the definitions that were in effect at the time of the census. The slow pace at which the new definitions are being put to use reflects in part the OMB's adoption of novel concepts such as micropolitan statistical areas, metropolitan divisions, and combined statistical areas. Revisions during the 1990s, by contrast, merely updated existing concepts with new population data. In any case, whatever effects the new classifications have, they are likely to occur over time as users gradually adapt to this new system.

Moving to the new classification scheme is, at its roots, a statistical policy change, not a programmatic one. In fact, in its guidance announcing the revised definitions, the OMB cautions government agencies against employing the definitions to develop and implement "nonstatistical programs and policies without full consideration of the effects of using these definitions for such purposes." Yet as the new system gains acceptance and wider use, policymakers, researchers, and even the average person may confront a new way of looking at the world—or at least their particular corners of it. Below we discuss the effects that these new metropolitan standards will have on federal policy, research, and the public at large.

Federal Policy

The federal government's use of the metropolitan area concept for purposes other than mere statistical reporting is widespread. This should not be surprising, because the distinctive economic character that metropolitan areas are designed to exhibit makes them good approximations for labor markets, commuter sheds, and air-quality regions. The U.S. Code alone—the federal government's body of law—contains over sixty unique mentions of the phrase "metropolitan statistical area."

Policymakers really put the concept to work, though, in the implementation of federal laws through regulation. Nearly every major federal agency—from those involved in agriculture to homeland security to education—oversees one or more programs that make use of OMB-defined metropolitan areas. Federal agencies typically use the metropolitan area concept as a basis for reporting information, establishing program eligibility, and/or setting program features; an example of each is offered below.[27]

—As a basis for reporting information: Home Mortgage Disclosure Act. Under the regulations that implement the Home Mortgage Disclosure Act (HMDA), federally insured depository institutions must collect information on applications for home mortgage loans. In addition to characteristics of the applicant, the institution must collect information about the property to which the application relates, including its location by metropolitan area, state, county, and census tract. Institutions must compile and report this information to the appropriate banking regulators (for example, the Federal Reserve, the Comptroller of the Currency) annually. Metropolitan areas typically represent the marketplaces within which banks and thrifts operate and thus serve as important geographic frames for evaluating lending performance under other laws related to HMDA, such as fair lending laws and the Community Reinvestment Act. As metropolitan areas change and grow in size, banks and thrifts must change their information and reporting procedures to bring their data—and lending practices—into line with the new metropolitan definitions.

27. State laws and regulations make use of OMB-defined metropolitan areas as well, but we focus on federal policy here to keep the scope reasonable and to comment on policies potentially applicable to all metropolitan areas.

—To establish program eligibility or applicability: Locality Pay Program. U.S. law requires federal pay rates to be comparable with non-federal pay rates for the same level of work within the same local area and for any existing pay disparities between federal and non-federal employees to be eliminated. "Locality pay areas" are places where the Federal Salary Council (FSC) has determined that wage rates should be adjusted. There are a total of thirty-two locality pay areas—thirty-one that coincide generally with metropolitan area definitions and one that encompasses the remainder of the United States. A review of the revised metropolitan standards by the FSC in December 2003 recommended that locality pay areas use the new metropolitan standards and, where available, the combined statistical area. Micropolitan areas are not used unless they are part of a combined metropolitan statistical area. As a result of boundary changes to several metropolitan areas under the new standards, the number of federal employees subject to locality pay adjustments increased.[28]

—To set program features: Medicare. Perhaps no federal program attracts more attention to the OMB's metropolitan definitions than Medicare. This is largely because many of the payments made to providers under Medicare rely on cost data specific to the area in which a provider is located. A hospital's location inside or outside a metropolitan area is used to determine eligibility for various special Medicare designations that can raise reimbursement rates.[29] The most notable example of metropolitan area usage within Medicare policy derives from program reimbursement for hospitals' operating costs based on prospectively set rates specific to each patient diagnosis. In making payments to a particular hospital, the Center for Medicare and Medicaid Services (CMS) adjusts each diagnostic rate by a wage index applicable to the area in which the hospital is located, in order to account for geographic differences in the labor costs hospitals bear. CMS previously defined these areas using MSAs, PMSAs, and NECMAs and used survey data to update the index annually for all metropolitan areas and statewide non-metropolitan areas. Generally, the wage index is higher in urban areas and lower in rural ones, so whether a hospital is located in a metropolitan area receives a great deal of scrutiny.[30]

Recognizing the significant effect that the new metropolitan standards could have on the calculation of the wage index, CMS analyzed the changes

28. The final rule was issued in December 2004. *Federal Register* 69, no. 242 (December 17, 2004): 75451–75453.

29. Many of these special designations afford rural hospitals additional reimbursement.

30. In fact, CMS oversees a Medicare Geographic Classification Review Board to consider special circumstances under which hospitals designated as "rural" can petition to receive an "urban" designation, and vice versa.

to each hospital's wage index that would result, first from constructing separate indexes for hospitals located in each MetroSA, metropolitan division, MicroSA, and statewide non-CBSA, and second from leaving hospitals in MicroSAs as part of a generalized statewide rural index.[31] The final rule opts for considering MicroSAs and statewide non-CBSAs together, in large part because moving to MicroSA-specific indexes could result in large one-time changes to many hospitals' payments, and because many MicroSAs are home to only one hospital, thus limiting the averaging effect of the index across providers. In addition, the final regulation considers metropolitan divisions as separate labor market areas, arguing that they represent the closest approximation to the PMSAs that defined labor market areas under the old system.[32]

Among these three types of uses, federal policymakers employ metropolitan areas most often in the same manner as the "locality pay program" example—to establish whether, by virtue of its location, an individual or community is eligible for a particular program or whether certain regulations apply to individuals, businesses, or governments. Programs that use metropolitan-area characteristics in formulas, as with Medicare, are rarer.[33] However, some agencies use the standards in more than one of these ways. In fact, the locality pay program uses metropolitan-area definitions to designate whether a metropolitan area is part of the program and then indexes pay levels according to local wages.

Nonetheless, the decision to change metropolitan definitions can have far-reaching consequences for these types of programs, and, as a result, some agencies are cautious about adopting the new standards. The Department of Housing and Urban Development (HUD), for example, is responsible for publishing annual "fair market rents" (FMRs) or payment standards for its major housing assistance program (commonly known as Section 8). When HUD announced the proposed FY2005 FMRs in 2004, which used the new metropolitan standards, they received public comments from key interest groups expressing concern that the new definitions produced drastic changes in FMRs in some communities. As a result, HUD decided not to switch immediately to the new OMB metropolitan definitions.

The impact that the new definitions will have on federal programs is still unclear. It will depend not only on the particular characteristics of the metro-

---

31. *Federal Register* 69, no. 96 (May 18, 2004): 28249–28252.
32. *Federal Register* 69, no. 154 (August 11, 2004): 48915–49781.
33. This is somewhat at odds with the notion that as metropolitan areas grow larger, they become eligible for more federal funds. See, for example, Chris Poynter, "Louisville Makes Gains on Federal Map; Area's Growth Opens Doors for More Funding, Businesses," *Louisville Courier-Journal,* June 10, 2003, p. 1A.

politan areas undergoing changes, but also on how lawmakers and rulemakers integrate the new concepts into existing systems. In this regard, the OMB offered more explicit guidance to federal agencies that use metropolitan areas for nonstatistical purposes.[34] The OMB urges agencies that had used PMSAs to now consider using metropolitan divisions, which it describes as the "comparable geographic units of classification." In addition, it suggests that in cases where old metropolitan areas divided into more than one new metropolitan area, the CSA may form a "more appropriate geographic unit for analytic and program purposes." Whether agencies will take these suggestions to heart or opt for the more straightforward use of MetroSAs alone may in the end dictate the pace at which the new definitions are adopted, and the extent to which programmatic changes result.

Research

As the OMB's suggestions indicate, one implication of the new metropolitan classification system is that researchers now have more choices. Under the old system, metropolitan researchers typically analyzed MSAs together with either CMSAs or PMSAs. The new system offers, at the local level, the opportunity to examine MetroSAs, metropolitan divisions, CSAs, and MicroSAs. In addition, the growth of metropolitan America has produced a greater number of MetroSAs than MSAs and PMSAs and more metropolitan principal cities than central cities.

A potentially expansive research community, including federal and state agencies, nonprofit research organizations, and private sector market researchers, will use the new metropolitan classifications. The federal statistical agencies themselves will influence the speed at which other researchers move toward the new system and the choices that researchers make within that system.

The greater number of choices available to researchers under the new system may carry both advantages and disadvantages. On the one hand, researchers may now have access to data that conform more closely to their geographic areas of interest. On the other hand, as different metropolitan researchers choose to focus on different classifications, it may become more difficult to compare across their findings. Some, as the OMB suggests, may choose to work with metropolitan divisions for comparability with PMSAs.[35]

---

34. Office of Management and Budget (2004).

35. One private sector firm, ACCRA, readily adopted metropolitan divisions to analyze cost-of-living differences among U.S. metropolitan areas. ACCRA and Fargo Cass County Economic Development Corporation (2004).

Others may work with MetroSAs alone, or in combination with MicroSAs. Rural experts may focus only on non-CBSAs or on non-CBSAs together with MicroSAs. This flexibility can enrich the field of inquiry, but it will become even more important for researchers to state their methodology clearly and explain why they have chosen a particular geographic frame. As discussed above, it is advised that national rankings of metropolitan areas and micropolitan areas employ the MetroSAs and MicroSAs rather than CSAs or metropolitan divisions.

Regardless of their views on the classification system itself, researchers should welcome the new metropolitan definitions for their basis in up-to-date census data on population, urbanization, and commuting patterns. These new areas exhibit a greater degree of economic and social cohesion today than do the old metropolitan definitions, which were rooted primarily in 1990 census data. The new methods for defining metropolitan areas and principal cities are also simpler than under the old system and help resolve some of the odder outcomes apparent in the 1999 definitions (such as King George County, Virginia, appearing in the Washington, D.C., metropolitan area).

What changes might the new system produce in actual research results? In this chapter, we have offered a look at how certain demographic and economic indicators at the metropolitan level differ when viewed through the old and new lenses. For the most part, the notable differences are limited to a few large metropolitan areas that underwent significant definitional changes, such as New York, San Francisco, Dallas, and Raleigh-Durham. In many other areas, such as Atlanta, Portland, Oregon, Wichita, and Washington, D.C., the addition, subtraction, or "relegation" to micropolitan areas of smaller counties at the metropolitan fringe does not do much to influence the overall empirical picture.

Popular Usage

The new system may, at least in the long run, exert as much influence on popular understanding of metropolitan areas as on researchers' understanding. Popular notions of metropolitan areas are shaped not only by their geographic makeup but also by name recognition. Both may contribute to the economic and social identity of local residents, businesses, and governments.

With respect to their geographic makeup, it is not surprising that the new metropolitan definitions are still "off the radar" in large swaths of metropolitan America, given that the policy and research communities have yet to completely embrace the changes. In part, this is because institutions such as regional media and chambers of commerce mediate between what the federal government decides is a metropolitan area and what average citizens consider to be their region. Newspaper "Metro" sections, for example, typically report on jurisdictions in which they have a substantial subscriber base. Thus, news in the *Washington Post* covers roughly fourteen counties rather than the eighteen that make up the Washington-Arlington-Alexandria, DC-MD-VA-WV MetroSA. The Mid-America Regional Council, the metropolitan planning organization for greater Kansas City, is composed of eight counties, whereas the new Kansas City, MO-KS MetroSA contains fifteen counties.

At the same time, several of the metropolitan areas that underwent significant changes might find more local receptivity than their older versions. The old New York PMSA, consisting of the five city boroughs and three upstate New York counties, bore little relation to the average citizen's conception of the metropolitan area. The revised New York MetroSA, which captures suburban Long Island and much of northern New Jersey, probably comes much closer. Similarly, the Los Angeles metropolitan area, which before included only Los Angeles County, now takes in Orange County as well, better reflecting the economic ties between these two jurisdictions.

Names, however, seem to carry even more weight than geographic composition in the public eye. The status of suburban places like Sandy Springs, Georgia, near Atlanta; Sugar Land, Texas, near Houston; Edison, New Jersey, outside New York; and Naperville, Illinois, outside Chicago, was immediately elevated when each found a spot in their respective metropolitan area's name.[36] Although some of those places might earn greater acceptance as a result, other revisions caused confusion and dismay. Consultations with local officials resulted in the OMB changing the New York-Newark-Edison, NY-NJ-PA MetroSA to the New York-Northern New Jersey-Long Island, NY-NJ-PA MetroSA in December 2003. Public opinion simultaneously dislodged Cheektowaga and Tonawanda, New York, both principal cities in the Buffalo metropolitan area, from that area's name in favor of the fourth-largest principal city, Niagara Falls, which is both a tourist destination and source of regional identity.

Of course, the power of a name is even more evident in micropolitan areas and new metropolitan areas. Hundreds of smaller counties and towns formerly part of "rural America" suddenly acquired their own identity and increased attention from researchers and businesses.[37] Even counties that

36. Haya El Nasser, "Metro Area's Suburbs Make Name for Themselves," *USA Today*, July 22, 2003, p. A3.

37. Laurent Belsie, "Small Rural Towns Get New Name—and New Attention," *Christian Science Monitor*, June 20, 3003, p. 2.

formerly resided at the fringe of large metropolitan areas, like Ashtabula, Ohio, formerly in the Cleveland metropolitan area, and Nye, Nevada, formerly in the Las Vegas metropolitan area, may gain more stature from a micropolitan label than they lost in separating from a metropolitan center.

These examples of definitional changes demonstrate that federal statistical policy can affect how we live and work. In the end, both research and policy have an important role to play in bridging the gap between the statistical versions of metropolitan areas and the popular notions of the regions in which metropolitan residents live. To the extent that research can narrow that gap over time, metropolitan-level research will provide greater insights for government and business decisions. The OMB's new metropolitan classification system thus presents both a unique challenge and a fresh opportunity for metropolitan research to make an impact.

APPENDIX 9A. DEFINITIONS OF METROPOLITAN CONCEPTS

Old Standards

Consolidated metropolitan statistical areas (CMSAs) consisted of a metropolitan area with at least 1 million people in which two or more primary metropolitan areas (PMSAs) had been identified. There were eighteen CMSAs in effect for Census 2000.

Primary metropolitan statistical areas (PMSAs) consisted of those counties or groups of counties within a large metropolitan area (at least 1 million people) that contained at least 100,000 people and met criteria for separate designations. There were seventy-three PMSAs in effect for Census 2000.

Metropolitan statistical areas (MSAs) contained cities or urbanized areas with at least 50,000 people. Counties were included or excluded in the MSA based on employment, commuting, and population density criteria. There were 258 MSAs in effect for Census 2000.

New England county metropolitan areas (NECMAs) were defined as county-based alternatives to the standard city- and town-based metropolitan areas in the six New England states (Connecticut, Maine, Massachusetts, New Hampshire, Rhode Island, and Vermont). There were twelve NECMAs in effect for Census 2000.

Central cities were defined for each MSA and CMSA. The largest incorporated place (or, in a few cases, census-designated place) in a metropolitan area was automatically designated a central city. Additional cities were included if they met population and employment criteria. There were 554 central cities in effect for Census 2000.

New Standards

Metropolitan statistical areas (MetroSAs) contain at least one urbanized area with at least 50,000 people (the "core"). Counties are included or excluded in the metropolitan area based on commuting criteria. There are 361 MetroSAs.

Metropolitan statistical areas of 2.5 million or more may be divided into *metropolitan divisions.* Metropolitan divisions consist of one or more counties that represent an employment center plus adjacent counties with strong commuting ties to the core. There are eleven MetroSAs with divisions, for a total of twenty-nine divisions.

Micropolitan statistical areas (MicroSAs) contain at least one urban cluster with between 10,000 and 50,000 people (the "core"). Counties are included or excluded in the micropolitan area based on commuting criteria. There are 573 micropolitan areas.

New England city and town areas (NECTAs) are defined as conceptually similar to the county-based metropolitan and micropolitan areas, but with cities and towns as the building blocks rather than counties. There are twenty-one metropolitan NECTAs and twenty-two micropolitan NECTAs.

Metropolitan statistical areas and micropolitan statistical areas may be joined to form *combined statistical areas (CSAs).* CSAs consist of two or more adjacent core-based statistical areas (CBSAs)—metropolitan or micropolitan or a combination of both—that meet employment interchange criteria. There are 120 CSAs.

Principal cities are defined for each CBSA. The largest city in a CBSA is automatically designated a principal city. Other cities may be designated if they meet certain criteria for population and employment. There are 1,255 principal cities.

TABLE 9A-1. Metropolitan Statistical Areas with Populations of 500,000 or Greater, New Standards, 2000

Rank	Metropolitan statistical area	Population
1	New York–Northern New Jersey–Long Island, NY-NJ-PA	18,323,002
2	Los Angeles–Long Beach–Santa Ana, CA	12,365,627
3	Chicago-Naperville-Joliet, IL-IN-WI	9,098,316
4	Philadelphia-Camden-Wilmington, PA-NJ-DE-MD	5,687,147
5	Dallas-Fort Worth-Arlington, TX	5,161,544
6	Miami-Fort Lauderdale-Miami Beach, FL	5,007,564
7	Washington-Arlington-Alexandria, DC-VA-MD-WV	4,796,183
8	Houston-Baytown-Sugar Land, TX	4,715,407
9	Detroit-Warren-Livonia, MI	4,452,557
10	Boston-Cambridge-Quincy, MA-NH	4,391,344
11	Atlanta-Sandy Springs-Marietta, GA	4,247,981
12	San Francisco-Oakland-Fremont, CA	4,123,740
13	Riverside-San Bernardino-Ontario, CA	3,254,821
14	Phoenix-Mesa-Scottsdale, AZ	3,251,876
15	Seattle-Tacoma-Bellevue, WA	3,043,878
16	Minneapolis-St. Paul-Bloomington, MN-WI	2,968,806
17	San Diego-Carlsbad-San Marcos, CA	2,813,833
18	St. Louis, MO-IL	2,698,687
19	Baltimore-Towson, MD	2,552,994
20	Pittsburgh, PA	2,431,087
21	Tampa-St. Petersburg–Clearwater, FL	2,395,997
22	Denver-Aurora, CO	2,157,756
23	Cleveland-Elyria-Mentor, OH	2,148,143
24	Cincinnati-Middletown, OH-KY-IN	2,009,632
25	Portland-Vancouver-Beaverton, OR-WA	1,927,881
26	Kansas City, MO-KS	1,836,038
27	Sacramento-Arden-Arcade-Roseville, CA	1,796,857
28	San Jose-Sunnyvale-Santa Clara, CA	1,735,819
29	San Antonio, TX	1,711,703
30	Orlando, FL	1,644,561
31	Columbus, OH	1,612,694
32	Providence-New Bedford-Fall River, RI-MA	1,582,997
33	Virginia Beach-Norfolk-Newport News, VA-NC	1,576,370
34	Indianapolis, IN	1,525,104
35	Milwaukee-Waukesha-West Allis, WI	1,500,741
36	Las Vegas-Paradise, NV	1,375,765
37	Charlotte-Gastonia-Concord, NC-SC	1,330,448
38	New Orleans-Metairie-Kenner, LA	1,316,510
39	Nashville-Davidson-Murfreesboro, TN	1,311,789
40	Austin-Round Rock, TX	1,249,763
41	Memphis, TN-MS-AR	1,205,204
42	Buffalo-Niagara Falls, NY	1,170,111
43	Louisville, KY-IN	1,161,975
44	Hartford-West Hartford-East Hartford, CT	1,148,618
45	Jacksonville, FL	1,122,750
46	Richmond, VA	1,096,957
47	Oklahoma City, OK	1,095,421
48	Birmingham-Hoover, AL	1,052,238
49	Rochester, NY	1,037,831
50	Salt Lake City, UT	968,858
51	Bridgeport-Stamford-Norwalk, CT	882,567
52	Honolulu, HI	876,156

(continued)

TABLE 9A-1. Metropolitan Statistical Areas with Populations of 500,000 or Greater, New Standards, 2000 (*continued*)

Rank	Metropolitan statistical area	Population
53	Tulsa, OK	859,532
54	Dayton, OH	848,153
55	Tucson, AZ	843,746
56	Albany-Schenectady-Troy, NY	825,875
57	New Haven-Milford, CT	824,008
58	Fresno, CA	799,407
59	Raleigh-Cary, NC	797,071
60	Omaha-Council Bluffs, NE-IA	767,041
61	Oxnard-Thousand Oaks-Ventura, CA	753,197
62	Worcester, MA	750,963
63	Grand Rapids-Wyoming, MI	740,482
64	Allentown-Bethlehem-Easton, PA-NJ	740,395
65	Albuquerque, NM	729,649
66	Baton Rouge, LA	705,973
67	Akron, OH	694,960
68	Springfield, MA	680,014
69	El Paso, TX	679,622
70	Bakersfield, CA	661,645
71	Toledo, OH	659,188
72	Syracuse, NY	650,154
73	Columbia, SC	647,158
74	Greensboro-High Point, NC	643,430
75	Poughkeepsie-Newburgh-Middletown, NY	621,517
76	Knoxville, TN	616,079
77	Little Rock-North Little Rock, AR	610,518
78	Youngstown-Warren-Boardman, OH-PA	602,964
79	Sarasota-Bradenton-Venice, FL	589,959
80	Wichita, KS	571,166
81	McAllen-Edinburg-Pharr, TX	569,463
82	Stockton, CA	563,598
83	Scranton-Wilkes-Barre, PA	560,625
84	Greenville, SC	559,940
85	Charleston-North Charleston, SC	549,033
86	Colorado Springs, CO	537,484
87	Harrisburg-Carlisle, PA	509,074
88	Madison, WI	501,774

Source: Authors' analysis of Census 2000 data.

REFERENCES

ACCRA and Fargo Cass County Economic Development Corporation. 2004. "ACCRA Cost of Living Index."

Berube, Alan, and William H. Frey. 2002. "A Decade of Mixed Blessings: Urban and Suburban Poverty in Census 2000." Brookings.

Brown, David L., and Louis E. Swanson, eds. 2004. *Challenges for Rural America in the Twenty-First Century.* State College: Pennsylvania State University Press.

Fitzsimmons, James D., and Michael R. Ratcliffe. 2004. "Reflections on the Review of Metropolitan Area Standards in the United States, 1990–2000." In *New Forms of Urbanization: Beyond the Urban-Rural Dichotomy,* edited by Tony Champion and Graeme Hugo. Burlington, Vt.: Ashgate Publishing.

Frey, William H. 2001. "Melting Pot Suburbs: A Census 2000 Study of Suburban Diversity." Brookings.

———. 2004a. "Micropolitan America: Small Is Interesting." *Milken Institute Review,* April.

———. 2004b. "The Fading of City-Suburb and Metro-Nonmetro Distinctions in the United States." In *New Forms of Urbanization: Beyond the Urban-Rural Dichotomy,* edited by Tony Champion and Graeme Hugo. Burlington, Vt.: Ashgate Publishing.

Frey, William H., and Alan Berube. 2002. "City Families and Suburban Singles: An Emerging Household Story from Census 2000." Brookings.

Frey, William H., and Alden Speare, 1995. "Metropolitan Areas as Functional Communities." In *Metropolitan And Nonmetropolitan Areas: New Approaches To Geographic Definition,* edited by Donald C. Dahmann and James D. Fitzsimmons. Washington: U.S. Department of Commerce.

Johnson, Kenneth M. 1999. "The Rural Rebound." *PRB Reports on America.* Washington: Population Reference Bureau.

Office of Management and Budget. 2000. "Standards for Defining Metropolitan and Micropolitan Statistical Areas." *Federal Register* 65, no. 249 (December 27): 82227–82238.

———. 2004. "Update of Statistical Area Definitions and Additional Guidance on Their Uses." Bulletin No. 04–03. February 18.

Singer, Audrey. 2004. "The Rise of New Immigrant Gateways." Brookings.

Suro, Roberto, and Audrey Singer. 2002. "Latino Growth in Metropolitan America: Changing Patterns, New Locations." Brookings.

U.S. General Accounting Office. 2004. *Metropolitan Statistical Areas: New Standards and Their Impact on Selected Federal Programs.* GAO-04–758.

10

Micropolitan America: A Brand New Geography

ROBERT E. LANG AND DAWN DHAVALE

"Micropolitan areas" represent a new category of places introduced by the U.S. Office of Management and Budget (OMB) in June 2003.[1] As the prefix "micro" implies, these places are generally (but not always) less populous than metropolitan areas. In particular, micropolitan principal cities are smaller than metropolitan cores; whereas the former range from 10,000 to 50,000 people, the latter must exceed 50,000 residents.[2] Because the concept is so recent, there is no significant literature on micropolitan areas. This chapter establishes baseline data on the size, growth rate, and location of micropolitan areas.

Micropolitan areas can be populous regions without big centers, whereas metropolitan areas may have big centers that are surrounded by little additional population. A place is defined as "metropolitan" or "micropolitan" based on the size of its center rather than total population. This raises an interesting question regarding the definition of "urban." The traditional view holds that a large core city anchors subsequent suburbanization and creates

1. OMB (2003). This new designation uses 2000 data as a reference point. In 2000, the new "core-based statistical area" (CBSA) replaced metropolitan statistical areas (MSAs), consolidated metropolitan statistical areas (CMSAs), and primary metropolitan statistical areas (PMSAs). CBSAs define both micropolitan and metropolitan areas.

2. The OMB definition for a micropolitan area is "at least one urban cluster of at least 10,000 but less than 50,000 in population," although more than 50,000 residents can live in the entire micropolitan statistical area. Like metropolitan areas, micropolitan areas are constructed from counties containing the population center, and those that have commuting relationships with the central county.

a metropolitan area. But micropolitan areas reverse this standard pattern: they grow to metropolitan scale without a large central city.

Some of the largest micropolitan areas are more than just overgrown small towns—they appear to be exemplars of a new decentralized or even countrified city. Most research on decentralized cities (for example, edge cities and edgeless cities) looks at the places that have grown next to traditional cores, such as Tysons Corner, Virginia, outside of Washington, D.C.[3] Yet the "suburban" growth in big micropolitan areas is not outside anything, because there is no real center, no urban area to be a suburb of. Micropolitan areas therefore represent a new metropolitan form with an expansive periphery and a relatively small core.

METHODOLOGY

In the study described in this chapter, we looked at the 567 micropolitan areas that lie within the continental United States, excluding those in Alaska, Hawaii, and Puerto Rico, which tend to be outliers. For example, there are remote Alaskan micropolitan areas that are actually closer to Seattle than Anchorage. In Hawaii, three entire islands are micropolitan areas.

This chapter focuses on three basic dimensions of place—size, growth, and location. Micropolitan area location is especially important because it significantly affects the first two qualities. Our analysis shows that micropolitan areas proximate to big metropolitan areas tend to be bigger and faster-growing, whereas the more remote places are often smaller and slower growing. This finding is consistent with geographer Calvin Beale's work that established remoteness as a critical indicator of metropolitan development.[4]

This chapter uses a remoteness indicator that measures the distance between the center of a micropolitan area and the center of a "big" metropolitan area. "Big" is defined as metropolitan areas with more than 1 million residents, which describes the fifty most populous U.S. regions, which range in size from Richmond, Virginia, with just 1 million, to New York, with over 21 million people.

Big metropolitan areas account for almost three-quarters of the U.S. population and are home to key transportation infrastructure, such as hub airports. Being distant from these places puts remote micropolitan areas at a distinct disadvantage. The twenty-five most remote micropolitan areas are at least 275 miles from a big metropolitan area, which means that their

---

3. Garreau (1991); Lang (2003).
4. Beale (1990).

residents must drive four or more hours to reach big-city services and amenities.

We can measure the suburb-to-city-center relationship in both metropolitan and micropolitan areas. The ratio of a center city's population to that of its suburbs has been tracked back to 1910.[5] In the first decade of the twentieth century, central cities dominated the metropolis, accounting for three-quarters of all people in the region. By 2000, the roles had been reversed, with just 37.7 percent of metropolitan residents living in central cities. But our analysis of micropolitan areas reveals that their central cities are even more modest relative to their suburbs: only 31.6 percent of micropolitan area residents live in their cores.

FINDINGS

With 567 micropolitan areas in the United States as a whole and one in nearly every state in the union, there is inevitably a great deal of variation in the geographic and demographic profile of micropolitan America.

Micros and Metros Together Cover More Than Half of the U.S. Land Area

The addition of micropolitan areas places more of the United States into urban areas (or "centered" as opposed to "noncentered" areas). In 1890, the U.S. census-designated frontier closed as settlement swept into remote corners of the nation. By the 1920s, the majority of the United States was, for the first time, urban. By 1950, more than half the U.S. population lived in metropolitan areas. As of the 1970 census, the United States had become a suburban-dominated nation, with more than half of all metropolitan residents living outside central cities.[6]

Now a new milestone has been reached: as of 2000, rural areas ("non-core-based areas") cover less than half the continental United States. The eastern half of the United States (east of the 98th meridian, which roughly divides the continental United States into equal east/west halves (see figure 9-2, page 194) is now substantially covered by metropolitan and micropolitan areas. The only expansive spaces left in the East without micropolitan areas are the upper Great Lakes, northern Maine, and the central Appalachian Mountains. A state such as Vermont, which has few metropolitan counties,

5. U.S. Census Bureau (2002).
6. Katz and Lang (2003).

is full of micropolitan ones. Midwestern and Southern states from Michigan to Mississippi now have their metropolitan areas complimented by substantial micropolitan zones. The urban coverage of the East is so extensive that those who travel Interstate 95 from Maine to Florida pass through only five counties that are not part of either metropolitan or micropolitan areas.

By contrast, major stretches of the West are without either micropolitan or metropolitan areas. The Great Plains and the northern Rockies maintain huge rural areas. However, the Interstate highways that pass through the Rockies and Great Plains often are lined with multiple micropolitan areas. This preliminary finding raises interesting questions regarding the role that transportation plays in micropolitan development. The differences between East and West also hint at the role that micropolitan areas play in regional development. In the East, micropolitan areas seem to be lower-density extensions of metropolitan areas, whereas many Western micropolitan areas are stand-alone central places with vast rural hinterlands.

Population Growth in Micropolitan Areas Lags National Average

Micropolitan "principal cities" range from 10,000 to 50,000 residents. Torrington, Connecticut (population 181,193), is the most populous micropolitan area in the United States, whereas Andrews, Texas (population 13,004), is the least populated one (see table 10A-1 in the appendix for the complete list of micropolitan areas). Most micropolitan areas lie in the South (43 percent) and the Midwest (34 percent). The West and Northeast together account for just one-fifth of all micropolitan areas (15 and 9 percent, respectively).

In terms of urban qualities, micropolitan areas fall between metropolitan and rural areas. They lack the large central city (over 50,000 residents) that satisfies the OMB's criterion for designation as a metropolitan area. In contrast, micropolitan areas have cities that compare with modest-sized towns. Yet big micropolitan areas can exceed small metropolitan areas in total population. In fact, Torrington, Conn., is larger than 103 metropolitan areas (out of 276).

Collectively, micropolitan areas account for 690 of the 3,141 U.S. counties. Over 28.3 million people, or one in ten Americans, live in micropolitan areas. Just over a fifth of U.S. counties are micropolitan, whereas metropolitan areas account for over a third. Most micropolitan areas (477) are made up of just one county. There are seventy-seven two-county micropolitan areas and seventeen three-county ones; just two have four counties.

Population growth in micropolitan areas lags significantly behind that of the United States as a whole. The United States grew 13.2 percent in the 1990s, whereas micropolitan areas gained just 7.9 percent more residents. Micropolitan areas were even further behind the nation's urban population (combining urbanized areas and urban clusters), which added 18.9 percent more people from 1990 to 2000. Despite the overall gains, just under a fifth (17 percent, or 93 out of 567) of micropolitan areas actually lost population between 1990 and 2000. This roughly corresponds to the performance of rural areas, where a quarter of counties also suffered population declines in the 1990s.[7]

In 2000, the average micropolitan area reached 51,179 in population (from 46,596 people in 1990); the median micropolitan area had 42,902 residents in 2000 (from 38,823 in 1990). The median distance of a micropolitan area to a big metropolitan area is 104 miles, whereas the average is 127 miles. Of course, there is considerable variation among micropolitan areas (see below).

Given the unwieldy number of micropolitan areas, the remainder of the analysis focuses on the top and bottom ten micropolitan areas by size, population change, and remoteness. Note that several micropolitan areas appear on more than one list.

Table 10-1 shows the ten most populated micropolitan areas as of 2000. As noted above, the top micropolitan area on the list outranks the 103 smallest metropolitan areas. Even the tenth-ranked micropolitan area is more populous than the fifty-nine least populated metropolitan areas. Almost half of the micropolitan areas on the list (including the top two) are in the Northeast, which is interesting because the region has the fewest micropolitan areas overall. We label these places "minimetros," because they are clearly not "micro" versions of the metropolis; in fact, the top few cases are more like medium-sized metropolitan areas.

The least populated micropolitan areas, or "smallvilles," are displayed at the bottom of table 10-1. None of these places is in the Northeast, whereas six are in Texas alone. Eight smallvilles lost population in the 1990s, which means that some could eventually lose their micropolitan status and become simply rural. Smallvilles are also remote—all ten are well past the median and average distance from big metropolitan areas.

The Fastest-Growing Micropolitan Areas Are Near Booming Metropolitan Areas

Most fast-growing micropolitan areas are in the shadow of big booming metropolitan areas like Las Vegas, Jacksonville, Florida, and Denver (table 10-2). Almost all are in fast-growing parts of the country, with none in the Northeast

7. McGranahan and Beale (2002).

TABLE 10-1. Largest and Smallest Micropolitan Areas, 2000

Rank	Micropolitan area	Population 1990	Population 2000	1990–2000 change (percent)	Closest metro area[a]	Distance (miles)
Minimetros						
1	Torrington, CT	174,092	182,193	4.7	Hartford	34.0
2	Lebanon, NH-VT	155,133	167,387	7.9	Boston	96.5
3	Seaford, DE	113,229	156,638	38.3	Baltimore	78.9
4	Lake Havasu City, AZ	93,497	155,032	65.8	Las Vegas	78.2
5	Ottawa-Streator, IL	148,331	153,098	3.2	Chicago	73.2
6	Pottsville, PA	152,585	150,336	−1.5	Philadelphia	72.1
7	Lexington, NC	126,677	147,246	16.2	Charlotte	47.8
8	Hilton Head Island, SC	101,912	141,615	39.0	Jacksonville	162.6
9	Daphne-Fairhope, AL	98,280	140,415	42.9	New Orleans	145.7
10	Jamestown-Dunkirk, NY	141,895	139,750	−1.5	Buffalo	53.2
Smallvilles						
558	Spirit Lake, IA	14,909	16,424	10.2	Minneapolis	154.7
559	Snyder, TX	18,634	16,361	−12.2	Dallas	248.0
560	Sweetwater, TX	16,594	15,802	−4.8	Austin	215.6
561	Heber, UT	10,089	15,215	50.8	Salt Lake City	45.4
562	Lamesa, TX	14,349	14,985	4.4	Austin	306.3
563	Vernon, TX	15,121	14,676	−2.9	Oklahoma City	133.8
564	Tallulah, LA	12,463	13,728	10.2	New Orleans	195.7
565	Vermillion, SD	13,186	13,537	2.7	Minneapolis	243.8
566	Pecos, TX	15,852	13,137	−17.1	San Antonio	328.7
567	Andrews, TX	14,338	13,004	−9.3	San Antonio	314.7

Source: Authors' calculations of Census 2000 and ArcView GIS analysis.
a. Top fifty metropolitan areas.

and only one in the Midwest. The biggest boomtown, Arizona's Lake Havasu City, is also a minimetro. This micropolitan area grew as a bedroom community to Laughlin, which is Nevada's southernmost gambling center. Another fast-growing micropolitan area includes Branson in southern Missouri, which is the nation's largest venue for country music and the only Midwestern boomtown.

The fastest-shrinking micropolitan areas ("dwindlevilles") are almost entirely in the South, with only one in the Midwest. Most are in the parts of these regions that are losing people, including the Great Plains (Pecos and Borger, Texas) and the Mid-South (Blytheville, Arkansas, and Fort Polk South, Louisiana). Many dwindlevilles are also more remote than average, including five that are more than 200 miles from the nearest big metropolitan area.[8]

8. For a discussion of Great Plains population loss, see Lang, Popper, and Popper (1997), and for population loss in the Mid-South see Lang and Rengert (2001).

TABLE 10-2. Fastest Growing and Declining Micropolitan Areas, 1990–2000

		Population				
Rank	Micropolitan aea	1990	2000	1990-2000 change (percent)	Closest metro area[a]	Distance (miles)
Boomtowns						
1	Silverthorne, CO	12,881	23,548	82.8	Denver	65.3
2	Pahrump, NV	17,781	32,485	82.7	Las Vegas	145.6
3	Edwards, CO	27,935	49,471	77.1	Denver	90.1
4	Palm Coast, FL	28,701	49,832	73.6	Jacksonville	62.1
5	The Villages, FL	31,577	53,345	68.9	Tampa	37.9
6	Jackson, WY-ID	14,611	24,250	66.0	Salt Lake City	242.2
7	Lake Havasu City, AZ	93,497	155,032	65.8	Las Vegas	78.2
8	Cedar City, UT	20,789	33,779	62.5	Las Vegas	160.2
9	Branson, MO	44,639	68,361	53.1	Kansas City	165.4
10	Heber, UT	10,089	15,215	50.8	Salt Lake City	45.4
Dwindlevilles						
558	Borger, TX	25,689	23,857	−7.1	Oklahoma City	221.1
559	Greenville, MS	67,935	62,977	−7.3	Memphis	136.1
560	Morgan City, LA	58,086	53,500	−7.9	New Orleans	98.3
561	West Helena, AR	28,838	26,445	−8.3	Memphis	69.6
562	Marquette, MI	70,887	64,634	−8.8	Milwaukee	227.8
563	Andrews, TX	14,338	13,004	−9.3	San Antonio	314.7
564	Blytheville, AR	57,525	51,979	−9.6	Memphis	46.5
565	Snyder, TX	18,634	16,361	−12.2	Dallas	248.0
566	Fort Polk South, LA	61,961	52,531	−15.2	Houston	164.0
567	Pecos, TX	15,852	13,137	−17.1	San Antonio	328.7

Source: Authors' calculations of Census 2000 and ArcView GIS analysis.
a. Top fifty metropolitan areas.

Western Micropolitan Areas Are the Most Remote, But Some Are Booming

Only one of the ten "nearburg" micropolitan areas closest to big metropolitan areas were losing population in the 1990s (table 10-3). In fact, five nearburgs are gaining at or above double-digit growth rates, including two just outside of Milwaukee. This finding hints at the possibility that nearburgs are really extensions of peripheral metropolitan development, which even in the Rust Belt often translates into fast population gains at the edge.[9] Interestingly, not one nearburg is in the West.

Although the West includes no nearburgs, all of the ten most remote "lonesometown" micropolitan areas are in the West or in the Great Plains section of the Midwest. That all of the lonesometowns are west of the 98th meridian is consistent with previous work that finds a big settlement split between East and West dating back to the 1840s. Lang argues that the East

9. Lang (2003).

TABLE 10-3. **Micropolitan Areas Nearest and Furthest from a Major Metropolitan Area**

Rank	Micropolitan area	Population 1990	Population 2000	1990–2000 change (percent)	Closest metro area[a]	Distance (miles)
Nearburgs						
1	Willimantic, CT	102,525	109,091	6.4	Providence	24.4
2	Albemarle, NC	51,765	58,100	12.2	Charlotte	25.2
3	Lancaster, SC	54,516	61,351	12.5	Charlotte	27.7
4	Batavia, NY	60,060	60,370	0.5	Rochester	31.1
5	Beaver Dam, WI	76,559	85,897	12.2	Milwaukee	31.3
6	Mount Vernon, OH	47,473	54,500	14.8	Columbus	32.6
7	Watertown, WI	67,783	74,021	9.2	Milwaukee	33.3
8	Torrington, CT	174,092	182,193	4.7	Hartford	34.0
9	Indiana, PA	89,994	89,605	−0.4	Pittsburgh	35.3
10	Marion, OH	64,274	66,217	3.0	Columbus	35.6
Lonesometowns						
558	Hobbs, NM	55,765	55,511	−0.5	San Antonio	371.7
559	Kalispell, MT	59,218	74,471	25.8	Seattle	376.9
560	Sheridan, WY	23,562	26,560	12.7	Salt Lake City	388.9
561	Carlsbad-Artesia, NM	48,605	51,658	6.3	San Antonio	401.4
562	Roswell, NM	57,849	61,382	6.1	Denver	417.6
563	Helena, MT	55,434	65,765	18.6	Salt Lake City	434.7
564	Minot, ND	67,609	67,392	−0.3	Minneapolis	449.0
565	Dickinson, ND	23,940	23,524	−1.7	Minneapolis	487.6
566	Williston, ND	21,129	19,761	−6.5	Minneapolis	539.6
567	Havre, MT	17,654	16,673	−5.6	Seattle	557.3

Source: Authors' calculations of Census 2000 and ArcView GIS analysis
a. Top fifty metropolitan areas

saw contiguous settlement that ran on a continuum from small towns to big cities, whereas the West experienced a more broken settlement pattern wherein big cities often remain surrounded by empty spaces.[10] This settlement split connects Eastern micropolitan areas to metropolitan areas and isolates Western ones.

Yet some of the West's isolated places are booming, such as Helena and Kalispell, Montana, due to their attraction as tourist destinations.[11] By contrast, the cold, flat, agriculture-dominated northern Great Plains micropolitan areas in North Dakota and Eastern Montana are losing people.

"Middleburgs" represent the average micropolitan area and can be used to gauge the extremes within each of these top-ten lists (table 10-4). The

10. Lang, Popper, and Popper (1995, 1997); Lang (2002).
11. For more discussion see Rengert and Lang (2001), who divided the Intermountain West into "cowboy" counties (or resource-based economies) and "cappuccino" counties (or places with tourism and retirees). They found that the cappuccino counties grew much faster than the cowboy ones.

T A B L E   1 0 - 4 .   Micropolitan Areas Between Mean and Median on Size, Growth, and Distance from a Major Metropolitan Area

		Population				
Rank	Micropolitan area	1990	2000	1990–2000 change (percent)	Closest metro area[a]	Distance (miles)
Middleburgs						
1	Coldwater, MI	41,502	45,787	10.3	Detroit	105.4
2	Glasgow, KY	42,964	48,070	11.9	Nashville	77.3
3	Jacksonville, TX	41,049	46,659	13.7	Dallas	112.4
4	McAlester, OK	40,581	43,953	8.3	Oklahoma City	104.1
5	Mount Vernon, IL	45,519	48,666	6.9	St. Louis	90.6
6	Paris, TX	43,949	48,499	10.4	Dallas	88.7
7	Plymouth, IN	42,182	45,128	7.0	Chicago	90.4
8	Rochelle, IL	45,957	51,032	11.0	Chicago	75.0
9	Sidney, OH	44,915	47,910	6.7	Columbus	70.8
10	Washington, NC	42,283	44,958	6.3	Virginia Beach	96.2

Source: Authors' calculations of Census 2000 and ArcView GIS analysis.

a. Top fifty metropolitan areas.

micropolitan areas on this list fall between the mean and the median on population, growth, and distance. Interestingly, they are located equally in the West and South, representing the larger geographic distribution of all micropolitan areas. Although these micropolitan areas all are average in terms of their characteristics, it should be noted that there is great diversity in micropolitan areas. Middleburgs are a useful reference point, but they should not be considered representative of the bulk of micropolitan areas in the United States.

CONCLUSION

The designation of micropolitan areas addresses a long-standing concern among rural advocates that many smaller—although important—cities fall below the Census Bureau's metropolitan area category. These advocates lobbied the Census Bureau to reclassify such places, and their efforts resulted in the micropolitan area concept and label. Thus the Census Bureau now recognizes a new category of quasi-urban place, presumably entitling formerly nonmetropolitan places to apply for metropolitan-based federal and state aid.

For research purposes, the micropolitan area label also allows a more sophisticated differentiation between what was "rural" and now is "deep rural." The Census Bureau's previous "nonmetropolitan" designation was too broad to be synonymous with rural areas. The remaining nonmetropolitan counties that fall below the micropolitan area level can now be seen as truly rural.

Micropolitan areas can use their new status as quasi-metropolitan areas to promote economic development. It is likely that micropolitan areas will form organizations and partnerships to better understand their conditions and lobby for improvements. Multiple research efforts will help micropolitan areas promote themselves as places for development and will provide a basis for directing federal and state aid.

With the introduction of the micropolitan concept, the unclassified United States (non-core-based areas) is not just rural, but *deeply* rural.[12] Most of these places are in the West and are dominated by public land, such as military lands, national parks, and Indian reservations. Some places, such as Moab, Utah, are doing fine due to an amenity-driven economy that is similar to tourism-dominated micropolitan areas. But the majority of remote rural places continue to suffer depopulation and distress, as they rely on declining industries such as agriculture and resource extraction.

12. Rowley (2003).

TABLE 10A-1. **Micropolitan Areas in the Continental United States, 2003**

Micropolitan area	State	Population		1990–2000 change (percent)	Closest metro area[a]	Distance (miles)
		1990	*2000*			
Albertville	AL	70,832	82,231	16.1	Birmingham	68.5
Alexander City	AL	49,889	53,677	7.6	Birmingham	64.3
Cullman	AL	67,613	77,483	14.6	Birmingham	43.2
Daphne-Fairhope	AL	98,280	140,415	42.9	New Orleans	145.7
Enterprise-Ozark	AL	89,873	92,744	3.2	Birmingham	154.6
Fort Payne	AL	54,651	64,452	17.9	Birmingham	94.4
Scottsboro	AL	47,796	53,926	12.8	Birmingham	101.3
Selma	AL	48,130	46,365	-3.7	Birmingham	77.2
Talladega-Sylacauga	AL	74,107	80,321	8.4	Birmingham	40.5
Troy	AL	27,595	29,605	7.3	Birmingham	124.1
Tuskegee	AL	24,928	24,105	-3.3	Birmingham	97.4
Valley	AL	36,876	36,583	-0.8	Atlanta	76.6
Eufaula	AL-GA	27,626	31,636	14.5	Atlanta	137.0
Arkadelphia	AR	21,437	23,546	9.8	Memphis	200.2
Batesville	AR	31,192	34,233	9.7	Memphis	104.9
Blytheville	AR	57,525	51,979	-9.6	Memphis	46.5
Camden	AR	36,400	34,534	-5.1	Memphis	191.5
El Dorado	AR	46,719	45,629	-2.3	Memphis	197.6
Forrest City	AR	28,497	29,329	2.9	Memphis	50.2
Harrison	AR	35,963	42,556	18.3	Memphis	200.2
Hope	AR	31,722	33,542	5.7	Dallas	194.5
Magnolia	AR	25,691	25,603	-0.3	Dallas	204.2
Mountain Home	AR	31,186	38,386	23.1	Memphis	162.2
Paragould	AR	31,804	37,331	17.4	Memphis	82.7
Russellville	AR	63,642	75,608	18.8	Memphis	191.4
Searcy	AR	54,676	67,165	22.8	Memphis	106.0
West Helena	AR	28,838	26,445	-8.3	Memphis	69.6
Lake Havasu	AZ	93,497	155,032	65.8	Las Vegas	78.2
Nogales	AZ	29,676	38,381	29.3	Phoenix	133.8
Payson	AZ	40,216	51,335	27.6	Phoenix	68.6
Safford	AZ	34,562	42,036	21.6	Phoenix	124.8
Sierra Vista-Douglas	AZ	97,624	117,755	20.6	Phoenix	158.0
Bishop	CA	18,281	17,945	-1.8	Las Vegas	134.4
Clearlake	CA	50,631	58,309	15.2	Sacramento	89.8
Crescent City	CA	23,460	27,507	17.3	Sacramento	251.7
Eureka-Arcata-Fortuna	CA	119,118	126,518	6.2	Sacramento	202.7
Phoenix Lake-Cedar	CA	48,456	54,501	12.5	Sacramento	81.1
Red Bluff	CA	49,625	56,039	12.9	Sacramento	112.7
Susanville	CA	27,598	33,828	22.6	Sacramento	122.8
Truckee-Grass Valley	CA	78,510	92,033	17.2	Sacramento	39.3
Ukiah	CA	80,345	86,265	7.4	Sacramento	130.5
Canon City	CO	32,273	46,145	43.0	Denver	66.6
Durango	CO	32,284	43,941	36.1	Denver	213.8
Edwards	CO	27,935	49,471	77.1	Denver	90.1
Fort Morgan	CO	21,939	27,171	23.8	Denver	87.7
Montrose	CO	24,423	33,432	36.9	Denver	190.7
Silverthorne	CO	12,881	23,548	82.8	Denver	65.3
Sterling	CO	17,567	20,504	16.7	Denver	135.6

(*continued*)

TABLE 10A-1. **Micropolitan Areas in the Continental United States, 2003** (*continued*)

		Population				
Micropolitan area	State	1990	2000	1990–2000 change (percent)	Closest metro area[a]	Distance (miles)
Torrington	CT	174,092	182,193	4.7	Hartford	34.0
Willimantic	CT	102,525	109,091	6.4	Providence	24.4
Seaford	DE	113,229	156,638	38.3	Baltimore	78.9
Arcadia	FL	23,865	32,209	35.0	Tampa	79.5
Clewiston	FL	25,773	36,210	40.5	Miami	61.1
Homosassa Springs	FL	93,515	118,085	26.3	Tampa	48.3
Key West-Marathon	FL	78,024	79,589	2.0	Miami	71.8
Lake City	FL	42,613	56,513	32.6	Jacksonville	46.6
Okeechobee	FL	29,627	35,910	21.2	Orlando	86.4
Palatka	FL	65,070	70,423	8.2	Jacksonville	45.2
Palm Coast	FL	28,701	49,832	73.6	Jacksonville	62.1
Sebring	FL	68,432	87,366	27.7	Orlando	79.4
The Villages	FL	31,577	53,345	68.9	Tampa	37.9
Wauchula	FL	19,499	26,938	38.2	Tampa	61.9
Americus	GA	33,816	36,966	9.3	Atlanta	110.4
Bainbridge	GA	25,511	28,240	10.7	Jacksonville	172.9
Calhoun	GA	35,072	44,104	25.8	Atlanta	59.3
Cedartown	GA	33,815	38,127	12.8	Atlanta	45.8
Cordele	GA	20,011	21,996	9.9	Atlanta	131.6
Cornelia	GA	27,621	35,902	30.0	Atlanta	82.5
Douglas	GA	35,805	45,022	25.7	Jacksonville	107.5
Dublin	GA	48,317	53,434	10.6	Atlanta	127.4
Fitzgerald	GA	24,894	27,415	10.1	Jacksonville	130.2
Fort Valley	GA	21,189	23,668	11.7	Atlanta	87.5
Jesup	GA	22,356	26,565	18.8	Jacksonville	93.8
LaGrange	GA	55,536	58,779	5.8	Atlanta	58.4
Milledgeville	GA	48,438	54,776	13.1	Atlanta	87.0
Moultrie	GA	36,645	42,053	14.8	Jacksonville	132.3
St. Marys	GA	30,167	43,664	44.7	Jacksonville	50.6
Statesboro	GA	43,125	55,983	29.8	Jacksonville	151.0
Summerville	GA	22,242	25,470	14.5	Atlanta	70.0
Thomaston	GA	26,300	27,597	4.9	Atlanta	61.2
Thomasville	GA	38,986	42,737	9.6	Jacksonville	132.7
Tifton	GA	34,998	38,407	9.7	Jacksonville	130.9
Toccoa	GA	23,257	25,435	9.4	Atlanta	88.6
Vidalia	GA	31,235	34,337	9.9	Jacksonville	136.5
Waycross	GA	48,799	51,119	4.8	Jacksonville	64.2
Boone	IA	25,186	26,224	4.1	Minneapolis	216.1
Clinton	IA	51,040	50,149	-1.7	Chicago	134.1
Fort Dodge	IA	40,342	40,235	-0.3	Minneapolis	192.1
Marshalltown	IA	38,276	39,311	2.7	Minneapolis	212.9
Mason City	IA	54,724	54,356	-0.7	Minneapolis	131.8
Muscatine	IA	51,499	53,905	4.7	Chicago	167.8
Newton	IA	34,795	37,213	6.9	Kansas City	206.6
Oskaloosa	IA	21,522	22,335	3.8	Kansas City	194.4
Ottumwa	IA	35,687	36,051	1.0	Kansas City	183.8
Pella	IA	30,001	32,052	6.8	Kansas City	183.3
Spencer	IA	17,585	17,372	-1.2	Minneapolis	171.1

(*continued*)

TABLE 10A-1. **Micropolitan Areas in the Continental United States, 2003** (*continued*)

Micropolitan area	State	1990	2000	1990–2000 change (percent)	Closest metro area[a]	Distance (miles)
Spirit Lake	IA	14,909	16,424	10.2	Minneapolis	154.7
Storm Lake	IA	19,965	20,411	2.2	Minneapolis	191.4
Burlington	IA-IL	50,710	50,564	-0.3	St. Louis	160.0
Keokuk-Fort Madison	IA-MO	46,234	45,468	-1.7	St. Louis	147.0
Blackfoot	ID	37,583	41,735	11.0	Salt Lake City	184.3
Burley	ID	38,893	41,590	6.9	Salt Lake City	162.4
Moscow	ID	30,617	34,935	14.1	Seattle	251.7
Mountain Home	ID	21,205	29,130	37.4	Salt Lake City	270.2
Rexburg	ID	34,611	39,286	13.5	Salt Lake City	250.1
Twin Falls	ID	68,718	82,626	20.2	Salt Lake City	181.9
Canton	IL	38,080	38,250	0.4	St. Louis	127.5
Carbondale	IL	61,067	59,612	-2.4	St. Louis	77.2
Centralia	IL	41,561	41,691	0.3	St. Louis	76.9
Charleston-Mattoon	IL	62,314	64,449	3.4	Indianapolis	103.3
Dixon	IL	34,392	36,062	4.9	Chicago	69.9
Effingham	IL	31,704	34,264	8.1	St. Louis	99.8
Freeport	IL	48,052	48,979	1.9	Milwaukee	96.3
Galesburg	IL	75,574	74,571	-1.3	Chicago	139.7
Harrisburg	IL	26,551	26,733	0.7	St. Louis	114.2
Jacksonville	IL	42,041	42,153	0.3	St. Louis	75.3
Lincoln	IL	30,798	31,183	1.3	St. Louis	116.3
Macomb	IL	35,244	32,913	-6.6	St. Louis	128.7
Marion-Herrin	IL	57,733	61,296	6.2	St. Louis	97.8
Mount Vernon	IL	45,519	48,666	6.9	St. Louis	90.6
Ottawa-Streator	IL	148,331	153,098	3.2	Chicago	73.2
Pontiac	IL	39,301	39,678	1.0	Chicago	67.0
Rochelle	IL	45,957	51,032	11.0	Chicago	75.0
Sterling	IL	60,186	60,653	0.8	Chicago	103.9
Taylorville	IL	34,418	35,372	2.8	St. Louis	88.0
Quincy	IL-MO	76,323	78,771	3.2	St. Louis	112.9
Angola	IN	27,446	33,214	21.0	Detroit	113.2
Auburn	IN	35,324	40,285	14.0	Detroit	124.5
Bedford	IN	42,836	45,922	7.2	Indianapolis	56.0
Connersville	IN	26,015	25,588	-1.6	Cincinnati	56.0
Crawfordsville	IN	34,436	37,629	9.3	Indianapolis	42.8
Decatur	IN	31,095	33,625	8.1	Indianapolis	106.3
Frankfort	IN	30,974	33,866	9.3	Indianapolis	47.6
Greensburg	IN	23,645	24,555	3.8	Indianapolis	49.2
Huntington	IN	35,427	38,075	7.5	Indianapolis	93.5
Jasper	IN	49,125	52,511	6.9	Louisville	77.2
Kendallville	IN	37,877	46,275	22.2	Indianapolis	130.6
Logansport	IN	38,413	40,930	6.6	Indianapolis	76.8
Madison	IN	29,797	31,705	6.4	Louisville	42.9
Marion	IN	74,169	73,403	-1.0	Indianapolis	70.7
New Castle	IN	48,139	48,508	0.8	Indianapolis	52.2
North Vernon	IN	23,661	27,554	16.5	Indianapolis	56.8
Peru	IN	36,897	36,082	-2.2	Indianapolis	81.3
Plymouth	IN	42,182	45,128	7.0	Chicago	90.4

(*continued*)

TABLE 10A-1. Micropolitan Areas in the Continental United States, 2003 (*continued*)

Micropolitan area	State	Population 1990	Population 2000	1990–2000 change (percent)	Closest metro area[a]	Distance (miles)
Richmond	IN	71,951	71,097	-1.2	Cincinnati	63.9
Scottsburg	IN	20,991	22,960	9.4	Louisville	36.9
Seymour	IN	37,730	41,335	9.6	Indianapolis	52.7
Vincennes	IN	39,884	39,256	-1.6	Indianapolis	90.5
Wabash	IN	35,069	34,960	-0.3	Indianapolis	88.1
Warsaw	IN	65,294	74,057	13.4	Chicago	112.0
Washington	IN	27,533	29,820	8.3	Indianapolis	77.7
Atchison	KS	16,932	16,774	-0.9	Kansas City	59.4
Coffeyville	KS	38,816	36,252	-6.6	Kansas City	136.2
Dodge City	KS	27,463	32,458	18.2	Oklahoma City	206.2
Emporia	KS	37,753	38,965	3.2	Kansas City	107.8
Garden City	KS	33,070	40,523	22.5	Denver	249.8
Great Bend	KS	29,382	28,205	-4.0	Oklahoma City	221.8
Hays	KS	26,004	27,507	5.8	Kansas City	259.3
Hutchinson	KS	62,389	64,790	3.8	Oklahoma City	177.2
Liberal	KS	18,743	22,510	20.1	Oklahoma City	225.1
Manhattan	KS	113,720	108,999	-4.2	Kansas City	109.3
McPherson	KS	27,268	29,554	8.4	Kansas City	173.9
Parsons	KS	23,693	22,835	-3.6	Kansas City	126.1
Pittsburg	KS	35,568	38,242	7.5	Kansas City	98.6
Salina	KS	54,935	59,760	8.8	Kansas City	169.5
Winfield	KS	36,915	36,291	-1.7	Oklahoma City	129.8
Campbellsville	KY	21,146	22,927	8.4	Louisville	60.0
Central City	KY	31,318	31,839	1.7	Nashville	78.7
Corbin	KY	33,326	35,865	7.6	Louisville	128.3
Danville	KY	45,686	51,058	11.8	Louisville	69.2
Frankfort	KY	58,352	66,798	14.5	Louisville	40.0
Glasgow	KY	42,964	48,070	11.9	Nashville	77.3
London	KY	43,438	52,715	21.4	Louisville	111.4
Madisonville	KY	46,126	46,519	0.9	Nashville	94.6
Mayfield	KY	33,550	37,028	10.4	Nashville	113.2
Maysville	KY	29,695	30,892	4.0	Cincinnati	62.6
Middlesborough	KY	31,506	30,060	-4.6	Louisville	144.9
Mount Sterling	KY	34,345	40,195	17.0	Cincinnati	77.9
Murray	KY	30,735	34,177	11.2	Nashville	90.6
Richmond	KY	72,311	87,454	20.9	Louisville	86.9
Somerset	KY	49,489	56,217	13.6	Louisville	93.3
Paducah	KY-IL	94,595	98,765	4.4	Nashville	128.6
Abbeville	LA	50,055	53,807	7.5	New Orleans	150.9
Bastrop	LA	31,938	31,021	-2.9	Memphis	190.3
Bogalusa	LA	43,185	43,926	1.7	New Orleans	71.1
Crowley	LA	55,882	58,861	5.3	New Orleans	156.0
De Ridder	LA	30,083	32,986	9.6	Houston	140.4
Fort Polk	LA	61,961	52,531	-15.2	Houston	164.0
Hammond	LA	85,709	100,588	17.4	New Orleans	65.7
Jennings	LA	30,722	31,435	2.3	Houston	162.4
Minden	LA	41,989	41,831	-0.4	Dallas	196.0
Morgan City	LA	58,086	53,500	-7.9	New Orleans	98.3

(*continued*)

TABLE 10A-1.   **Micropolitan Areas in the Continental United States, 2003**
(*continued*)

Micropolitan area	State	Population 1990	Population 2000	1990–2000 change (percent)	Closest metro area[a]	Distance (miles)
Natchitoches	LA	36,689	39,080	6.5	Houston	196.0
New Iberia	LA	68,297	73,266	7.3	New Orleans	118.8
Opelousas-Eunice	LA	80,331	87,700	9.2	New Orleans	144.5
Pierre Part	LA	22,753	23,388	2.8	New Orleans	73.7
Ruston	LA	57,450	57,906	0.8	Memphis	237.2
Tallulah	LA	12,463	13,728	10.2	New Orleans	195.7
Cambridge	MD	30,236	30,674	1.4	Baltimore	63.1
Easton	MD	30,549	33,812	10.7	Baltimore	43.9
Lexington Park	MD	75,974	86,211	13.5	Washington	58.5
Ocean Pines	MD	35,028	46,543	32.9	Baltimore	99.5
Augusta-Waterville	ME	115,904	117,114	1.0	Boston	146.1
Rockland	ME	36,310	39,618	9.1	Boston	147.2
Adrian	MI	91,476	98,890	8.1	Detroit	67.4
Allegan	MI	90,509	105,665	16.7	Chicago	121.1
Alma	MI	38,982	42,285	8.5	Detroit	79.6
Alpena	MI	30,605	31,314	2.3	Detroit	163.9
Big Rapids	MI	37,308	40,553	8.7	Detroit	123.0
Cadillac	MI	38,507	44,962	16.8	Detroit	154.7
Coldwater	MI	41,502	45,787	10.3	Detroit	105.4
Escanaba	MI	37,780	38,520	2.0	Milwaukee	195.1
Houghton	MI	37,147	38,317	3.1	Minneapolis	275.8
Marquette	MI	70,887	64,634	-8.8	Milwaukee	227.8
Midland	MI	75,651	82,874	9.5	Detroit	87.3
Mount Pleasant	MI	54,624	63,351	16.0	Detroit	103.6
Owosso	MI	69,770	71,687	2.7	Detroit	47.8
Sault Ste.	MI	34,604	38,543	11.4	Detroit	259.8
Sturgis	MI	58,913	62,422	6.0	Chicago	124.5
Traverse City	MI	106,497	131,342	23.3	Detroit	175.5
Iron Mountain	MI-WI	31,421	32,560	3.6	Milwaukee	194.1
Albert Lea	MN	33,060	32,584	-1.4	Minneapolis	99.5
Alexandria	MN	28,674	32,821	14.5	Minneapolis	124.5
Austin	MN	37,385	38,603	3.3	Minneapolis	101.7
Bemidji	MN	34,384	39,650	15.3	Minneapolis	218.8
Brainerd	MN	66,040	82,249	24.5	Minneapolis	130.3
Fairmont	MN	22,914	21,802	-4.9	Minneapolis	120.1
Faribault-Northfield	MN	49,183	56,665	15.2	Minneapolis	51.2
Fergus Falls	MN	50,714	57,159	12.7	Minneapolis	152.7
Hutchinson	MN	32,030	34,898	9.0	Minneapolis	56.2
Mankato-North Mankato	MN	82,120	85,712	4.4	Minneapolis	85.2
Marshall	MN	24,789	25,425	2.6	Minneapolis	139.4
New Ulm	MN	26,984	26,911	-0.3	Minneapolis	94.5
Owatonna	MN	30,729	33,680	9.6	Minneapolis	75.2
Red Wing	MN	40,690	44,127	8.4	Minneapolis	52.7
Willmar	MN	38,761	41,203	6.3	Minneapolis	89.2
Winona	MN	47,828	49,985	4.5	Minneapolis	106.2
Worthington	MN	20,098	20,832	3.7	Minneapolis	161.6
Branson	MO	44,639	68,361	53.1	Kansas City	165.4
Farmington	MO	48,904	55,641	13.8	St. Louis	52.9

(*continued*)

TABLE 10A-1. **Micropolitan Areas in the Continental United States, 2003** (*continued*)

Micropolitan area	State	Population 1990	2000	1990–2000 change (percent)	Closest metro area[a]	Distance (miles)
Fort Leonard	MO	41,307	41,165	-0.3	St. Louis	115.9
Hannibal	MO	36,158	37,915	4.9	St. Louis	95.0
Kennett	MO	33,112	33,155	0.1	Memphis	88.2
Kirksville	MO	28,813	29,147	1.2	Kansas City	140.4
Lebanon	MO	27,158	32,513	19.7	Kansas City	135.0
Marshall	MO	23,523	23,756	1.0	Kansas City	73.2
Maryville	MO	21,709	21,912	0.9	Kansas City	102.5
Mexico	MO	23,599	25,853	9.6	St. Louis	91.7
Moberly	MO	24,370	24,663	1.2	Kansas City	112.9
Poplar Bluff	MO	38,765	40,867	5.4	Memphis	119.1
Rolla	MO	35,248	39,825	13.0	St. Louis	93.2
Sedalia	MO	35,437	39,403	11.2	Kansas City	66.7
Sikeston	MO	39,376	40,422	2.7	St. Louis	115.7
Warrensburg	MO	42,514	48,258	13.5	Kansas City	38.4
West Plains	MO	31,447	37,238	18.4	St. Louis	152.7
Cape Girardeau-Jackson	MO-IL	82,878	90,312	9.0	St. Louis	98.0
Brookhaven	MS	30,278	33,166	9.5	New Orleans	125.1
Clarksdale	MS	31,665	30,622	-3.3	Memphis	70.0
Cleveland	MS	41,875	40,633	-3.0	Memphis	102.9
Columbus	MS	59,308	61,586	3.8	Birmingham	93.9
Corinth	MS	31,722	34,558	8.9	Memphis	75.0
Greenville	MS	67,935	62,977	-7.3	Memphis	136.1
Greenwood	MS	46,578	48,716	4.6	Memphis	105.2
Grenada	MS	21,555	23,263	7.9	Memphis	86.4
Indianola	MS	32,867	34,369	4.6	Memphis	105.4
Laurel	MS	79,145	83,107	5.0	New Orleans	145.9
McComb	MS	50,210	52,539	4.6	New Orleans	106.5
Meridian	MS	103,224	106,569	3.2	Birmingham	128.8
Oxford	MS	31,826	38,744	21.7	Memphis	51.9
Picayune	MS	38,714	48,621	25.6	New Orleans	65.9
Starkville	MS	38,375	42,902	11.8	Birmingham	118.0
Tupelo	MS	107,835	125,251	16.2	Memphis	84.9
Vicksburg	MS	47,880	49,644	3.7	New Orleans	184.7
West Point	MS	21,120	21,979	4.1	Birmingham	111.3
Yazoo City	MS	25,506	28,149	10.4	Memphis	159.1
Natchez	MS-LA	56,184	54,587	-2.8	New Orleans	146.6
Bozeman	MT	50,463	67,831	34.4	Salt Lake City	331.2
Butte-Silver Bow	MT	33,941	34,606	2.0	Salt Lake City	369.9
Havre	MT	17,654	16,673	-5.6	Seattle	557.3
Helena	MT	55,434	65,765	18.6	Salt Lake City	434.7
Kalispell	MT	59,218	74,471	25.8	Seattle	376.9
Albemarle	NC	51,765	58,100	12.2	Charlotte	25.2
Boone	NC	36,952	42,695	15.5	Charlotte	94.3
Brevard	NC	25,520	29,334	14.9	Charlotte	121.4
Dunn	NC	67,822	91,025	34.2	Charlotte	102.7
Elizabeth City	NC	47,649	53,150	11.5	Virginia Beach	37.3
Forest City	NC	56,918	62,899	10.5	Charlotte	75.9
Henderson	NC	38,892	42,954	10.4	Richmond	90.5

(continued)

TABLE 10A-1. **Micropolitan Areas in the Continental United States, 2003**
(*continued*)

Micropolitan area	State	Population		1990–2000 change (percent)	Closest metro area[a]	Distance (miles)
		1990	2000			
Kill Devil Hills	NC	22,746	29,967	31.7	Virginia Beach	87.7
Kinston	NC	57,274	59,648	4.1	Virginia Beach	129.3
Laurinburg	NC	33,754	35,998	6.6	Charlotte	69.8
Lexington-Thomasville	NC	126,677	147,246	16.2	Charlotte	47.8
Lincolnton	NC	50,319	63,780	26.8	Charlotte	38.8
Lumberton	NC	105,179	123,339	17.3	Charlotte	95.0
Morehead City	NC	52,556	59,383	13.0	Virginia Beach	141.2
Mount Airy	NC	61,704	71,219	15.4	Charlotte	85.7
New Bern	NC	102,399	114,751	12.1	Virginia Beach	125.4
North Wilkesboro	NC	59,393	65,632	10.5	Charlotte	78.7
Roanoke Rapids	NC	76,314	79,456	4.1	Virginia Beach	71.3
Rockingham	NC	44,518	46,564	4.6	Charlotte	53.0
Salisbury	NC	110,605	130,340	17.8	Charlotte	37.2
Sanford	NC	41,374	49,040	18.5	Charlotte	87.6
Shelby	NC	84,714	96,287	13.7	Charlotte	51.1
Southern Pines	NC	59,013	74,769	26.7	Charlotte	70.8
Statesville-Mooresville	NC	92,931	122,660	32.0	Charlotte	44.8
Washington	NC	42,283	44,958	6.3	Virginia Beach	96.2
Wilson	NC	66,061	73,814	11.7	Virginia Beach	112.6
Dickinson	ND	23,940	23,524	-1.7	Minneapolis	487.6
Jamestown	ND	22,241	21,908	-1.5	Minneapolis	308.7
Minot	ND	67,609	67,392	-0.3	Minneapolis	449.0
Williston	ND	21,129	19,761	-6.5	Minneapolis	539.6
Wahpeton	ND-MN	25,664	25,136	-2.1	Minneapolis	192.8
Beatrice	NE	22,794	22,993	0.9	Kansas City	149.4
Columbus	NE	29,820	31,662	6.2	Kansas City	242.5
Fremont	NE	34,500	36,160	4.8	Kansas City	215.2
Grand Island	NE	63,022	68,305	8.4	Kansas City	244.6
Hastings	NE	36,748	38,190	3.9	Kansas City	229.8
Kearney	NE	44,076	49,141	11.5	Kansas City	272.7
Lexington	NE	21,868	26,508	21.2	Denver	287.9
Norfolk	NE	46,726	49,538	6.0	Kansas City	268.5
North Platte	NE	33,932	35,939	5.9	Denver	254.0
Scottsbluff	NE	36,877	37,770	2.4	Denver	174.9
Claremont	NH	38,592	40,458	4.8	Boston	72.5
Concord	NH	120,005	136,225	13.5	Boston	54.0
Keene	NH	70,121	73,825	5.3	Boston	57.3
Laconia	NH	49,216	56,325	14.4	Boston	64.6
Berlin	NH-VT	41,233	39,570	-4.0	Boston	145.7
Lebanon	NH-VT	155,133	167,387	7.9	Boston	96.5
Alamogordo	NM	51,928	62,298	20.0	Phoenix	368.6
Carlsbad-Artesia	NM	48,605	51,658	6.3	San Antonio	401.4
Clovis	NM	42,207	45,044	6.7	Denver	336.3
Deming	NM	18,110	25,016	38.1	Phoenix	253.5
Espanola	NM	34,365	41,190	19.9	Denver	217.0
Gallup	NM	60,686	74,798	23.3	Phoenix	261.7
Grants	NM	23,794	25,595	7.6	Phoenix	249.6
Hobbs	NM	55,765	55,511	-0.5	San Antonio	371.7

(*continued*)

TABLE 10A-1. **Micropolitan Areas in the Continental United States, 2003** (*continued*)

Micropolitan area	State	Population 1990	Population 2000	1990–2000 change (percent)	Closest metro area[a]	Distance (miles)
Las Vegas	NM	25,743	30,126	17.0	Denver	267.8
Los Alamos	NM	18,115	18,343	1.3	Denver	249.9
Portales	NM	16,702	18,018	7.9	Oklahoma City	355.6
Roswell	NM	57,849	61,382	6.1	Denver	417.6
Silver City	NM	27,676	31,002	12.0	Phoenix	212.7
Taos	NM	23,118	29,979	29.7	Denver	199.0
Elko	NV	35,077	46,942	33.8	Salt Lake City	184.5
Fallon	NV	17,938	23,982	33.7	Sacramento	161.7
Gardnerville Ranchos	NV	27,637	41,259	49.3	Sacramento	80.6
Pahrump	NV	17,781	32,485	82.7	Las Vegas	145.6
Amsterdam	NY	51,981	49,708	-4.4	Hartford	129.3
Auburn	NY	82,313	81,963	-0.4	Rochester	55.3
Batavia	NY	60,060	60,370	0.5	Rochester	31.1
Corning	NY	99,088	98,726	-0.4	Rochester	45.1
Cortland	NY	48,963	48,599	-0.7	Rochester	80.2
Gloversville	NY	54,191	55,073	1.6	Hartford	140.6
Hudson	NY	62,982	63,094	0.2	Hartford	69.3
Jamestown-Dunkirk	NY	141,895	139,750	-1.5	Buffalo	53.2
Malone	NY	46,540	51,134	9.9	Rochester	198.7
Ogdensburg-Massena	NY	111,974	111,931	0.0	Rochester	163.6
Olean	NY	84,234	83,955	-0.3	Buffalo	44.5
Oneonta	NY	60,517	61,676	1.9	Rochester	132.2
Plattsburgh	NY	85,969	79,894	-7.1	Boston	191.8
Seneca Falls	NY	33,683	33,342	-1.0	Rochester	41.9
Watertown-Fort Drum	NY	110,943	111,738	0.7	Rochester	114.3
Ashland	OH	47,507	52,523	10.6	Cleveland	52.5
Ashtabula	OH	99,821	102,728	2.9	Cleveland	52.2
Athens	OH	59,549	62,223	4.5	Columbus	69.3
Bellefontaine	OH	42,310	46,005	8.7	Columbus	49.1
Bucyrus	OH	47,870	46,966	-1.9	Columbus	52.7
Cambridge	OH	39,024	40,792	4.5	Columbus	76.6
Celina	OH	39,443	40,924	3.8	Columbus	94.9
Chillicothe	OH	69,330	73,345	5.8	Columbus	52.3
Coshocton	OH	35,427	36,655	3.5	Columbus	55.8
Defiance	OH	39,350	39,500	0.4	Detroit	114.7
East Liverpool-Salem	OH	108,276	112,075	3.5	Pittsburgh	59.1
Findlay	OH	65,536	71,295	8.8	Columbus	73.3
Fremont	OH	61,963	61,792	-0.3	Cleveland	75.7
Greenville	OH	53,619	53,309	-0.6	Cincinnati	76.3
Marion	OH	64,274	66,217	3.0	Columbus	35.6
Mount Vernon	OH	47,473	54,500	14.8	Columbus	32.6
New Philadelphia-Dover	OH	84,090	90,914	8.1	Cleveland	68.5
Norwalk	OH	56,240	59,487	5.8	Cleveland	51.3
Portsmouth	OH	80,327	79,195	-1.4	Cincinnati	84.1
Sidney	OH	44,915	47,910	6.7	Columbus	70.8
Tiffin-Fostoria	OH	59,733	58,683	-1.8	Columbus	72.3
Urbana	OH	36,019	38,890	8.0	Columbus	45.0
Van Wert	OH	30,464	29,659	-2.6	Columbus	101.1

(continued)

TABLE 10A-1. **Micropolitan Areas in the Continental United States, 2003** (*continued*)

Micropolitan area	State	Population		1990–2000 change (percent)	Closest metro area[a]	Distance (miles)
		1990	*2000*			
Wapakoneta	OH	44,585	46,611	4.5	Columbus	72.4
Washington	OH	27,466	28,433	3.5	Columbus	47.5
Wilmington	OH	35,415	40,543	14.5	Cincinnati	44.9
Wooster	OH	101,461	111,564	10.0	Cleveland	42.2
Zanesville	OH	82,068	84,585	3.1	Columbus	51.6
Ada	OK	34,119	35,143	3.0	Oklahoma City	65.5
Altus	OK	28,764	28,439	-1.1	Oklahoma City	126.1
Ardmore	OK	51,076	54,452	6.6	Oklahoma City	91.2
Bartlesville	OK	48,066	48,996	1.9	Oklahoma City	125.0
Duncan	OK	42,299	43,182	2.1	Oklahoma City	68.4
Durant	OK	32,089	36,534	13.9	Dallas	84.8
Elk City	OK	18,812	19,799	5.2	Oklahoma City	125.8
Enid	OK	56,735	57,813	1.9	Oklahoma City	68.2
Guymon	OK	16,419	20,107	22.5	Oklahoma City	243.3
McAlester	OK	40,581	43,953	8.3	Oklahoma City	104.1
Miami	OK	30,561	33,194	8.6	Kansas City	143.9
Muskogee	OK	68,078	69,451	2.0	Oklahoma City	115.9
Ponca City	OK	48,056	48,080	0.0	Oklahoma City	96.6
Shawnee	OK	58,760	65,521	11.5	Oklahoma City	36.9
Stillwater	OK	61,507	68,190	10.9	Oklahoma City	53.7
Tahlequah	OK	34,049	42,521	24.9	Oklahoma City	140.3
Woodward	OK	18,976	18,486	-2.6	Oklahoma City	125.2
Albany-Lebanon	OR	91,227	103,069	13.0	Portland	79.4
Astoria	OR	33,301	35,630	7.0	Portland	56.3
Brookings	OR	19,327	21,137	9.4	Portland	231.3
City of the Dalles	OR	21,683	23,791	9.7	Portland	80.5
Coos Bay	OR	60,273	62,779	4.2	Portland	187.3
Grants Pass	OR	62,649	75,726	20.9	Portland	230.6
Hood River	OR	16,903	20,411	20.8	Portland	48.4
Klamath Falls	OR	57,702	63,775	10.5	Portland	203.6
La Grande	OR	23,598	24,530	3.9	Portland	229.3
Pendleton-Hermiston	OR	66,874	81,543	21.9	Portland	179.5
Prineville	OR	14,111	19,182	35.9	Portland	153.4
Roseburg	OR	94,649	100,399	6.1	Portland	162.1
Ontario	OR-ID	42,472	52,193	22.9	Portland	312.9
Bloomsburg-Berwick	PA	80,937	82,387	1.8	Philadelphia	98.2
Bradford	PA	47,131	45,936	-2.5	Buffalo	77.3
Chambersburg	PA	121,082	129,313	6.8	Baltimore	79.5
DuBois	PA	78,097	83,382	6.8	Pittsburgh	79.2
East Stroudsburg	PA	95,709	138,687	44.9	New York	57.1
Gettysburg	PA	78,274	91,292	16.6	Baltimore	54.8
Huntingdon	PA	44,164	45,586	3.2	Pittsburgh	93.9
Indiana	PA	89,994	89,605	-0.4	Pittsburgh	35.3
Lewisburg	PA	36,176	41,624	15.1	Philadelphia	117.9
Lewistown	PA	46,197	46,486	0.6	Baltimore	107.7
Lock Haven	PA	37,182	37,914	2.0	Rochester	117.6
Meadville	PA	86,169	90,366	4.9	Cleveland	84.7
New Castle	PA	96,246	94,643	-1.7	Pittsburgh	47.8

(continued)

TABLE 10A-1. **Micropolitan Areas in the Continental United States, 2003** (*continued*)

Micropolitan area	State	Population 1990	Population 2000	1990–2000 change (percent)	Closest metro area[a]	Distance (miles)
Oil City	PA	59,381	57,565	-3.1	Pittsburgh	65.9
Pottsville	PA	152,585	150,336	-1.5	Philadelphia	72.1
Sayre	PA	60,967	62,761	2.9	Rochester	96.2
Selinsgrove	PA	36,680	37,546	2.4	Baltimore	108.8
Somerset	PA	78,218	80,023	2.3	Pittsburgh	48.7
St. Marys	PA	34,878	35,112	0.7	Pittsburgh	87.9
Sunbury	PA	96,771	94,556	-2.3	Philadelphia	96.6
Warren	PA	45,050	43,863	-2.6	Buffalo	79.6
Bennettsville	SC	29,361	28,818	-1.8	Charlotte	69.9
Chester	SC	32,170	34,068	5.9	Charlotte	43.9
Dillon	SC	29,114	30,722	5.5	Charlotte	90.6
Gaffney	SC	44,506	52,537	18.0	Charlotte	54.6
Georgetown	SC	46,302	55,797	20.5	Charlotte	140.0
Greenwood	SC	59,567	66,271	11.3	Charlotte	106.0
Hilton Head	SC	101,912	141,615	39.0	Jacksonville	162.6
Lancaster	SC	54,516	61,351	12.5	Charlotte	27.7
Newberry	SC	33,172	36,108	8.9	Charlotte	80.8
Orangeburg	SC	84,803	91,582	8.0	Charlotte	119.0
Seneca	SC	57,494	66,215	15.2	Atlanta	105.7
Union	SC	30,337	29,881	-1.5	Charlotte	64.2
Walterboro	SC	34,377	38,264	11.3	Charlotte	160.3
Aberdeen	SD	39,936	39,827	-0.3	Minneapolis	279.1
Brookings	SD	25,207	28,220	12.0	Minneapolis	185.2
Huron	SD	18,253	17,023	-6.7	Minneapolis	256.0
Mitchell	SD	20,497	21,880	6.7	Minneapolis	257.5
Pierre	SD	17,270	19,253	11.5	Minneapolis	358.7
Spearfish	SD	20,655	21,802	5.6	Denver	353.4
Vermillion	SD	13,186	13,537	2.7	Minneapolis	243.8
Watertown	SD	27,672	31,437	13.6	Minneapolis	197.9
Yankton	SD	19,252	21,652	12.5	Minneapolis	256.4
Athens	TN	42,383	49,015	15.6	Atlanta	119.6
Brownsville	TN	19,437	19,797	1.9	Memphis	52.1
Columbia	TN	54,812	69,498	26.8	Nashville	38.3
Cookeville	TN	78,306	93,417	19.3	Nashville	73.2
Crossville	TN	34,736	46,802	34.7	Nashville	100.8
Dyersburg	TN	34,854	37,279	7.0	Memphis	74.2
Greeneville	TN	55,853	62,909	12.6	Charlotte	142.2
Harriman	TN	47,227	51,910	9.9	Nashville	127.0
Humboldt	TN	46,315	48,152	4.0	Memphis	85.8
La Follette	TN	35,079	39,854	13.6	Nashville	147.6
Lawrenceburg	TN	35,303	39,926	13.1	Nashville	71.8
Lewisburg	TN	21,539	26,767	24.3	Memphis	107.9
McMinnville	TN	32,992	38,276	16.0	Nashville	63.7
Newport	TN	29,141	33,565	15.2	Charlotte	147.5
Paris	TN	27,888	31,115	11.6	Nashville	84.7
Sevierville	TN	51,043	71,170	39.4	Atlanta	152.9
Shelbyville	TN	30,411	37,586	23.6	Nashville	46.0

(*continued*)

TABLE 10A-1. **Micropolitan Areas in the Continental United States, 2003** (*continued*)

Micropolitan area	State	Population 1990	Population 2000	1990–2000 change (percent)	Closest metro area[a]	Distance (miles)
Tullahoma	TN	79,785	93,024	16.6	Nashville	62.7
Union City	TN-KY	39,988	40,202	0.5	Memphis	103.7
Alice	TX	37,679	39,326	4.4	San Antonio	125.4
Andrews	TX	14,338	13,004	-9.3	San Antonio	314.7
Athens	TX	58,543	73,277	25.2	Dallas	59.7
Bay City	TX	36,928	37,957	2.8	Houston	74.2
Beeville	TX	25,135	32,359	28.7	San Antonio	86.5
Big Spring	TX	32,343	33,627	4.0	San Antonio	264.2
Borger	TX	25,689	23,857	-7.1	Oklahoma City	221.1
Brenham	TX	26,154	30,373	16.1	Houston	63.2
Brownwood	TX	34,371	37,674	9.6	Austin	128.3
Corsicana	TX	39,926	45,124	13.0	Dallas	50.7
Del Rio	TX	38,721	44,856	15.8	San Antonio	160.4
Dumas	TX	17,865	20,121	12.6	Oklahoma City	251.3
Eagle Pass	TX	36,378	47,297	30.0	San Antonio	119.2
El Campo	TX	39,955	41,188	3.1	Houston	60.1
Gainesville	TX	30,777	36,363	18.1	Dallas	69.8
Granbury	TX	34,341	47,909	39.5	Dallas	74.8
Hereford	TX	19,153	18,561	-3.1	Oklahoma City	292.6
Huntsville	TX	50,917	61,758	21.3	Houston	65.4
Jacksonville	TX	41,049	46,659	13.7	Dallas	112.4
Kerrville	TX	36,304	43,653	20.2	San Antonio	63.4
Kingsville	TX	30,734	31,963	4.0	San Antonio	169.1
Lamesa	TX	14,349	14,985	4.4	Austin	306.3
Levelland	TX	24,199	22,716	-6.1	Oklahoma City	305.9
Lufkin	TX	69,884	80,130	14.7	Houston	113.8
Marshall	TX	57,483	62,110	8.0	Dallas	136.2
Mineral Wells	TX	25,055	27,026	7.9	Dallas	95.5
Mount Pleasant	TX	24,009	28,118	17.1	Dallas	103.8
Nacogdoches	TX	54,753	59,203	8.1	Houston	127.7
Palestine	TX	48,024	55,109	14.8	Dallas	90.7
Pampa	TX	24,992	23,631	-5.4	Oklahoma City	189.7
Paris	TX	43,949	48,499	10.4	Dallas	88.7
Pecos	TX	15,852	13,137	-17.1	San Antonio	328.7
Plainview	TX	34,671	36,602	5.6	Oklahoma City	265.7
Raymondville	TX	17,705	20,082	13.4	San Antonio	213.7
Rio Grande City	TX	40,518	53,597	32.3	San Antonio	200.2
Snyder	TX	18,634	16,361	-12.2	Dallas	248.0
Stephenville	TX	27,991	33,001	17.9	Dallas	97.7
Sulphur Springs	TX	28,833	31,960	10.8	Dallas	69.7
Sweetwater	TX	16,594	15,802	-4.8	Austin	215.6
Uvalde	TX	23,340	25,926	11.1	San Antonio	69.2
Vernon	TX	15,121	14,676	-2.9	Oklahoma City	133.8
Brigham City	UT	36,485	42,745	17.2	Salt Lake City	80.1
Cedar City	UT	20,789	33,779	62.5	Las Vegas	160.2
Heber	UT	10,089	15,215	50.8	Salt Lake City	45.4
Price	UT	20,228	20,422	1.0	Salt Lake City	101.3
Vernal	UT	22,211	25,224	13.6	Salt Lake City	133.9

(*continued*)

TABLE 10A-1. Micropolitan Areas in the Continental United States, 2003 (*continued*)

Micropolitan area	State	Population 1990	Population 2000	1990–2000 change (percent)	Closest metro area[a]	Distance (miles)
Martinsville	VA	73,104	73,346	0.3	Charlotte	115.3
Staunton-Waynesboro	VA	97,687	108,988	11.6	Richmond	98.4
Barre	VT	54,928	58,039	5.7	Boston	133.8
Bennington	VT	35,845	36,994	3.2	Boston	98.1
Rutland	VT	62,142	63,400	2.0	Boston	115.1
Aberdeen	WA	64,175	67,194	4.7	Seattle	92.8
Centralia	WA	59,358	68,600	15.6	Portland	67.9
Ellensburg	WA	26,725	33,362	24.8	Seattle	61.0
Moses Lake	WA	54,758	74,698	36.4	Seattle	113.3
Oak Harbor	WA	60,195	71,558	18.9	Seattle	57.7
Port Angeles	WA	56,464	64,525	14.3	Seattle	101.7
Pullman	WA	38,775	40,740	5.1	Seattle	207.0
Shelton	WA	38,341	49,405	28.9	Seattle	61.8
Walla Walla	WA	48,439	55,180	13.9	Seattle	181.7
Baraboo	WI	46,975	55,225	17.6	Milwaukee	91.9
Beaver Dam	WI	76,559	85,897	12.2	Milwaukee	31.3
Manitowoc	WI	80,421	82,887	3.1	Milwaukee	66.4
Menomonie	WI	35,909	39,858	11.0	Minneapolis	64.6
Merrill	WI	26,993	29,641	9.8	Milwaukee	168.1
Monroe	WI	30,339	33,647	10.9	Milwaukee	81.4
Platteville	WI	49,264	49,597	0.7	Milwaukee	135.3
Stevens Point	WI	61,405	67,182	9.4	Milwaukee	111.5
Watertown-Fort Atkinson	WI	67,783	74,021	9.2	Milwaukee	33.3
Whitewater	WI	75,000	93,759	25.0	Milwaukee	41.2
Wisconsin Rapids	WI	73,605	75,555	2.6	Milwaukee	128.2
Marinette	WI-MI	65,468	68,710	5.0	Milwaukee	159.1
Beckley	WV	76,819	79,220	3.1	Charlotte	181.3
Clarksburg	WV	91,509	92,144	0.7	Pittsburgh	87.7
Fairmont	WV	57,249	56,598	-1.1	Pittsburgh	69.2
Oak Hill	WV	47,952	47,579	-0.8	Columbus	172.4
Point Pleasant	WV-OH	56,132	57,026	1.6	Columbus	99.9
Bluefield	WV-VA	110,940	107,578	-3.0	Charlotte	150.8
Evanston	WY	18,705	19,742	5.5	Salt Lake City	91.1
Gillette	WY	29,370	33,698	14.7	Denver	340.5
Laramie	WY	30,797	32,014	4.0	Denver	169.8
Riverton	WY	33,662	35,804	6.4	Salt Lake City	243.3
Rock Springs	WY	38,823	37,613	-3.1	Salt Lake City	183.8
Sheridan	WY	23,562	26,560	12.7	Salt Lake City	388.9
Jackson	WY-ID	14,611	24,250	66.0	Salt Lake City	242.2

Source: Authors' calculations of Census 2000 and ArcView GIS analysis.

a. Top fifty metropolitan areas.

REFERENCES

Beale, Calvin L. 1990. "A Characterization of Types of Metropolitan Areas." In *A Taste of the Country: A Collection of Calvin Beale's Writings,* edited by Peter A. Morrison. Pennsylvania State University Press.

Garreau, Joel. 1991. *Edge City: Life on the New Frontier.* New York: Anchor.

Katz, Bruce, and Robert E. Lang. eds. 2003. *Redefining Urban and Suburban America: Evidence from Census 2000,* vol. 1. Brookings.

Lang, Robert E. 2002. "Open Spaces, Bounded Places: Does the American West's Arid Landscape Yield Dense Metropolitan Growth?" *Housing Policy Debate* 13 (4): 755–78.

———. 2003. *Edgeless Cities: Exploring the Elusive Metropolis.* Brookings.

Lang, Robert E., Deborah Epstein Popper, and Frank J. Popper. 1995. "Progress of the Nation: The Settlement History of the Enduring American Frontier." *Western Historical Quarterly* 23 (3): 289–307.

———. 1997. "Is There Still a Frontier? The 1890 Census and the Modern West." *Journal of Rural Studies* 13 (4): 377–86.

Lang, Robert E., and Kristopher M. Rengert. 2001. "The Hot and Cold Sunbelts: Comparing State Growth Rates, 1950–2000." Census Note Series. Washington: Fannie Mae Foundation.

McGranahan, David and Calvin Beale. 2002. "Understanding Rural Population Loss." *Rural America* 17 (4): 2–11.

Office of Management and Budget. 2003. OMB Bulletin No. 03–04. June 6.

Rengert, Kristopher M., and Robert E. Lang. 2001. "Cowboys and Cappuccino: The Emerging Diversity of the Rural West." Census Note Series. Washington: Fannie Mae Foundation.

Rowley, Thomas D. 2003. *The Rural Identity Crisis.* Columbia, Mo.: Rural Policy Research Institute.

U.S. Census Bureau. 2002. *Demographic Trends in the 20th Century.* Government Printing Office.

Contributors

Alan Berube
Brookings Institution

Thomas Bier
Cleveland State University

Eugenie L. Birch
University of Pennsylvania

Jason Booza
Wayne State University

Colleen Casey
St. Louis University

Dawn Dhavale
Virginia Polytechnic Institute

Peter Dreier
Occidental College

David Fasenfest
Wayne State University

Benjamin Forman
District of Columbia Department of Parks and Recreation

William H. Frey
Brookings Institution

Meghan Zimmerman Gough
Ohio State University

Bruce Katz
Brookings Institution

Robert E. Lang
Virginia Polytechnic Institute

Kurt Metzger
United Way for Southeastern Michigan

Charlie Post
Cleveland State University

Robert Flack
St. Louis University

Steven Raphael
University of California, Berkeley

Audrey Singer
Brookings Institution

Michael A. Stoll
University of California, Los Angeles

Todd Swanstrom
St. Louis University

Jennifer S. Vey
Brookings Institution

Jill H. Wilson
Brookings Institution

Index

African Americans. *See* Black
    populations
Agriculture, Department of, 198
Akron (OH), 176
Alaska, 236
Albuquerque (NM), 38, 45, 48, 56
Allentown (PA), 22
Anaheim (CA), 87, 88
Anchorage (AK), 223
Andrews, TX MicroSA, 202, 238
Ann Arbor, MI MetroSA, 223
Ann Arbor, MI PMSA, 214, 223
Anne Arundel County (MD), 66
Annexation, 17, 62, 149–50
Apache Junction (AZ), 91
Appalachian Mountains, 237
Arizona, 66–67, 85
Arlington (TX), 87, 90
Ashtabula County (OH), 230
Asians: city growth and, 22; in down-
    towns, 43–44, 45; household
    ownership, numbers, and
    composition, 45; in metropolitan
    areas, 96, 107–10; neighborhood
    segregation and, 5; population
    growth of, 102, 104, 106, 111, 114;
    spatial isolation from jobs,
    123–24, 126, 135, 141. *See also*
    Racial and ethnic issues
Atlanta (GA), 35, 45, 51, 55, 87
Atlanta metropolitan area (GA): addi-
    tion or subtraction of counties to,
    206, 228; boomburbs in, 84; coun-

ties of, 63, 69, 70, 71, 72; racial and
    ethnic issues, 99, 105, 107, 113
Atlanta-Sandy Springs-Gainesville,
    GA-AL CSA, 206, 208f
Atlanta-Sandy Springs-Marietta, GA
    MetroSA, 206
Aurora (CO), 87, 88
Aurora (IL), 16
Austin (TX), 38, 43, 51, 56, 67
Austin-Round Rock, TX MetroSA, 218

Baby boomers, 47
Baltimore (MD), 43, 55, 177, 182, 192,
    196
Baltimore, MD PMSA, 196
Banks and banking, 224
Beale, Calvin, 236
Beale Codes. *See* Rural-Urban
    Continuum Codes
Berkeley (CA), 14
Berkeley County (WV), 208
Berube, Alan, 191–234
Bethesda-Frederick-Gaithersburg, MD
    Metropolitan Division, 201
Birch, Eugenie L., 29–59
Black populations: city growth and, 20;
    in downtowns, 43, 44, 45; employ-
    ment issues, 120; housing and,
    120; in metropolitan areas, 96,
    107–10; in multigroup neighbor-
    hoods, 94; neighborhood and resi-
    dential segregation and, 5, 125;
    population growth of, 102, 111;